STUDIES IN PHILOSOPHY

Edited by
Robert Bernasconi
University of Memphis

A ROUTLEDGE SERIES

Studies in Philosophy

Robert Bernasconi, *General Editor*

The Rights of Woman as Chimera

The Political Philosophy of Mary Wollstonecraft

Natalie Fuehrer Taylor

Routledge
New York & London

Routledge
Taylor & Francis Group
711 Third Avenue,
New York, NY 10017

Routledge
Taylor & Francis Group
2 Park Square,
Milton Park, Abingdon,
Oxfordshire OX14 4RN

First issued in paperback 2014

Routledge is an imprint of the Taylor and Francis Group, an informa business

© 2007 by Taylor & Francis Group, LLC

ISBN 978-0-415-97853-8 (hbk)
ISBN 978-1-138-87986-7 (pbk)

Library of Congress Cataloging-in-Publication Data

Taylor, Natalie Fuehrer.
  The rights of woman as chimera : the political philosophy of Mary Wollstonecraft.
    p. cm. -- (Studies in philosophy)
  Includes bibliographical references and index.
  ISBN 978-0-415-97853-8 (alk. paper)
    1. Wollstonecraft, Mary, 1759-1797--Criticism and interpretation. 2.
Wollstonecraft, Mary, 1759-1797. Vindication of the rights of woman. 3. Women's
rights--Philosophy. 4. Women--Education--Philosophy. 5. Woman (Philosophy) I.
Title.

HQ1595.W64T39 2006
305.42092--dc22   2006028287

Visit the Taylor & Francis Web site at
http://www.taylorandfrancis.com

and the Routledge Web site at
http://www.routledge-ny.com

Contents

Acknowledgments

The Rights of Woman as Chimera began as my dissertation in the Department of Political Science at Fordham University. I appreciate the financial support from the Fordham, as well as from the Bradley, Earhart, and Olin Foundations. I am profoundly grateful to many people, who offered me their thoughts and their encouragement during that time. Michael Zuckert introduced me to Mary Wollstonecraft during a course he taught at Fordham in the fall of 1996. My mentor at Fordham, Mary Nichols, has been most generous with her time and with her suggestions for improving my work. She has also been very generous with the green cottage, where I could work, distracted only by games of Taboo and music from Lee and Lauren. I am also indebted to my dissertation committee, Daryl Tress, David Nichols, and Pamela Jensen for the great care they gave my dissertation. Since beginning this project Denise Schaeffer read and commented on my work in many and various forms. I am also very fortunate to have had bright, thoughtful, and fun fellow graduate students. Their formal and informal conversation in the Bronx and at Hatch Lake provided me with great insight and warm, heartfelt memories.

Since leaving Fordham I have enjoyed the support of my colleagues at both Oglethorpe University and Skidmore College. Joe Knippenberg was very kind and helpful to me as I worked through the chapters on Wollstonecraft's intellectual relationship to John Locke. Alan Woolfolk was gracious enough to invite me to present my work to Oglethorpe's faculty, who gather on Friday afternoons for the purpose of sharing their research. The lively response my talk received was thought provoking and serves as a wonderful example of academic collegiality.

My dissertation was revised for publication at Skidmore. I am grateful to my friends and colleagues in the Government department and the Women Studies program. Steve Hoffman, Roy Ginsberg, Aldo Vacs, Ron Seyb, Tim

Burns, Beau Breslin, Kate Graney, Bob Turner, and Barbara McDonough have been cheerful supporters of my efforts since my arrival. Tim carefully read early drafts of my manuscript and has offered his sharp insight on Rousseau. Conversations with Kate on the once and future state of feminism have always been interesting and challenging. Roy and Beau offered me good advice on preparing this manuscript and have been eager to share my excitement as I worked toward publishing it. Barbara's level-headed, practical approaches to my difficulties have never failed to be efficient and effective. And, although Grace Burton is not a political scientist by training, but married into our department, she has joined her husband, Ron, in tirelessly providing their good, sound advice and frequent pep talks. Such interested and friendly colleagues are indeed a great luxury.

I appreciate the thoughtful attention my work has received from other Wollstonecraft scholars. Wendy Gunther-Canada served as a panel discussant, commenting on an earlier version of chapter six. Eileen Hunt Botting read not only chapter six, but also chapter seven. Eileen promptly obliged me with her insights even in the very last weeks before the manuscript was due. Both women made suggestions, which improved not only my manuscript, but my understanding and appreciation of Mary Wollstonecraft.

I am grateful to Max Novick and Jennifer Genetti, my editors at Routledge, and Robert Bernasconi, series editor for Studies in Philosophy. They have been professional, patient, and helpful throughout the process.

During the years that I have been working on my book about marriage and the family, my family has been my greatest support and my greatest happiness. My parents, Walt and Jean Fuehrer, have inspired in me a real admiration for the institution of marriage and have been models of loving parents, as well as models of dedicated children and siblings. As a result, I have benefited from the examples of grandparents, aunts and uncles, and cousins. My twin sister, Diana, is my dearest friend and continues to inspire wonder in me about the equality and difference among human beings. My husband, Flagg, has been unceasingly kind as I worked on my book, patiently doing whatever I—or our new baby—needed so that I might "unfold my faculties." May I always be "an affectionate wife and a rational mother" to him and to our son.

Introduction

THE HYENA IN PETTICOATS

In 1790 Mary Wollstonecraft published her first political treatise, *A Vindication of the Rights of Men*. Hastily written, it is Wollstonecraft's spirited response to Edmund Burke's *Reflections on the Revolution in France*. In his well known treatise Burke argues that legitimate government rests on honored traditions and habits, rather than on individual rights—a notion that had gained philosophical and political currency by the eighteenth century. Wollstonecraft's answer to Burke's *Reflections* came just twenty-eight days after *Reflections* was published and it was the first of forty-five responses to Burke's treatise within the first year of its publication. Wollstonecraft's answer to Burke is often overshadowed by *The Rights of Man*, written by eighteenth-century radical luminary, Tom Paine. Yet, one of Wollstonecraft's most spirited verbal attacks against Burke captured the attention of Wollstonecraft's contemporaries and has continued to interest scholars today. In what seems to Wollstonecraft to be "empty, rhetorical flourishes," Burke laments the lowly treatment given to the Queen of France by the market women, who had slogged through the mud in the October rain in order to escort the King and Queen from Versailles to Paris. To Burke, the Queen of France is the epitome of feminine beauty and virtue. To Wollstonecraft, the Queen of France is the epitome of contemptible feminine weakness and vice. In *A Vindication of the Rights of Men* Wollstonecraft refutes Burke's characterization of Marie Antoinette, suggesting the Queen is as wretched as the women who made up the vulgar mob. Reminding Burke of his description of the market women as "the furies of hell, in the abused shape of the vilest of women," Wollstonecraft replies to Burke, "Probably you mean women who gained a livelihood by selling vegetables or fish, who never had had the advantages of education; or their vices might have lost part of their abominable deformity, by losing part of their grossness. The queen of France—the great and small vulgar, claim our pity; they have almost insuperable obstacles to surmount in their progress towards true dignity of character."[1] This attack on Marie Antoinette is motivated by Wollstonecraft's belief that woman, as well as man, may aspire to reason and virtue, eschewing the superficial feminine charms, pervasive in Wollstonecraft's day and seemingly epitomized in the Queen of France.

For her attack on Marie Antoinette, Horace Walpole called Wollstonecraft "a hyena in petticoats."[2] It is ironic that Wollstonecraft's implicit (in this instance) demand that women aspire to the dignity of human beings was met, not simply with an affront to her femininity, but with an assault on her character as a human being as well. Walpole reduces Wollstonecraft to a heinous, shrill, flesh-eating animal dressed in women's clothes. Implicit in Walpole's insult is the notion that woman must be comprised of two parts: the feminine and the human. A corruption of one or both of these parts results in "a hyena in petticoats," a *chimera* or a monster comprised of two parts, which is not found in nature.

Chimera has a second meaning, which is more common in eighteenth-century writings. Not only does *chimera* mean a mythological creature comprised of incongruent parts, but it also means a utopian or fanciful dream. Wollstonecraft appreciates the ambivalence of this word and uses it to convey both a monster and a utopian dream throughout her second and better known political treatise, *A Vindication of the Rights of Woman*. Seemingly undaunted by Walpole's insult, Wollstonecraft takes up her pen to write *A Vindication of the Rights of Woman*. In more explicit and elaborate arguments than her attack on the Queen of France, Wollstonecraft calls "with the firm tone of humanity"[3] for the education of woman so that, like man, she may exercise reason and virtue. Though Wollstonecraft hopes to establish equality among man and woman, she hopes to do so while still preserving the differences between them. Wollstonecraft acknowledges that her pursuit of woman, comprised of both human and feminine virtues "may be termed utopian dreams" (*VRW*, 36). Wollstonecraft also understands that the wrong combination of the feminine and the human may well lead to a chimera in the mythological sense, a monster. This book is a study of Mary Wollstonecraft's philosophical pursuit of her utopian dream on the pages of *A Vindication of the Rights of Woman*.

Wollstonecraft begins by making her case for the equality of man and woman with arguments which seem to resonate with the natural rights doctrine, popular in Wollstonecraft's intellectual and political circles. However, in her attempt to extend a natural rights doctrine to women, Wollstonecraft runs into theoretical difficulties which point to the incompatibility of these

Enlightenment principles with the lives of women. I shall argue that the tensions which Wollstonecraft recognizes in the natural rights doctrines come to light in the consideration of "the woman question," but point to the fundamental limits of natural rights theory itself. In other words, in pursuing her utopian dream, her chimera, of equality between the sexes, Wollstonecraft appreciates that the natural rights doctrine of Rousseau and Locke creates "half-beings" (*VRW*, 39), chimeras in a mythological sense. I shall then argue that Wollstonecraft's political philosophy can be more fully elaborated and refined by a consideration of Aristotle's treatment of sexual difference. Finally, I will examine the fulfillment of Mary Wollstonecraft's utopian dream. She recognizes her chimera as a citizen, as well as a rational, virtuous, wife and mother.

I.

There are two perennial inquiries within the scholarship on Mary Wollstonecraft, which are not mutually exclusive. The first inquiry revolves around the extent to which Wollstonecraft's personal and biographical circumstances inform her political and feminist philosophy. Reviewing Claire Tomlin's *The Life and Death of Mary Wollstonecraft*, E.P. Thompson suggests Wollstonecraft's intellectual accomplishments are often overlooked in favor of her compelling, unconventional life. "She is seen less as a significant intellectual . . . than an Extraordinary Woman. And the moral confusions, or personal crises, of a woman are always somehow more interesting than those of a man: they engross all other aspects of the subject."[4] Susan Kin Zaw recognizes the negative impact that Wollstonecraft's unconventional life had on her philosophy. She writes, "I believe that Wollstonecraft developed her early moral philosophy and psychology in response to her struggles to get her own reason and feeling into alignment . . . philosophy is not the pursuit of knowledge for its own sake but a search for understanding that can direct action by making sense of personal experience."[5] Motivated by an attempt to overcome her personal struggles, Wollstonecraft draws from a number of other philosophers to explain her own experience. As a thinker, Zaw finds Wollstonecraft to be "a cherry picker and a personalizer" (Zaw, 109).

Other scholars consider the influence of Wollstonecraft's personal life on her philosophy to be an important and necessary element of her feminist and political philosophy. Barabara Taylor insists that although her work, *Mary Wollstonecraft and the Feminist Imagination*, is "not a biography—anyone looking for new revelations about her [Wollstonecraft's] private life will be disappointed—it does seek to uncover the pressures of her life and times exerted in her thought, and her imaginative responses to them" (Taylor, 4). Drawing a distinction between the private life of an author and her public writings, Taylor argues, is contrary to both the eighteenth-century mind and the feminist mind (Taylor, 18, 20).

Many of the full length treatments of Wollstonecraft are biographical. These scholars are primarily concerned with Wollstonecraft's attempt to transform literary practices in order to give women a voice. They consider Wollstonecraft's confrontation with the intellectual traditions of her time. Ralph Wardle's *Mary Wollstonecraft: A Critical Biography* and Gary Kelly's *Revolutionary Feminism: The Mind and Career of Mary Wollstonecraft* are examples of such work. Wardle pays particular attention to the influences on Wollstonecraft as she wrote each work and notes the way in which she may have experimented with others' thought. For example, Wardle tells us that Wollstonecraft was reading Rousseau's *Emile* as she began her work as governess with an aristocratic Irish family. Wollstonecraft imagines a similarity between herself and the author of *Emile.* "Rousseau 'rambles into that *chimerical* world in which I have too often wandered.'"[6] Like Rousseau, Wollstonecraft imagines "not the man of man," but the "man of nature" (*Emile,* 253). As a result, Wollstonecraft soon produces a sentimental novel, *Mary, A Fiction.* The heroine is a chimera, a fanciful illusion. Wollstonecraft declares at the outset of her novel that the heroine is no Sophie. Instead, Mary is an independent, determined woman, who is touched by sensibility. Kelly's treatment of Wollstonecraft is also helpful in the respect that he considers each one of her works as he follows the course of her life. He appreciates that Wollstonecraft's experiences bear upon her writings and he documents the changes in her writing style in order to accommodate a particular objective.

Not all commentators have explained Wollstonecraft's thought by her personal or historical circumstances. A second inquiry, which occupies Wollstonecraft scholars, is whether Wollstonecraft is able to engage in the philosophic debate with canonical thinkers or whether she must create a new, feminist discourse in the face of the hostile, masculine cannon. There are those commentators who see Wollstonecraft's thought as derivative of earlier, male thinkers. These scholars fall into two categories: those who identify Wollstonecraft with Lockean liberalism and those who identify her with Rousseau's romanticism. Zillah Eisenstein is the most well known proponent of the position that Wollstonecraft is a Lockean. In her book, *The Radical Future of Liberalism,* Eisenstein cites Wollstonecraft's support of the new bourgeois order, economic independence for women, and emphasis on individual achievement and usefulness as evidence of Locke's influence on Wollstonecraft. Virginia Muller also identifies Wollstonecraft as a Lockean liberal. In her essay, "What Can Liberals Learn from Mary Wollstonecraft?" Muller points out the ways in which Wollstonecraft must revise some fundamental Lockean tenets. For example, Wollstonecraft rejects property rights as the core of democracy and she rejects a distinction between the public and the private sphere, which liberalism generally insists upon. Muller must admit that Wollstonecraft and Lockean liberalism are not a comfortable fit. However, Muller defends her claim by reminding us that Wollstonecraft believes in reason, the possibility of change and progress, modern democracy, and individual liberty.

I disagree that Lockean liberalism provides an adequate theoretical framework for Wollstonecraft's *A Vindication of the Rights of Woman*. Though John Locke's political thought would have permeated eighteenth-century British intellectual circles, Ralph Wardle tells us in his biography of Wollstonecraft that it is unlikely that she read Locke's political works (there is evidence that she read Locke's educational treatise). More importantly, Wollstonecraft does not base her claim for equality on natural rights. Rather, her demand for equality is based on the character of the human soul. Human beings, male or female, are rational creatures. Furthermore, Wollstonecraft does not suggest that the political community is instituted for the protection of natural rights. Rather, consistent with her understanding of the human soul, Wollstonecraft tells her readers that we live in a political community so that we may unfold our rational capacities. In a similar vein as Aristotle, Wollstonecraft suggests that we are rational animals and, therefore, we are political animals. For these reasons, Wollstonecraft's political thought resonates more with Aristotle than it does with John Locke.[7]

In the second category of scholars, who consider Wollstonecraft as continuing the project of an earlier thinker, are those who believe Wollstonecraft was primarily influenced by Rousseau. Many of them are scholars of literature and are interested in Wollstonecraft's fictional works. Wollstonecraft's fictions, *Mary, A Fiction* and *Cave of Fancy* are early works and are considered largely autobiographical. Wollstonecraft wrote these fictions just after enthusiastically reading Rousseau's *Emile*. Though Wollstonecraft warns at the outset of her novel that Mary is no Sophie, Wollstonecraft idealizes the heroine's sensibility. Many would argue that Wollstonecraft's later works belie a conversion to the faith of reason. However, Wollstonecraft always defended Rousseau. She writes, "A defense of Rousseau appears to us unnecessary— for surely he speaks to the heart, and whoever reading his works can doubt whether he wrote from it—had better take up some other book . . . It is impossible to pursue his simple descriptions without loving the man in spite of the weaknesses of character that he himself depicts" (Wardle, 131). Meena Alexander suggests that the inner-outer dichotomy of Romantic literature presupposed a centralized self that was not compatible with the lives of women. In her book, *Women in Romanticism*, Alexander demonstrates that Romantic subjectivity is questioned and then refashioned by female Romantic authors, such as Wollstonecraft. Alexander's work is instructive in that it demonstrates the connection that women have to other people (Alexander credits maternity). Although both Virginia Muller and Meena Alexander recognize significant incompatibilities between Wollstonecraft's thought and liberalism and Romanticism, neither Muller nor Alexander move beyond their respective frameworks in order to fully explain Wollstonecraft's political philosophy.

Other scholars have demonstrated the important differences between Mary Wollstonecraft and her male predecessors. In her treatment of Wollstonecraft's thought, *A Vindication of Political Virtue: the Political Theory of Mary Wollstonecraft*, Virgina Sapiro urges her readers to consider Wollstonecraft's place in the history of political theory. [8] Identifying various philosophical strains to Wollstonecraft's thought, Sapiro reveals the complexity to Wollstonecraft's philosophy. In this instance, Wollstonecraft's biographical details and the influence of earlier thinkers are eclipsed by her own intellectual accomplishments. More recently, Eileen Hunt Botting's interpretation of Wollstonecraft's philosophy of the family belies those that see Wollstonecraft as simply derivative of earlier, male philosophers. In her book, *Family Feuds: Wollstonecraft, Burke, and Rousseau on the Transformation of the Family*, Botting examines the philosophies of these three thinkers and observes unexpected similarities between them. Rousseau, Burke, and Wollstonecraft all identify the family as the occasion for fostering the moral, social, and political virtues that would sustain the political community. While Rousseau and Burke preserve the patriarchal structure of the family, Botting observes that Wollstonecraft recognizes the necessity of eliminating the patriarchal structure of the family in order to assure a more egalitarian political community. In this respect, Botting demonstrates the ways in which Wollstonecraft's thought surpasses that of her most important influences.

Wendy Gunther-Canada also turns her attention to Wollstonecraft's struggle to enter the political discourse of her day. However, Gunther-Canada sees greater tension between Wollstonecraft and the political discourse of her time than Sapiro and Botting do. In her essay, "Mary Wollstonecraft's 'Wild Wish': Confounding Sex in the Discourse on Political Rights," Gunther-Canada argues that *Vindications of the Rights of Men* is exactly that: a treatise about the rights of men. In writing her first political treatise, it becomes clear to Wollstonecraft that women were not included in the debate, either as participants or subjects of it. In order to discuss the rights of woman, a second treatise must be written. In Gunther-Canada's recent, full length treatment of Wollstonecraft's thought, *Rebel Writer*, she pursues her observation that Enlightenment humanism is limiting in terms of gender. "The goal of [Gunther-Canada's] analysis is to demonstrate how Wollstonecraft's writing subverted the patriarchal plot of political theory."[9] Gunther-Canada characterizes Wollstonecraft's writings as "oppositional discourse" (Gunther-Canada, 11).

Following Sapiro, Botting, and Gunther-Canada, I am concerned with the extent to which Wollstonecraft's engagement with the canonical thinkers helps her in the pursuit of her utopian dream. I would suggest that Wollstonecraft does enter the canonical discourse and that she learns many lessons from these male thinkers. However, Wollstonecraft's engagement with them in not uncritical. Wendy Gunther-Canada rightly observes that in order to fully include women in political debate and participation, a new ideal of womanhood and a new ideal of citizenship must be put forward by the female philosopher. Understanding Wollstonecraft's departures form her male predecessors gives us a greater appreciation for Wollstonecraft's political philosophy—and a deeper understanding of the canonical philosophers.

I am particularly indebted to Virginia Sapiro for my reading of Mary Wollstonecraft's *A Vindication of the Rights of Woman*. Sapiro's book, *A Vindication of Political Virtue*, is a thoughtful and comprehensive thematic presentation of Wollstonecraft's political philosophy. Sapiro avoids understanding Wollstonecraft as simply a liberal or a Romantic. She tells her readers, "Those who make Wollstonecraft sound like a late eighteenth-century John Locke in drag mistake her. But she is also not the backward-looking seeker of a lost golden age. She was forthright in her contempt for Rousseau's 'golden age of stupidity' (*Scand.* 288)" (Sapiro, xx). Sapiro argues that Wollstonecraft's conception of reason differs from her contemporaries. For Wollstonecraft, reason is not cold logic or calculation, but rather the capacity for virtue. Furthermore, Sapiro points out that social life is not a utilitarian field in which private interests are mutually pursued. Social life is the means of improving individual and social character. Sapiro goes so far as to compare Mary Wollstonecraft's understanding of the ideal social relationship to the ancient Greek conception of friendship.[10] However, Sapiro quickly dismisses this comparison based on the assumption that Wollstonecraft probably did not read the ancient Greek philosophers.

Though my interpretation of *A Vindication of the Rights of Woman* is consistent with that put forth by Sapiro, it moves beyond Sapiro's work in two significant respects. In the first case, I devote a significant amount of attention to Wollstonecraft's explicit and implicit critique of state of nature theories, in particular those put forth by Jean-Jacques Rousseau and John

Locke. In the state of nature it is obvious that men are physically stronger than women—a generality Wollstonecraft does not deny in *A Vindication of the Rights of Woman* (*VRW*, 8). To Locke, the physical difference is relatively unimportant. It does not suggest any further difference between men and women and it becomes less and less evident as scientific progress is made and man gains greater control over nature. To Rousseau, on the other hand, the initial difference in physical strength has important ramifications. In response to their relative weakness, women cultivate other qualities in order to put them on a more even footing with men. As men and women enter into civil society and become more and more civilized these differences are fostered, rather than mitigated. While Locke emphasizes the similarity and, as a consequence, the equality of men and women, Rousseau emphasizes the difference. Albeit in different respects, both Locke and Rousseau suggest that woman is a "half-being" (*VRW*, 39). And, so, neither Locke nor Rousseau provide the philosophical foundation for the utopian dream Wollstonecraft pursues. In rejecting the state of nature theories of Locke and Rousseau, Wollstonecraft seeks a political philosophy, which incorporates both the equality between men and women and the differences between them.

Secondly, I think Sapiro is too quick to dismiss the comparison that she introduces between Wollstonecraft and ancient Greek thinkers. There is some evidence in Wollstonecraft's writing that she was familiar with Greek texts. For example, in her famous attack on Burke, *A Vindications of the Rights of Men*, Wollstonecraft accuses Burke of only quoting Aristotle partially, implying she had some familiarity with Aristotle's *Politics* (*VRM*, 19). In addition, Wollstonecraft refutes Burke's conception of femininity and the quality of love, which results from it. Wollstonecraft argues that if Burke's conception is correct, then the character of love presented in Plato's *Symposium* must be wrong (*VRM*, 48). Even if Wollstonecraft had not read ancient philosophy, Wollstonecraft's friends and foes certainly had. It is entirely possible that Wollstonecraft had been indirectly influenced by Aristotle's ideas.[11] But the issue is not the historical one of demonstrating the specifics of her acquaintance with ancient philosophy. Rather, I wish to indicate that there is a plausible basis for an extended analysis of her thought in light of Aristotle's political principles. Therefore, I retrieve Sapiro's discarded observation and explore the affinities between Mary Wollstonecraft and Aristotle. This exploration elaborates and clarifies her political philosophy, in particular shedding considerable light on the apparently chimerical product of her critique of Rousseau and Locke. Although recognizing the affinities between Wollstonecraft and Aristotle gives us a better appreciation of Wollstonecraft's utopian dream, there are limits to Aristotle's ability to help her pursue it.

Wollstonecraft moves beyond Aristotle's treatment of friendship and predicts the salutary benefits that marriage, based on such a conception of friendship, and the family will have on the political community. Wollstonecraft moves beyond Rousseau and Locke, as well as Aristotle, by introducing woman into politics. Wollstonecraft's chimera is a citizen, as well as a wife and mother.

II.

My study of Mary Wollstonecraft's *A Vindication of the Rights of Woman* divided into three sections. The first section considers Mary Wollstonecraft's political philosophy in light of the political thought of Rousseau. From the outset of her most famous treatise, *A Vindication of the Rights of Woman*, it is clear that Rousseau is Wollstonecraft's primary interlocutor. While her spirited condemnation of Rousseau and his ideal woman, Sophie, garner the attention of scholars, I suggest Wollstonecraft learns a great deal from the "Solitary Walker." The first chapter is devoted to the lessons Wollstonecraft learns from Rousseau. Despite the very important lessons Wollstonecraft does learn from Rousseau, Wollstonecraft must finally reject his state of nature theory as the foundation for her own political thought. Chapter two examines the reasons for Wollstonecraft's departure from Rousseau.

The second section of this book examines the influence of John Locke on Wollstonecraft. Following the organization of the first section, the third chapter considers the lessons Locke may have imparted to Wollstonecraft. In his educational treatise, *Some Thoughts Concerning Education*, Locke encourages parents to educate their daughters in a similar manner as their sons. The result is young girls and mothers, who are strong in body and in mind. However, Locke's conception of human reason differs significantly from Wollstonecraft's conception and Wollstonecraft must be dissatisfied with Locke's framework as well. The important differences between Locke and Wollstonecraft are considered in the fourth chapter. While there are murmurs of both similarity and difference to both Rousseau and Locke in Wollstonecraft's thought, neither thinker's account of women can fully elaborate Mary Wollstonecraft's understanding of the character of women and the character of marriage. Wollstonecraft's rejection of Rousseau's and Locke's frameworks is, finally, a rejection of the state of nature theories.

After considering Wollstonecraft's political thought in light of Rousseau and Locke, I will turn my attention to the benefit Wollstonecraft may have gained by a study of Aristotle. This will comprise the third and final section of the book. In the fifth chapter I defend my claim that Aristotle's political philosophy is an alternative to the state of nature theories put forth by Locke and Rousseau. In his *Discourse on the Origin and the Foundations of Inequality Among Men* (or the *Second Discourse*), Rousseau criticizes Hobbes' and Locke's inquiry into the state of nature. According to Rousseau, these thinkers did not go back far enough into history to have arrived at the state of nature. Instead, both Hobbes and Locke describe social man at an early stage of civilization. In this way, Rousseau sets himself up as an alternative to early modern thinkers. However, Rousseau also sets up his state of nature theory as an alternative to Aristotle's political philosophy. The *Second Discourse* begins with an epigram from Aristotle's *Politics*. "What is natural has to be investigated not in beings that are depraved, but in those that are good according to nature."[12] Rousseau goes on to tell his readers in the Preface that his inquiry into natural man is worthy of the Aristotle's of his century (*Second Discourse*, 125). Rousseau begins his speculation on natural man by dismissing Aristotle's description of man outside of society (*Second Discourse*, 134), offering instead his own image of savage man. Given Wollstonecraft's dissatisfaction with Rousseau, Rousseau's suggestion to consider Aristotle as an alternative to his political philosophy may have been particularly inviting. In the remainder of the third section, I will consider the ways in which Wollstonecraft's thought may be more fully elaborated in an Aristotelian framework. In the chapter five, I shall consider Aristotle's explanation of the biological differences between male and female and the extent to which Aristotle's explanation supports Wollstonecraft's claim that women are meant to pursue virtue, despite their physical differences from men. In large part, I utilize the work of Daryl Tress, "The Metaphysical Science of Aristotle's *Generation of Animals* and Its Feminist Critics." Tress demonstrates that both the male and the female make necessary, though unique, contributions to the generation of offspring. Yet, Aristotle holds, neither male nor female are limited to their parental roles. Both are obliged to pursue virtue. In the sixth and final chapter I turn my attention to Wollstonecraft's understanding of marriage. Wollstonecraft's hope for marriage, I shall argue, can be more fully elaborated and refined by a consideration of the teaching on friendship put forth by Aristotle in the *Nicomachean Ethics*. It is by considering Wollstonecraft's political philosophy in light of Arisitotle's philosophy that we may begin to see how the "hyena in petticoats" is to fulfill her utopian dream. In the seventh and final chapter of this book I demonstrate the ways in which Wollstonecraft's political philosophy moves beyond Aristotle's. Although Aristotle offers his readers an example of a rational, virtuous woman, who is the friend of her husband, he does not elaborate her importance to the political community. And, he certainly does not allow her to participate as a citizen. The female philosopher does both. In doing so, Mary Wollstonecraft introduces a new ideal of womanhood and a new ideal of citizenship.

Chapter One

The Land of Chimeras

It is virtually impossible to consider any of Mary Wollstonecraft's works, fiction or nonfiction, without reflecting on Jean-Jacques Rousseau. Scholars of British Literature, writing on Wollstonecraft's novels, are typically concerned with the extent to which her works can be identified with Romanticism and, in this respect, with Jean-Jacques Rousseau. Though *A Vindication of the Rights of Woman* is dedicated to a French diplomat, it is immediately clear that Wollstonecraft's fire is aimed at Rousseau. Throughout the *Vindication*, Wollstonecraft takes every opportunity to condemn the notion of woman as it is represented by his character, Sophie, in *Emile*. Wollstonecraft's spirited attack on Rousseau in her political treatise may suggest that Rousseau's influence extends only to her novels. On the contrary, I shall argue that Wollstonecraft learns important political lessons from Rousseau. In particular, Rousseau teaches Wollstonecraft that all individuals are not only human beings, but also either male or female. The second half of their being, their sex, is that which attaches one human being to another and adds a complexity to the individual's natural independence or wholeness. Furthermore, Rousseau teaches Wollstonecraft the importance of natural differences between the sexes and the corrosive effect that the unnatural, corrupted male or female sex can have on the political community. Wollstonecraft, like Rousseau before her, appreciates that a woman's roles of wife and mother, contribute to a healthy individual, family, and community. After considering the valuable lessons that Wollstonecraft gains from Rousseau, I will turn my attention to Wollstonecraft's rejection of Rousseau's political philosophy as the basis for her own. It would be wrong to think this rejection is simply the result of her disagreement about the character of Sophie, or with Rousseau's understanding of women more generally. Wollstonecraft's criticism of Sophie reveals her departure from the fundamental tenets of natural rights theory. Wollstonecraft rejects the notion that women, or human beings more generally, are motivated by self-preservation and that human communities are formed out of a desire to protect oneself from the aggression of others. In contrast to natural rights theorists, Wollstonecraft believes human beings are motivated by their desire for virtue and that human beings live in civil society in order to foster virtue. While Sophie is the occasion for her engagement with Rousseau, Wollstonecraft's departure from Rousseau is due to a fundamental disagreement on the nature of human beings and the character of their political relationships.

To be sure, Rousseau is one of Wollstonecraft's favorite foes. However, scholars have not overlooked the fact that Rousseau is also one of Wollstonecraft's favorite friends. In considering Rousseau's relationship to his readers, Carol Blum and Mary Seidman Trouille have both remarked on the unique sympathy Rousseau's readers felt for the author. "It was his moral superiority and the moral superiority one could enjoy by adoring him which were important, not any specific doctrine he had put forth."[1] While Blum is primarily concerned with the influence of Rousseau's explicitly political works on the French Revolutionaries, Trouille notices the same affection and sympathy in the female readers of *La Nouvelle Heloise* and *Emile*.[2] Even if their views on women were incompatible with Rousseau's sexual politics, "his women readers still identified with him and with his characters of his novels because they expressed . . . their deepest aspirations and longings—for ideal love, self-fulfilling motherhood, and domestic felicity" (Trouille, 4).

And, indeed, Wollstonecraft is loyal to Rousseau on the basis of her affection for the Solitary Walker. When given the chance, Wollstonecraft defends Rousseau against his critics. She writes,

> A defense of Rousseau appears to us unnecessary—for surely he speaks
> to the heart, and whoever reading his works can doubt whether he wrote
> from it—had better take up some other book . . . It is impossible to
> pursue his simple descriptions without loving the man in spite of the
> weakness of character that he himself depicts. (Wardle, 131)

Despite their philosophical differences, Wollstonecraft harbors a personal affection for Rousseau.

Other scholars have noted a more substantive connection between Wollstonecraft and Rousseau. Jean Grimshaw argues, "it is above all the philosophy and other writings of Rousseau which form a backdrop of Wollstonecraft's work, and central to this is Rousseau's account, in *Emile*, of female nature, his prescriptions for female upbringing and female virtue."[3] Grimshaw gives an account of Rousseau's presentation of the feminine condition in *Emile* and discusses Wollstonecraft's disagreement with it. "In the *Vindication*, it was perhaps above all the idea that virtue was *gendered*, that it should be different for women and men, that Wollstonecraft attacked" (Grimshaw, 16). Any suggestion that women are dependent creatures, meant solely for the pleasure of men—a view that some of Rousseau's observations and prescriptions for Sophie seem to endorse—outrages Wollstonecraft. Yet, Grimshaw points out, despite Wollstonecraft's objections, "Wollstonecraft remained attracted to the idea that women have special qualities, which while not in themselves virtues, could lead to virtue" (Grimshaw, 18). Putting aside the *Vindication*, Grimshaw takes up Wollstonecraft's fiction in order to consider evidence that Wollstonecraft fell under the sway of Rousseau's teaching on the differences between the sexes.

Grimshaw's essay is typical of the scholarship on Wollstonecraft's relationship to Rousseau. In her full length treatment of Wollstonecraft's life and works, *Mary Wollstonecraft and the Language of Sensibility*, Syndy Conger understands Rousseau's influence in a similar manner.[4] Conger considers the influence of eighteenth-century Romantic novels on Wollstonecraft. From novelists, such as Goethe, Samuel Richardson, and Rousseau, Wollstonecraft adopts the language and ethics of sensibility. Conger tells her readers that in the eighteenth century, sensibility had come to mean "emotional consciousness, a capacity for refined emotion; readiness to feel compassion for suffering."[5] Sensibility was considered the particular trait of women and a complement to men's greater rationality. Conger argues that sensibility plays a steady role in Wollstonecraft's life and works and demonstrates Wollstonecraft's commitment to sensibility in her novels. However, by the time Wollstonecraft writes *A Vindication of the Rights of Woman*, she has come to appreciate the political dangers of feminine sensibility and rejects it as a means to women's improvement. Wollstonecraft's "*Rights of Woman* represents the moment of greatest crisis in that faith [in sensibility] . . . here she tries to disentangle herself entirely from the notion" (Conger, 114).

Eileen Hunt Botting differs from Grimshaw and Conger in that she appreciates the continued influence of Rousseau on Wollstonecraft as Wollstonecraft is writing her treatise on women. Wollstonecraft and Rousseau, Botting explains in *Family Feuds*, are friendly critics of the Enlightenment insofar as they both appreciate that human beings may be motivated by affection for others, rather than merely by self-interest or self-preservation as Thomas Hobbes contends. Wollstonecraft and Rousseau "also argued that the stability, independence, and ethical quality of any political society depended on the cultivation and direction of the affections toward the social formation of future subjects or citizens."[6] Yet, Botting does not see

Wollstonecraft as simply echoing Rousseau's philosophy of the family. "Wollstonecraft persuasively argues that Rousseau and Burke's patriarchal conceptions of the family hinder, rather than foster, the affections that inspire the social virtues, and that her model of the egalitarian family provides a more practical and ethical foundation for affective-social formation, especially in the rising democratic culture of the late Enlightenment" (Botting, 11). It is the sex-role differentiation in Rousseau's philosophy of the family that gives it its patriarchal character and that Wollstonecraft cannot abide in her model of the egalitarian family.

In a similar vein to Eileen Hunt Botting, I suggest that Wollstonecraft continues to appreciate Rousseau's teaching on the importance of the family to the political community. However, in contrast to Botting, I argue that Wollstonecraft also recognizes the importance of the natural differences between the sexes. In particular, Wollstonecraft echoes Rousseau's appreciation for motherhood and domestic felicity and makes use of it in her own demand for political reform in *A Vindication of the Rights of Woman*. In this chapter, I will examine those aspects of Rousseau's thought with which Wollstonecraft agrees and which offer support for her own views, in particular, Rousseau's criticism of the corrosive effects of society on the human beings of his day and the great potential for virtue as wife and mother.

I. THE CHIMERA

Rousseau begins Book IV of the *Emile* by declaring, "We are, so to speak, born twice: once to exist and once to live; once for our species and once for our sex."[7] Rousseau goes on to make the point that this is true of females as well as males. "Everything is equal: girls are children, boys are children; the same name suffices for beings so much alike" (*Emile*, 211). In other words, all individuals are comprised of two parts: that part which is human and that part which is male or female. In his *Second Discourse*, Rousseau tells us,

> Every general idea is purely intellectual; if the imagination is at all involved, the idea immediately becomes particular. Try to outline the image of a tree in general to yourself, you will never succeed; in spite of yourself it will have been seen as small or large, bare or leafy, light or dark, and if you could see in it only what there is in every tree, the image would no longer resemble a tree.[8]

The same may be said of human beings. Though we may try to imagine the abstract idea of human being, we always have either a man or a woman in our mind's eye. Rousseau's project in the *Emile* is, in large part, the task of putting the two parts of the individual together in a way that preserves both the species and the sex and avoids a creature which no longer resembles a human being.

At the outset of the *Emile*, Rousseau promises to educate Emile to be a natural man, as opposed to civil man. "Natural man is entirely for himself. He is a numerical unity, the absolute whole, which is relative only to itself or its kind. Civil man is only a fractional unity dependent on the denominator; his value is determined by his relation to the whole, which is the social body" (*Emile*, 39–40). In his book, *Rousseau, Nature & the Problem of the Good Life,* Lawrence Cooper argues that this numerical unity, or what Cooper calls psychic unity, is the primary attribute of natural man.[9] In contrast to natural man, Rousseau presents us with the man of his day, a fractional man.

> Always in contradiction with himself, always floating between his incli-
> nations and his duties, he will never be either a man or a citizen. He
> will be good neither for himself nor for others. He will be one of these
> men of our days: a Frenchman, and Englishman, a bourgeois. He will
> be nothing. (*Emile*, 40)

Cooper tells his readers that Rousseau presents five types of human beings in his corpus: the divided, corrupt, social man; the virtuous citizen of the ancient austere polis; the inhabitant of the pure state of nature; Jean-Jacques Rousseau of *The Reveries of A Solitary Walker*; and Emile (Cooper, 67). Of these five types of human beings presented by Rousseau, he explicitly names three as natural men: the Savage, the Solitary Walker, and Emile.[10] These three men distinguish themselves from the others by their numeri-cal unity. Although these natural men all enjoy numerical unity, they are not simply identical. As we shall see, the differences between the Savage and Emile become evident at the time of the birth of their sex. This suggests a difference in the degree to which each is affected by his social passions. The numerical unity each enjoys varies in its complexity as a result. I would point out that Sophie is absent from Cooper's list of five human types, which appear in Rousseau's corpus. She is certainly not listed as one of the three natural human beings. In fact, Sophie is conspicuously absent from Cooper's book, leaving the reader with the nagging suspicion that women are unable to attain Rousseau's ideal unity. If women are capable of Rousseau's numer-ical unity, able to combine the human with the female sex, just as Emile combines the human and the male sex, then woman's unity will differ in its complexity from both the Savage and Emile.

Of the three types of human beings, which Lawrence Cooper identifies as natural, I am particularly interested in the Savage of the pure state of nature and, of course, Emile. Commentators have noticed a certain parallel between the Savage and Emile.[11] By way of introduction to the subject of his treatise, Rousseau tells readers of the *Second Discourse*, "It is so to speak, the life of your species that I will describe to you in terms of the qualities you received, which your education and your habits could deprave, but which they could not destroy" (*Discourses*, 133). Rousseau describes the *Emile* in similar terms. Against the charge that his work is merely a romance, Rousseau tells his critics, "A fair romance it is indeed, the romance of human nature. If it is to be found only in this writing, is that my fault? This ought to be the history of my species. You who deprave it, it is you who make a romance of my book" (*Emile*, 416). While Masters points out the distinction between the two (i.e. the *Second Discourse* is concerned with the development of the species and the *Emile* traces the development of natural man), I would suggest that the similarities, as well as the differences, between the Savage and Emile are instructive.

In the Preface to the *Emile*, Rousseau tells his readers "Childhood is unknown . . . They [the wisest men] are always seeking the man in the child without thinking of what he is before being a man" (*Emile*, 33–34). Rousseau expresses a similar regret in the Preface to the *Second Discourse*.

> How will man ever succeed in seeing himself as Nature formed him, through all the changes which the succession of times and of things must have wrought to his original constitution, and to disentangle what he owes to his own stock from what circumstances and his progress have added to or changed in his primitive state? (*Discourses*, 124)

Like "the wisest men," who seek the man in the child, "the Philosophers who have examined the foundations of society have all felt the necessity of going back as far as the state of Nature, but none of them has reached it . . . They spoke of Savage man and depicted civil man" (*Discourses*, 132). Indeed, Rousseau explicitly identifies the Savage in the earliest stages of the state of nature with childhood. In describing the incredibly slow rate of movement out of the state of nature, Rousseau tells his readers, "Centuries went by in all the crudeness of the first ages, the species had already grown old, and man remained ever a child" (*Discourses*, 157). If childhood, in particular that of Emile, can be compared to the Savage in the pure state of nature, then Emile's subsequent development can be compared to the Savage's gradual movement to civil society. It is important to note that, for Rousseau, the natural is determined by the beginning (Masters, 5). If Rousseau's task in the *Second Discourse* is "to explain by what chain of wonders the strong could resolve to serve the weak, and the People to purchase an idea of repose at the price of real felicity" (*Discourse*, 131), his challenge in the *Emile* is to imagine a strong individual, who remains free from social passions and, therefore, free from enslavement to the weak. In other words, Rousseau attempts to break "the chain of wonders" in Emile's development and allow him to live as if in an "age at which the individual human being would want to stop development [of the life of the species]" (*Discourses*, 133). Yet, Rousseau does not expect that Emile will ever live as a solitary being, isolated from the political community. Therefore, Emile has something in common with the civil man as well as the Savage in the state of nature. Just as the *Second Discourse* ends with the Savage's entrance into society, so the *Emile* ends by Emile becoming a citizen. This is accomplished by Emile's marriage to Sophie.[12] Rousseau's success in breaking "the chain of wonders" will be measured, therefore, by the character of Emile's marriage to Sophie.

Up until the time of Emile's second birth, the birth of his sex, Rousseau admits that his work has been relatively easy. Emile, like the Savage in the pure state of nature, has few desires. Rousseau is primarily concerned with keeping it that way and with ensuring that Emile satisfies his few desires by himself. Both Emile and the Savage do not feel dependent on anyone. Rousseau has nurtured a healthy *amour de soi* in Emile. *Amour de soi* or self-love, "regards only ourselves" and "is contented when our true needs our satisfied" (*Emile*, 213). This type of self-love is characteristic of the natural man. However, with the birth of his sex, Emile's passions become more numerous. Furthermore, the sexual desires cannot be satisfied by oneself. The second part of our being, our sex, be it male or female, suggests a dependence on or an attachment to at least one other human being. The wholeness, which is to be comprised of the species and the sex is a rather complex unity, due to this fractured character of the sex. The unity is not comprised of two, simple and equal parts. This complexity varies between the Savage and Emile (and, presumably, the complexity will vary in Sophie as well). The Savage undergoes a similar experience. In the pure state of nature, man's sexual desires are general. "Any woman suits him." It is only after a certain degree of contact with other human beings that man's desires become attached to a single object (*Discourses*, 155). The Savage becomes dependent on a particular woman to satisfy his desires. Emile, on the other hand, does not enjoy a time of sexual freedom during which any woman would suit Emile. As fortified by his natural education as he may be, Emile is born into civil society and his sexual desires will be attached to single object. This will make the birth of Emile's sex more significant than the birth of the Savage's sex. In both the *Second Discourse* and the *Emile*, Rousseau identifies the sexual desire for a particular female as a time of revolution (though for Emile, not the Savage, the desire for a particular object is coincident with the birth of the sex). "This was the period of a first revolution which brought about the establishment and the differentiation of families . . . the habit of living together gave rise to the sweetest sentiments known to man, conjugal love, and Paternal love" (*Discourses*, 164). Rousseau tells us that the Savage man loses some vigor, but his numerical unity is preserved. For Emile, a natural man living in society, the situation is much more precarious.

> As the roaring of the sea precedes a tempest from afar, this story of revolution is proclaimed by the murmur of the nascent passions. A mute fermentation warns of danger's approach. A change in humor, frequent anger, a mind in constant agitation, makes the child almost unmanageable . . . His feverishness turns him into a lion. (*Emile*, 211)

The birth of Emile's sex, the birth of the second half of his being, is a greater threat to Emile's numerical unity than the birth of the Savage's sex. He no longer resembles the ideal human being, but appears to be a beast. The threat to our numerical unity comes primarily from *amour-propre*. "But *amour-propre*, which makes comparisons, is never content and never could be, because this sentiment, preferring ourselves to others, also demands others to prefer us to themselves, which is impossible" (*Emile*, 213–214). The birth of *amour-propre* is not necessarily coincident with the birth of the sex. Emile is unique in that Rousseau's natural education deters the emergence of *amour-propre* until puberty. In fact, in the corrupt eighteenth century society, which Rousseau observes, *amour-propre* is often awakened quite early in a person's life. However, with the birth of our sex and the attempt to "obtain the preference that one grants" (*Emile*, 214), the birth of *amour-propre* in Emile can no longer be deterred. With the birth of his sex, and inevitably the birth of *amour propre*, Emile is in danger of losing his wholeness, his independence from the opinions of others. "From the bosom of so many diverse passions I see opinion raising an unshakable throne, and stupid mortals, subjected to its empire, basing their own existence on the judgements of others" (*Emile*, 215). Emile is in danger of becoming a fraction. Rather than a human being, Emile would resemble an unnatural creature, comprised of two incompatible parts.

The natural education of Emile offers Rousseau's readers a means to achieve numerical unity, or wholeness, overcoming social vanity. This is a utopian vision, which Rousseau knows will not be immediately appreciated by his readers. Nonetheless, he perseveres.

> I go forward by the force of things without gaining credibility in the judgment of my readers. For a long while they have seen me in the land of chimeras. I always see them in the land of prejudices . . . Every time that this reasoning forces me to separate myself from those opinions, I have learned from experience to take it for granted that my readers will not imitate me (*Emile*, 253).

Rousseau is wrong to take for granted that he would have no imitators. In a letter to her sister, Wollstonecraft tells her that she is reading Rousseau's *Emile* and that she feels a certain affinity to the author. "He chuses [sic] a *common* capacity to educate—and gives as a reason, that genius will educate itself—however he rambles into that *chimerical* world in which I have often [wand]ered—and draws the usual conclusion that all is vanity and vexation of spirit [in the eighteenth century]."[13] Like Rousseau, Wollstonecraft recognizes the damage that vanity and social prejudices have on human beings and, in particular, on the women of her day.

> One cause of this barren blooming I attribute to a false system of education, gathered from the books written on this subject by men, who considering females rather as women than human creatures, have been more anxious to make them alluring mistresses than affectionate wives and rational mothers; and the understanding of the sex has been so bubbled by this specious homage, that the civilized women of the present century, with few exceptions, are only anxious to inspire love, when they ought to cherish a nobler ambition, and by their abilities and virtues exact respect. (*VRW*, 7)

Unlike Emile, whose education has protected him from social prejudices, women in the eighteenth century have been educated simply as fractional beings, "basing their own existence on the judgment of others" (*Emile*, 215).

Rousseau imparts to Wollstonecraft the lesson that all individuals consist of the human as well as their sex. The proper combination of these two parts creates a wholeness and independence from the opinion of others. With this understanding, Wollstonecraft outlines her project. "I shall first consider women in the grand light of human creatures, who, in common with men, are placed on this earth to unfold their faculties; and afterwards I shall more particularly point out their [women's] peculiar designation" (*VRW*, 8). Like

Rousseau, Wollstonecraft recognizes that her efforts to establish the humanity of women will not be readily appreciated by all of her readers. She admits
her treatise "may be termed Utopian dreams" (*VRW*, 36). Yet, Wollstonecraft
follows her chimera, knowing that individuals, who are not comprised of
both the human and their sex are likely to be vicious, unnatural creatures.

II. NATURAL DISTINCTIONS

The first lesson that Rousseau imparts to readers of the *Emile* is the importance of motherhood. The neglect of this natural distinction has grave consequences not only for particular women, but also for marriages and the
community. Though Wollstonecraft tirelessly argues against the notion that
the sexes are different in nature, Wollstonecraft is in agreement with Rousseau on the importance of motherhood. This natural distinction has great
potential to protect women from vanity and social prejudices and it contributes to a strong healthy political community.

After condemning the fractional, civilized man, Rousseau begins to
consider the education of man beginning at birth. "Civil man is born, lives,
and dies in slavery. At birth he is sewed in swaddling clothes, at his death he
is nailed in a coffin. So long as he keeps his human shape, he is enchained
by our institutions" (*Emile*, 42–43). This declaration echoes Rousseau's well
known premise of the *Social Contract*. "Man was/is born free, and everywhere is in chains."[14] In this instance, Rousseau does not go on to consider
the threat of political institutions to our freedom, but turns his attention to
the social customs of caring for children. Rousseau begins with the rather
common practice of swaddling infants. Swaddling clothes, though ostensibly well intentioned, have important consequences on children's bodies and
souls. In the *Second Discourse*, Rousseau follows the gradual transformation
of the vigorous, robust Savage into a relatively weak civil man. In part, civil
man's weakness may be attributed to the practice of swaddling infants and
the use of wet nurses, or as Rousseau will call them in the *Emile*, mercenary
women. "The original weakness they owe to their Parents' constitution, the
care taken to swaddle and cramp all their limbs, the softness in which they
are reared, perhaps the use of another milk than their Mother's, everything
thwarts and delays in them the first progress of Nature" (*Discourses*, 215).
In the *Emile*, Rousseau's concern is correcting the ways in which civil society has cramped man's soul. Again, he condemns the practice of swaddling
infants. "Their first sentiment is a sentiment of pain and suffering . . . The
first gifts they receive from you is chains" (*Emile*, 43). Rousseau wonders
where the practice of swaddling children comes from and attributes it to a

"denatured practice" (*Emile*, 44). Mothers, refusing to breast-feed their children, place them in the care of nurses. Rousseau calls these nurses mercenary women. Just as hiring soldiers is an indication of a weak, corrupt regime, so too is hiring women to breastfeed its children a sign of corruption. Like mercenary soldiers, these mercenary women care more for money than they do for the vitality of the citizenry. In an effort to prevent injury and to save themselves trouble, the mercenary women swaddle the infants. The infants receive their chains and the mothers "devote themselves gaily to the entertainments of the city" (*Emile*, 44). Far from a fanciful, utopian vision, the eighteenth century French woman is a chimera in the mythological sense, a creature which is comprised of two incongruous parts, divided between her inclination and her natural duty.

Rousseau goes on to tell his readers that these corrupt mothers are rather cunning in their abdication of their duty. "I have sometimes seen the little trick of young women who feign to want to nurse their children. They know how to have pressure put on them to give up this whim. Husbands, doctors, especially mothers, are adroitly made to intervene. A husband who dared to consent to his wife's nursing her child would be a man lost" (*Emile*, 45). Despite his greater strength and authority, a husband allows his wife's feigned weakness and yields to her feminine manipulation, allowing her to disregard her natural duty. With this example, Rousseau shows us a link in the "chain of wonders" by which "the strong could resolve to serve the weak, and the people to purchase an idea of repose at the price of real felicity" (*Discourses*, 131). The decision to delegate the natural care of a child to a stranger dissolves the bonds of the family. "Prudent husbands, paternal love must be immolated for the sake of peace; and you are fortunate that women more continent than yours can be found in the country, more fortunate yet if the time your wives save is not destined for others than you!" (*Emile*, 45). Not only does a father forfeit his relationship to his child, but he also forfeits his wife's fidelity.

The continual seeking of pleasure and the attempt to satisfy grotesque, unnatural passions take its toll on the individual, marriage, and also the political community. Rousseau fears that these fractional creatures will eventually stop having babies.

> As soon as the condition of motherhood becomes burdensome, the means to deliver oneself from it completely is soon found. They want to perform a useless act so as always to be able to start over again, and they turn to the prejudice of the species the attraction given for the sake of multiplying it. This practice, added to the other causes of depopulation,

presages the impending fate of Europe. The sciences, the arts, the philosophy, and the morals that this practice engenders will not be long in making a desert of it. It will be peopled with ferocious beasts. The change of inhabitants will not be great. (*Emile*, 44–45)

Abstracting what is natural to the sex (in this case, the natural duties of motherhood) from the individual does not create the general idea of the human being. Instead, it creates beasts that no longer resembles the human at all.[15]

Breastfeeding one's own child holds great promise for Rousseau. He allows us to glimpse the salutary effects it has on the mother, her marriage, and for the larger political community. The mother, who breastfeeds her child fulfills her natural duty and enjoys contentment, which is unknown to the fractious, pleasure seeking women Rousseau sees in eighteenth century France. Rousseau goes on to promise that the marriage and family of the mother, who breastfeeds, will be improved. Breastfeeding, and the subsequent care of children begins as a duty assigned to a woman by nature, but it turns out to be her source of happiness. It also appears to fortify the marriage bond and protect it from infidelity, which results from the attempt of a woman to satisfy her vanity. "When the family is lively and animated, the domestic cares constitute the dearest occupation of the wife and the sweetest enjoyment of the husband. Thus, from the correction of this single abuse would soon result the general reform; nature would soon have reclaimed its rights. Let women once again become mothers, men will soon become fathers and husbands again" (*Emile*, 46).

Rousseau does not stop there. He implicitly promises his readers that breastfeeding will restore the political community, as well as the individual and marriage. Breastfeeding creates certain affection between woman and child. Although the corrupted women of Rousseau's day do not want to trouble themselves with the care of their children, they do not want their children's affection to go to another. And, so, the wet nurse is sent away from the child just as soon as her services are no longer needed and the vicious mother "inspire[s] contempt in the children for their nurses by treating them as veritable servants" (*Emile*, 45). The trouble is the mother is unable to replace the wet nurse. Rousseau observes the worst possible outcome. "The mother who believes she replaces the nurse and makes up for her neglect by her cruelty is mistaken. Instead of making a tender son out of a denatured nursling, she trains him in ingratitude, she teaches him one day to despise her who gave him life, as well as her who nursed him with her milk" (*Emile*, 45). Feeling no obligation to the woman who gave him birth or to the woman, who nourished him with her milk, the child will not learn to feel any bond to other human beings. "Everything follows from this depravity [a mother's refusal to breastfeed]. The whole moral order degenerates" (*Emile*, 46). We may infer then, that if mothers were to breastfeed their children, the degeneration of the moral order would not occur. Children would learn the proper respect and affection for their mothers, their fathers, and their siblings, which would prepare them for their relationship to other citizens

Like Rousseau, Wollstonecraft begins her treatise by indicting the French and in particular French women. In her dedicatory letter to Talleyrand-Perigord, Wollstonecraft regrets he did not include women in his plan for public education. In the wake of the French Revolution, which many believed would be the triumph of equality for all human beings, women remained subject to the same old hierarchies. Wollstonecraft bemoans the corruption of French morals and attributes it to the continued inequality between men and women. Much to the reader's surprise, Wollstonecraft begins her radical work on the rights of women by encouraging their traditional roles. Wollstonecraft suggests that improved character of wives and mothers will benefit the political community (*VRW*, 4). Throughout her treatise on the equality of women, Wollstonecraft returns again and again to the differentiation between the sexes and, in particular, to the importance of motherhood. "The care of children in their infancy is one of the grand duties annexed to the female character by nature" (*VRW*, 151). Yet, this natural duty is not so compelling that it will be sustained under corrupt circumstances. Rather than caring for their children as nature would dictate, fractional mothers bend to social conventions. In the eighteenth century, this means giving preference to the first born son, the presumed heir, and often neglecting daughters and younger sons.

> Woman, however, a slave in every situation to prejudice, seldom exerts enlightened maternal affection; for she either neglects her children, or spoils them by improper indulgence . . . Justice, truth, everything is sacrificed by these Rebekah's, and for the sake of their *own* children they violate the most sacred duties, forgetting the common relationship that binds the whole family on earth together. (*VRW*, 151)

The fractional, weak mother who cares only for her own social position is grossly unnatural. She is unable to raise healthy virtuous children.

"But the nature of the poison points out the antidote" (*VRW*, 19). Wollstonecraft joins Rousseau in suggesting a seemingly simple solution. Mothers should breastfeed their children. Not only will breastfeeding serve to excite a mother's natural affection for all of her children (rather than the over indulgent attention to the presumed heir), but it will also encourage greater affection between husband and wife.

> After having been fatigued with the sight of insipid grandeur and the slavish ceremonies that with cumberous [sic] pomp supplied the place of domestic affections, I have turned to some other scene to relieve my eye by resting it on the refreshing green every where scattered by nature. I have viewed with pleasure a woman nursing her children . . . I have seen her prepare herself and her children, with only the luxury of cleanliness, to receive her husband, who returning weary home in the evening found smiling babes and a clean hearth. (*VRW*, 142)

Though *A Vindication of the Rights of Woman* is often cited as Wollstonecraft's departure from the tenets of Romanticism and the works of Rousseau, Wollstonecraft depends on the feelings of husband and wife to restore the integrity of the individual, the family, and, as a consequence, the political community. The "delight at seeing his child suckled by its mother" is "the natural way of cementing the matrimonial tie" (*VRW*, 142). The alleged convert to the faith of reason is unabashed in telling her readers that her "heart has loitered in the midst of the group, and has even throbbed with sympathetic emotion" (*VRW*, 142–143). The scene Wollstonecraft describes is "the happiest as well as the most respectable situation" (*VRW*, 143).

While Wollstonecraft agrees with Rousseau that the corruption of eighteenth century Europe may be abated by respecting the distinctive traits of women, we begin to see that Wollstonecraft goes beyond Rousseau. Rousseau is confident that if mothers would return to their natural duties, fathers would match their concern for their children. Although Rousseau maintains that the prejudices and practices of his day corrupt men and women alike, from Wollstonecraft's perspective, he places too much responsibility for change on the women. Wollstonecraft holds men, as well as women, responsible for moral change. Because social convention has designated women responsible for sexual propriety, men have been given license to concern themselves only with pleasure. From Wollstonecraft's point of view, they have taken advantage of this license and have neglected their families.

> But 'til men become attentive to the duty of a father, it is vain to expect women to spend that time in their nursery which they "wise in their generation" choose to spend at their glass; for this exertion of cunning is only an instinct of nature to enable them to obtain indirectly a little of that power of which they are unjustly denied a share: for, if women are

not permitted to enjoy legitimate rights, they will render both men and themselves vicious, to obtain illicit privileges. (*VRW*, 6)

Women, financially and emotionally dependent on their husbands, care only for pleasing them.

Men are not aware of the misery they cause, and the vicious weakness they cherish, by only inciting women to render themselves pleasing; they do not consider that they thus make natural and artificial duties clash, by sacrificing the comfort and the respectability of a woman's life to voluptuous notions of beauty, when in nature they all harmonize. (*VRW*, 142)

Divided between her socially determined inclinations for pleasing her husband (and, therefore, the fleeting satisfaction of her *amour propre*) and the natural inclination that is distinctive to her sex, woman is deformed. Rather than the Utopian dream, the chimera that Wollstonecraft pursues, woman appears as a chimera in the mythological sense: she is comprised of two incompatible parts, which do not fit together by nature.

In a similar vein to Rousseau, Wollstonecraft notices that the lack of maternal affection will have negative effects on society as well as on the individual and the family. In fact, it reduces mankind to the condition of animals. "The want of natural affection, in many women, who are drawn from their duty by the admiration of men, and the ignorance of others, render the infancy of man a much more perilous state than that of the brutes" (*VRW*, 177). Again, Wollstonecraft's concern is not simply a philosophical one, but also, above all, a real concern for the viability of the species. Indeed, these concerns are linked. "In public schools women, to guard against errors of ignorance, should be taught the elements of anatomy and medicine, not only to enable them to take proper care of their health, but to make them rational nurses of their infants, parents, and husbands; for the bills of mortality are swelled by the blunders of self-willed old women" (*VRW*, 177).

While breastfeeding is a good start to the care of children, raising healthy children and preserving strong families require that women foster their initial maternal instincts and supplement these maternal instincts with human reason. We can begin to identify a fundamental difference in the disposition of Rousseau and Wollstonecraft to nature. Rousseau's understanding of nature depends on human beings' beginnings. In his initial discussion of the importance of motherhood in Book I of the *Emile*, Rousseau is content with the natural inclinations of women to breastfeed and places his hopes for reform in these simple passions. Wollstonecraft, on the other hand, believes the cultivation of woman's initial maternal stirrings will encourage women to develop their rational faculties. It is only through woman's natural capacity to reason and by applying reason to the care of her family that woman is able to find fulfillment in motherhood. This suggests that Wollstonecraft, in contrast to Rousseau, takes her bearings from a human being's end or perfection. If so, Wollstonecraft will have a much different understanding of human nature and the political community than Rousseau.

Although Rousseau's initial consideration of motherhood relies on the simplest passions, in Book V of the *Emile* Rousseau does suggest that Sophie requires practical reasoning in order to be a compatible companion to Emile. Sophie's ability to distinguish the relative merits of various opinions will contribute to the happiness of the married couple as the family as a whole. In order to appreciate the difference between Rousseau's conception of a woman's capacity to reason and Wollstonecraft's understanding, it is helpful to consider to what end each thinker attributes rationality to women. Rousseau insists Sophie's reasoning is for the sake of others. "A man from the first of these two classes [a man who thinks] ought not to make an alliance in the other [the class of people who do not think], for the greatest charm of society is lacking to him when despite having a wife, he is reduced to thinking alone" (*Emile*, 408). Although Sophie's life is made more pleasant by her ability to reason, Sophie's cultivation of her rationality serves what is good for Emile. After all, "It is not good for man to be alone . . . We have promised [Emile] a companion. She must be given to him" (*Emile*, 357). Not only is a rational woman good for the man who thinks, but it is good for the children of such a couple. "Besides, how will a woman who has no habit of reflecting raise her children? . . . How will she incline them toward virtues she does not know?" (*Emile*, 409, *VRW*, 88). Again, Sophie's capacity for reason is for the sake of others and not for the sake of her own completion.[16] This does not escape Wollstonecraft's notice. Responding directly to this passage from the *Emile*, Wollstonecraft reminds her readers that Sophie's practical reasoning is meant for finding means to an end, but not contemplating the end itself. It is necessarily incomplete and is dependent on Emile's more philosophical reasoning (*Emile*, 377). She is not convinced that Sophie's reasoning will benefit herself or her children. Wollstonecraft considers this "a direct and exclusive appropriation of reason . . . leaving woman in a state of the most profound ignorance" (*VRW*, 87). Wollstonecraft acknowledges no difference between Sophie and Emile—the couple who is Rousseau's hope for political reform— and the fractured, eighteenth-century couples she condemns.

How indeed should she [make her children "sensible and amiable"], when her husband is not always at hand to lend her his reason?—when they both together make but one moral being . . . and perchance his abstract reason, that should concentrate the scattered beams of her practical reason, may be employed in judging of the flavor of wine, descanting on the sauces most proper for turtle; or more profoundly intent at a card-table, he may be generalizing his ideas as bets away his fortune, leaving all the minutiae of education to his helpmate, or to chance. (*VRW*, 89)

Together Sophie and Emile comprise one moral being. Rousseau intends them to be utopian visions, but to Wollstonecraft they appear to be half-beings who are comprised of the parts from two creatures, but do not make a natural whole. "For surely [Rousseau] speaks to the heart" (Wardle, 131) and Wollstonecraft appreciates his efforts to express women's longings for ideal love and domestic felicity. However, Wollstonecraft will not sacrifice woman's wholeness for the sake of Sophie's domestic happiness as it is offered by Rousseau. For Wollstonecraft, woman must be allowed to develop the full use of her reason. It completes her as an individual. Because motherhood is an occasion for rational activity, motherhood contributes to the wholeness of the woman.

Wollstonecraft is sincere in her hope that women will find greater happiness in motherhood and marriage. She is also hopeful that domestic felicity will go a long way to improving the political community. Yet, Wollstonecraft knows that the wholeness of the individual, as well as the health of the political community, cannot be restored by simply fostering one half of the being, the sex. "And whilst women are educated to rely on their husbands for judgment, this [womanish follies] must ever be the consequence, for there is no improving an understanding by halves, nor can any being act wisely from imitation" (*VRW*, 177). Wollstonecraft appreciates that care must be given to that part of woman, which is human. For Wollstonecraft, like Rousseau, the human is dignified by a freedom from social prejudices and the opinion of others. And, so Wollstonecraft is willing to follow Rousseau farther into "the land of chimeras" in her effort to restore the unity or the wholeness, which women lack.

II. UNNATURAL DISTINCTIONS

Rousseau educates Emile with the intention of preserving his numerical unity, his independence from the opinion of others. Rousseau has been at

great pains to ensure that Emile is able to satisfy his (relatively few) desires by
his own power. As Emile becomes a young man, Rousseau further prepares
Emile to live among other human beings. Despite Rousseau's apparently
nostalgic longing for the state of nature, Emile lives in eighteenth century
society and Rousseau recognizes the impossibility of returning to the pure
state of nature. "A man who wanted to regard himself as an isolated being,
not depending at all on anything and sufficient unto himself, could only be
miserable . . . Finding the whole earth covered with thine and mine and
having nothing belonging to him except his body, where would he get his
necessities? By leaving the state of nature, we force our fellows to leave it,
too" (*Emile*, 193).

Rousseau's challenge is to preserve Emile's independence from others
as Emile forms relations with a greater number of people. To this end, Rousseau insists Emile learn a trade. It is in his discussion of the importance of
learning a trade that Rousseau levels his most damning political criticism
against his contemporaries. Though Emile may be of "common genius," he
is not of common wealth and, therefore, he is expected to enjoy a genteel
leisure. Rousseau anticipates and responds to the protests of the aristocracy.
Over and over again, Rousseau justifies a trade for the young aristocrat by
promising it will protect him from the reversal of fortune. In this respect,
Rousseau takes advantage of his contemporaries' social vanities and their fear
of suffering. However, Rousseau offers other reasons for learning a trade. The
arguments Rousseau puts forth follow Rousseau's egalitarian, social contract
theory of the political community, beginning with the state of nature.

The first reason that Emile must learn a trade is the simple need for
self-preservation. Self-preservation is the first law of nature (*Emile*, 193 and
the *Discourses*, 127). All human beings are equal in their concern for it and
their right to ensure it. Up until this point in Emile's education, Rousseau
has been careful not to make a distinction of social rank to Emile. Rousseau
will be faithful to this practice in teaching Emile a trade. He gives as his reason that

> man is the same in all stations; the rich man does not have a bigger
> stomach than the poor one . . . a man of great family is no greater
> than a man of the people; and finally, as the natural needs are every-
> where the same, the means of providing for them ought to be equal
> everywhere. (*Emile*, 194)

Practicing a trade is one way by which Emile can feed himself. However,
Rousseau knows that in the decaying gentry of eighteenth-century France,

material needs are more easily obtained by using other human beings to one's own advantage, by being "pliable and groveling with rascals" (*Emile*, 197). In this regard, readers of both the *Emile* and the *Second Discourse* may notice a parallel between the most precarious stage of the state of nature and the conditions of the eighteenth century France, verging on revolution. Rousseau describes the condition of man in the last epoch of the state of nature. Living among other human beings has multiplied and amplified the desires of man. Despite the varying degrees of wealth, all human beings find themselves grossly dependent on others: "rich, he needs their services; poor, he needs their help, and moderate means do not enable him to do without them. He must therefore constantly try to interest them in his fate and to make them really or apparently find their own profit in working for his" (*Discourses*, 170). Like the corrupted civil man, the Savage in the last epoch of the state of nature will humiliate himself to satisfy his needs. Man's constant attempt to force others to work for his own interest "makes him knavish and artful with some, imperious and harsh with the rest" (*Discourses*, 170). Eventually, the savages in the last epoch of the state of nature will harm others in an attempt to satisfy their desires and the social contract must be instituted.

Civil man, most particularly the aristocratic and the bourgeois man, of the eighteenth century is in the same predicament as the Savage in the last stage of the state of nature. Civil man has numerous desires, which seem to multiply with his wealth. He becomes more and more dependent on others to satisfy these desires. So, his wealth serves to degrade and weaken man. Rousseau admonishes his contemporaries for feeling invulnerable to the coming revolution.

> You trust in the present order of society without thinking that this order is subject to inevitable revolutions . . . Who can answer for what will become of you then? All that men have made, men can destroy. The only ineffaceable characters are those printed by nature; and nature does not make princes, rich men, or great lords. (*Emile*, 194)

Far from being protected from the revolution by their wealth and power, the aristocracy is the most vulnerable. "That vanquished king who, full of rage, wants to be buried under the debris of his throne may be praised as much as one pleases; I despise him. I see that he exists only by his crown, and that he is nothing at all if he is not a king" (*Emile*, 194). To those who consider themselves empowered by their social rank and hereditary power, Rousseau asks, "How will you despise the baseness and the vices which you need to subsist? You depended only on riches, and now you depend on the rich. You have only worsened your slavery and added your poverty on top of it. Now you are poor without being free" (*Emile*, 197). Rousseau distinguishes between the man who has recourse to a trade and the rascal who lives at the expense of others.

> You no longer need to be a coward and a liar with the nobles, pliable and groveling with rascals, basely obliging to everyone, a borrower or a thief . . . The opinion of others does not touch you. You do not have to pay court to anyone; no fool to flatter . . . That rogues have the conduct of great affairs is of little importance to you. (*Emile*, 197)

The reversal of fortune, in the extreme case of revolution, or even the threat of a reversal renders a man weak and dependent. As we will soon see, Rousseau identifies a dependence on public opinion with effeminacy.

On the verge of a new civil society, Rousseau promises freedom and independence to those who will minimize their desires and provide for them with their own labor. It is a promise that he makes to the Savage entering the social contract, as well as the civil man of his own time. Stripped of their claims to material wealth, a man enters civil society. "A man and a citizen, whoever he may be, has no property to put into society than himself" (*Emile*, 195). This is also true of Emile, who is entering the already formed civil society. Rousseau knows that Emile will claim the wealth that his father has already acquired and Rousseau is quick to disregard it.

> You owe others more than if you were born without property since you were favored at birth. It is not just that what one man has done for society should relieve another for what he owes it; for each, owing himself wholly can pay for himself and no father can transmit to his son the right to be useless to his fellows. (*Emile*, 195)

To live by the riches of another is to diminish that other person's means of self preservation and degrade oneself. If equality is to be maintained in civil society, all men must work for their own self-preservation and respect that right of others. "To work is therefore an indispensable duty for social man. Rich or poor, powerful or weak, every idle citizen is a rascal" (*Emile*, 195).

Throughout the *Vindication*, Wollstonecraft joins Rousseau in his condemnation of the eighteenth-century aristocracy. Wollstonecraft appreciates the political lessons taught by Rousseau in the *Emile:* artificial power serves to weaken men rather than to strengthen them.

> Birth, riches and every extrinsic advantage that exalt a man above his fellows, without any mental exertion, sink him in reality below them. In proportion to his weakness, he is played upon by designing men, till the bloated monster has lost all traces of humanity. (*VRW*, 45)

Seeking a chimera, a fanciful, utopian vision of human beings, Wollstonecraft meets instead with chimeras in the mythological sense, fractional creatures that do not exist by nature. Wollstonecraft shares Rousseau's fear that human beings have been so degraded by their eighteenth-century civilization that they are unable to restore their natural dignity. "Educated in slavish dependence, and enervated by luxury and sloth, where shall we find men who will stand forth to assert the rights of man; or claim the privilege of moral beings, who should have but one road to excellence?" (*VRW*, 45)

Wollstonecraft's reproach of eighteenth-century society does not end with the decrepit male aristocracy. She explicitly compares women to the aristocracy and condemns them as well. Wollstonecraft turns to Rousseau's critique of aristocracy and the solution he outlines for Emile as a guide for the women of her day. "Consequently, the most perfect education, in my opinion, is such an exercise of the understanding as is best calculated to strengthen the body and form the heart . . . This was Rousseau's opinion respecting men: I extend it to women" (*VRW*, 21).[17] In putting forth this solution for women, Wollstonecraft faces the same difficulties from women as Rousseau anticipates when insisting Emile learn a trade. Women enjoy their power, however degrading it may be.

> Still the regal homage which they receive is so intoxicating . . . it may be impossible to convince them that the illegitimate power, which they obtain, by degrading themselves, is a curse, and that they must return to nature and equality, if they wish to secure the placid satisfaction that unsophisticated affections impart. (*VRW*, 21–22)

Despite women's dependence on the good esteem of their husbands, Wollstonecraft appreciates that women of her day have been educated to see their weakness as a source of power. "Taught from infancy that beauty is woman's scepter, the mind shapes itself to the body, and roaming round its gilt cage, seeks only to adorn its prison" (*VRW*, 44).

Wollstonecraft has been attentive to the tutor Rousseau and learns her lesson well. Rousseau issues parents the difficult task of caring for their children without turning them into little tyrants. Parents must be on guard immediately upon the birth of their child. Because the infant cannot satisfy his desires, he cries. "From these tears we might think so little worthy of attention is born man's first relation to all that surrounds him; here is formed the first link in that long chain of which the social order is formed" (*Emile*, 65). As the child gets older, Rousseau suggests never allowing a child to give orders. "But if he is allowed to give orders to adults, the child will feel 'how pleasant it is to act with the hands of others and to need only to stir [his tongue] to make the universe move' (p. 68)."[18] Women, who Rousseau suggests remain children (*Emile*, 211), are also weak and, as Wollstonecraft constantly points out, enjoy acting with the hands of others. The fractional, weak character of eighteenth-century men gives women power over men.

> Women, it is true, obtaining power by unjust means, by practicing or fostering vice, evidently lose the rank which reason would assign them, and they become either abject slaves or capricious tyrants. They lose all simplicity, all dignity of mind, in acquiring power, and act as men are observed to act when they have been exalted by the same means. (*VRW*, 45)

Again, Wollstonecraft describes the women of her day in chimerical, monstrous terms. Concerned only with her beauty, women seem part human being and part exotic bird.

> And, why do they not discover, when "in the noon of beauty's power," that they are treated like queens only to be deluded by hollow respect, till they are led to resign, or not assume, their natural prerogatives? Confined then in cages like the feathered race, they have nothing to do but to plume themselves, and stalk with mock majesty from perch to perch. It is true that they are provided with food and raiment, for which they neither toil nor spin; but health, liberty, and virtue, are given in exchange. (*VRW*, 55–57)

Just as Rousseau recognizes the decline of Europe's aristocracies and anticipates their inevitable demise, Wollstonecraft knows the woman who reigns by her beauty is also vulnerable to a reversal of fortunes. And, like Rousseau, she wonders what type of woman will replace the feathered creatures. "But, where amongst mankind, has been found sufficient strength of mind to enable a being to resign these adventitious prerogatives; one who, rising with the calm dignity of reason above opinion, dared to be proud of the privileges inherent in man?" (*VRW*, 56).

"It is time to effect a revolution in female manners—time to restore to them their lost dignity—and make them, as part of the human species, labour by reforming themselves to reform the world" (*VRW*, 45). Wollstonecraft appreciates that the fate of humanity depends on liberating men and women from their passions that enslaves them to others. Their constant attempt to satisfy their vanity, or to use Rousseau's word, *amour propre*, has made men and, particularly, women vicious, fractional creatures. Wollstonecraft regrets that women, unlike men, have nothing to do, but seek pleasure.

> Men have various employments and pursuits which engage their attention, and give a character to the opening of the mind; but women, confined to one, and having their thoughts constantly directed to the most insignificant parts of themselves, seldom extend their views beyond the triumph of the hour. (*VRW*, 44)

In a similar vein to Rousseau's project of educating a strong and whole, independent, natural man, Wollstonecraft is confident that woman can also be revitalized. "But were the understanding once emancipated from the slavery to which the pride and sensuality of man and their short-sighted desire, like that of the dominion in tyrants, of present sway, has subjected them, we should probably read of their weakness with surprise" (*VRW*, 44).

In her attempt to apply Rousseau's education for Emile to the women of her day, Wollstonecraft adopts Rousseau's suggestion that Emile learn a trade. Just as Emile is to liberate himself from social prejudices, Wollstonecraft expects that women will liberate themselves from their husbands and their own vanity through occupation. Rather than expecting women to "loiter with easy grace" throughout the long day, Wollstonecraft suggests that "[W]omen might certainly study the art of healing, and be physicians as well as nurses" (*VRW*, 147–148). She goes on to suggest that women may even pursue occupation in politics and business. She is primarily concerned with saving women from both "common and legal prostitution" (*VRW*, 148). Were women able to support themselves, they

> would not marry for support, as men accept places under government, and neglect the implied duties; nor would an attempt to earn their

subsistence, a most laudable one! sink them almost to the level of those poor abandoned creatures who live by prostitution. For are not milliners and mantua-makers reckoned the next class? (*VRW*, 148)

In advocating women's employment, Wollstonecraft hopes to free them from their constant concern for the opinions of others, in particular those of their husbands, and foster an independent, whole person.

It is worth stopping to consider whether or not Wollstonecraft would consider managing a household and caring for children suitable occupation for women. As I have already demonstrated, Wollstonecraft has a true appreciation for marriage and motherhood. By adhering to the natural duty of women to care for their infants, women develop a concern for their children and other members of society. By turning their attention away from themselves, women keep a check on their social passions. In the simplest terms, motherhood gives women something else to do than vainly soliciting the fawning attention of their all too often indifferent husbands. For this reason alone, motherhood can be understood to be noble occupation. In addition to keeping in check women's social passions, Wollstonecraft understands motherhood as an opportunity to develop what is natural, but unique to human beings: reason. Mothers, indeed fathers, may feel a primal love for their children. For Wollstonecraft, these emotions are simply not enough. The tasks of caring for one's family require the guidance of reason and scientific investigation. In this way, women are able to develop their own reason. Under the right conditions, the family has great potential to restore humanity.

However, wives and mothers are unable to exert a positive influence if they are weak and fractional creatures, consumed by their passions and constantly trying to please. Depending on another person for subsistence encourages this character. As we will see in the last chapter of this book, this is reason enough for Wollstonecraft to argue for married women's employment. There is further reason for Wollstonecraft to advocate that women seek employment, one less philosophical and more practical. Wollstonecraft knows, even in the eighteenth century, that women cannot count on marriage. Unmarried women, either spinsters or widows, were left to the mercy of other men, most likely brothers. Wollstonecraft describes this as an "equivocal and humiliating situation" and the problem continuously emerges throughout her treatise on women's rights (*VRW*, 48, 65, 148). This is an important difference between Rousseau and Wollstonecraft. To be sure, Rousseau's political reform depends on the improved character of women. However, Rousseau places his hopes for reform in the marriages they will make. Indeed, we only know Sophie through her relationship to Emile and it is difficult to imagine her without Emile. Wollstonecraft also appreciates the importance of the virtue of women in political reform. However, she expects that they will contribute to their communities as individuals as well as wives and mothers.

Wollstonecraft has followed Rousseau into "the land of chimeras." Wollstonecraft recognizes that we are born twice: once for the species and once for our sex. A whole individual, as well as a strong political community, depends on the proper combination of these two halves. If one half or the other is perverted by its passions, the individual becomes less than human and the political community is populated by beasts. Wollstonecraft, along with Rousseau, encourages the natural affection women have for their children. Sacrificing women's conventional pleasures for the sake of their children is sure to bring about a healthier individual and society. In addition to this Wollstonecraft imitates Rousseau's lessons for Emile and suggests that women find means to support themselves, liberating themselves from the esteem of others. As we further consider Rousseau's prescriptions for Emile's trade, it begins to look as if Wollstonecraft can proceed no farther into Rousseau's land of chimeras.

Not just any trade will do for Emile. The trade that Emile chooses must foster his numerical unity. Rousseau immediately rules out the possibility of Emile becoming an embroiderer, a gilder, or a varnisher, like Locke's pupil (*Emile*, 197). Emile's trade "must not demand from those practicing it qualities of soul that are odious and incompatible with humanity . . . But let us always remember that there is no decency without utility" (*Emile*, 197). Anticipating the corrupted responses of his eighteenth century readers, Rousseau is strict in his definition of utility. He excludes the possibility of "professions that are idle, futile, or subject to fashion, such as a that of a wigmaker, which is never necessary and can become useless from one day to the next, so long as nature does not cease providing us with hair" (*Emile*, 198). There is one principle by which to judge the utility of Emile's trade. "He has to have a trade that could serve Robinson Crusoe on his island" (*Emile*, 198).

Rousseau places what, at first, seems to be a further demand on Emile's trade. Not only must Emile choose a trade which is compatible with humanity, he must choose a trade which is compatible with his sex.

> Give a man a trade which suits his sex . . . Every sedentary and indoor profession which effeminates and softens the body neither pleases nor suits him. Never did a young boy by himself aspire to be a tailor. Art is required to bring to this woman's trade the sex for which it is not made.

The needle and the sword cannot be wielded by the same hands. (*Emile*, 199)

As it turns out, the trades which are incompatible with humanity are the same as the trades, which are incompatible with Emile's sex: the embroiderer, the wigmaker, the tailor. These trades are all subject to fashion.

Rousseau briefly considers the trade of farmer for Emile, but he rejects it on the ground that the farmer is more dependent on fortune and men than the artisan. The latter "is as free as the farmer is slave. [The farmer] is dependent on his field, whose harvest is at another's discretion. The enemy, the prince, a powerful neighbor, or a lawsuit can take his field away from him" (*Emile*, 195). It is decided that Emile is to be a carpenter instead. It is important to note that at this point, Emile's development differs quite radically from the Savage. The Savage experiences a second revolution, which Emile, does not (not yet, at least). "Metallurgy and agriculture were the two arts the invention of which brought about this great revolution. For the Poet it is gold and silver, but for the Philosopher it is iron and wheat that civilized men, and ruined Mankind" (*Discourses*, 168). Thanks to Rousseau's decision that Emile is to be a carpenter, Emile is protected from further, devastating corruption.[19]

Rousseau's plan to preserve Emile's wholeness, his independence from the opinion of others, seems to work. Sophie and her mother visit Emile at the carpentry shop where he is employed and they ask Emile to leave with them. Emile refuses based on the commitment he made to the older carpenter. If he were to leave work, his master's livelihood would be at risk. Breaking his promise to his master would violate the fundamental law of nature: each individual has a right to self-preservation. Sophie's mother suggests that Emile use some of his inherited wealth to compensate Emile's master for the work would leave unfinished. "Doesn't this young man, who is so prodigal and who pours out money without necessity, any longer know how to find money on suitable occasions?" (*Emile*, 438). Even if her mother does not, Sophie appreciates that use his wealth in order to avoid honest labor would "enslave his soul to riches; Emile would accustom himself to putting his riches in the place of his duties and to believing that one is excused from everything provided one pays" (*Emile*, 438). Just as Rousseau predicts, Emile's trade protects his wholeness, his numerical unity. He does not submit to the will of another nor does he depend on his riches.

It is worth returning to and emphasizing the implication that the activities Rousseau deems appropriate for women are those, which are subject to fashion, such as the tailor.[20] It is not entirely clear how Rousseau imagines that Sophie will avoid corruption, for these are the trades that he has called "odious and incompatible with humanity" (*Emile*, 197). Of course, Sophie engages in them for her own pleasure and not for financial profit, and so the possibility of her becoming, as a result, dependent on the whims of others is diminished. Still, Sophie's occupation, her sewing and embroidery, is not one that Rousseau would permit Emile. Wollstonestract, who agrees with Rousseau about the dangers associated with these occupations (even suggesting that hatmakers and dressmakers are just barely more respectable than prostitutes! [*VRW*, 148]), rejects them for women as well as men. Rousseau, on the other hand, not only permits these activities to women, but he also suggests that women are better suited for the activities, which are odious to humanity. Rousseau offers his readers an example of women's inability to perform those trades that are compatible with humanity. While visiting Emile at the carpentry shop, Sophie takes an interest in Emile's work. "The silly girl even tries to imitate Emile. With her frail white hand she pushes a plane along a plank. The plane slides and does not bite" (*Emile*, 438). Sophie, who "ought to be a woman as Emile is a man—that is say, she ought to have everything which suits the constitution of her species and her sex in order to fill her place in the physical and moral order" (*Emile*, 357), is unable to perform the trade which preserves Emile's wholeness.[21] At the very least, this suggests that the wholeness or the unity which is forged by combining the species and the female sex cannot be formed in the same manner as the wholeness comprised of the species and the male sex.

Wollstonecraft appreciates that Rousseau's prescription for wives and mothers are a strong palliative for the fractured, corrupt women of the eighteenth century. Yet, Wollstonecraft also knows what Rousseau recognizes as well, being unable to provide for oneself, being dependent on another or on public opinion is humiliating and degrading. In designating to women the trades, which are subject to fashion, Rousseau suggests women are unable to achieve the same numerical unity that Rousseau prescribes for Emile. In order to determine, how and if numerical unity is forged for the female, it is necessary to turn to Rousseau's treatment of women in the *Emile* and in the state of nature. Furthermore, Rousseau insists that Emile learn a trade in order to protect himself from certain social revolution. Emile's trade allows Emile to live in a more egalitarian social order, based on natural rights, rather than conventional hierarchies. Rousseau seems to exclude women from this regime. Rousseau's treatment of Sophie is disappointing to Wollstonecraft, for it reveals a fundamental problem in Rousseau's egalitarian philosophy of *The Discourse on Inequality* and *The Social Contract*.

Chapter Two

Rousseau's Half-Being

Rousseau's project to educate Emile to be a natural man—a numerical unity— promises to free him from the opinion of others. While numerical unity is certainly good for the individual, we have also seen its benefit to the family and to the political community. Wealth and beauty simply mask the fractional creatures, which populate the aristocracies of the eighteenth century. Those, like Emile, who enjoy numerical unity and preserve it by limiting their desires and by satisfying those desires through their own efforts, will find themselves independent of others and free. They are the promise of Rousseau's egalitarian political community, founded on his natural rights theory.

Wollstonecraft, as we have seen, adopts Rousseau's project and hopes to educate women to numerical unity or wholeness. She shares Rousseau's hopes that whole human beings will restore the political community. I have attempted to demonstrate that Wollstonecraft heeds Rousseau's teaching on the complexity of wholeness. It is comprised of the species and the sex. Indeed, Rousseau imparts an important lesson to Wollstonecraft on the education of the sexes. An individual's sex is the source of his or her attachment to others and, therefore, the source of his or her social passions. Rousseau and Wollstonecraft appreciate the ability of the sex to bring the individual outside of him or herself. Therefore, the political community depends on the character of the relationship between the sexes. This half of our being is more complex and requires protection from fracture. Like Rousseau, Wollstonecraft's ideas for political reform depend on domestic felicity and self-fulfilling motherhood. However, our sex is but one half of our being. Numerical unity or wholeness requires that the species or the human half of Rousseau's chimera be properly educated as well. Otherwise, his utopian vision is likely to turn into a chimera in the mythological sense, an ugly, vicious creature comprised of incongruous parts, which do not make a natural whole. Following

Rousseau into the land of chimeras, Wollstonecraft is disappointed by the woman she finds there. Rousseau has not afforded Sophie the same whole-ness that he has bestowed on Emile through his education. Quite the con-trary, it seems to Wollstonecraft that Rousseau denies women the possibility to "acquire human virtues (or perfections) by the *same* means as men, instead of being educated like a fanciful kind of *half* being—one of Rousseau's wild chimeras" (*VRW*, 39, Wollstonecraft's emphasis).

Echoing Rousseau's critique of the aristocracy, Wollstonecraft con-demns the "unnatural distinctions" and the "hereditary honors," which make "cyphers" of women (*VRW*, 24). Wollstonecraft tells her readers that those who encourage women's pleasing feminine graces under the pretense of hon-oring them actually foster the fractional character of women.

> I now principally allude to Rousseau, for his character of Sophia is, undoubtedly, a captivating one, though it appears to me grossly unnat-ural; however it is not the superstructure, but the foundation of her character, the principles on which her education was built, that I mean to attack; nay, warmly as I admire the genius of that able writer, whose opinions I shall often have occasion to cite. (*VRW*, 24)

Following Rousseau into the land of chimeras Wollstonecraft has misjudged the possibility that Rousseau's egalitarian political philosophy is able to pro-vide a framework for the independence or wholeness of women. Rousseau affords Sophie an education, which forms only one half of her being, the sex. Rousseau insists that Sophie, in particular and women more generally, should make themselves pleasing to men. This means manipulating male pride and exploiting woman's relative physical weakness, which Wollstone-craft finds degrading to women. In a rather lengthy footnote to this passage, Wollstonecraft quotes Rousseau's *Emile*, faithfully, I might add (*Emile*, 387). She objects to Rousseau's teaching that women's relative weakness renders them dependent on men. This dependency forces women to "base their exis-tence on the judgments of others" (*Emile*, 215). In this respect, Rousseau encourages woman's fractional character.

Some scholars have commented on Wollstonecraft's disappointment with Rousseau's understanding of women, arguing that it points to an incon-sistency between the *Emile* and his explicitly political works, *The Discourse on Inequality* (the so called *Second Discourse*) and the *Social Contract.* Clau-dia Johnson suggests that Wollstonecraft's vehement objection to Rousseau's character of Sophie is based on his appropriation of the courtly woman into bourgeois culture.[1] Johnson understands Wollstonecraft's "scorn" toward

Rousseau to be an appropriate response to such an inconsistency in Rousseau's political philosophy.

> Rousseau's commitment to a voluptuous "male aristocracy" (*VRW*, 87) in the private sphere seems so maddeningly inconsistent with the "manly" inservility she is glad to admire elsewhere in his work that he stands as an object lesson in danger of trying to abolish the tyranny of rank without sweeping away the tyranny of sex along with it. (Johnson, 32)

Johnson is not alone in this presumption. Trouille also credits Wollstonecraft with identifying "the contradictions between the egalitarian philosophy elaborated by Rousseau in the *Social Contract* and the *Discourse on Inequality* and the unequal, oppressed status of women that he defends and attempts to justify, even idealize, in *Emile*" (Trouille, 224). Although Rousseau devotes significant attention to women in the *Second Discourse*, neither Johnson nor Trouille pause to consider how Rousseau's natural rights theory informs his conception of Sophie. I shall argue that Wollstonecraft must reject Rousseau's character of Sophie, not because Sophie is inconsistent with the "egalitarian" principles of Rousseau's explicitly political writings, but rather because Sophie is consistent with the "egalitarian" principles of the *Second Discourse*. Upon closer consideration, we will see that Sophie is consistent with the female Savage in the state of nature. Despite Rousseau's claim that human beings in the state of nature are free from social passions and enjoy wholeness, we will see that the female Savage is fractured even in the state of nature. As a result, Rousseau's natural woman—be it the female Savage or Sophie—embodies the very principles of natural rights theory to which Wollstonecraft objects: the premise that human beings are naturally solitary beings, motivated by self-preservation and, consequentially, the suggestion that the relationship between human beings (either marriage or the larger political community) is marked by tension or hostility. Wollstonecraft's critique of Sophie, thus, points to a much deeper critique of Rousseau's state of nature, and the political philosophy which ensues.

I. FIRST PRINCIPLES

After an introduction, Wollstonecraft begins her treatise on the rights of woman with a chapter entitled "The Rights and Involved Duties of Mankind." It is in these pages that we would expect an author so steeped in Rousseau's works and in the political life of the British Radical Whigs, to offer her own, more female friendly, version of a natural rights theory. However, we are disappointed in this expectation.[2] Instead, Wollstonecraft makes a metaphysical inquiry. "In the present state of society it appears necessary to go back to first principles in search of the most simple truths, and to dispute with some prevailing prejudice every inch of ground" (*VRW*, 11). These first principles upon which Wollstonecraft is to build her plan for political reform are rather straightforward, though not the basic tenets of natural rights theory. Wollstonecraft first puts forth her understanding of the human condition. While sharing their passions with animals, human beings are distinguished from animals by their reason. And reason, she asserts, controls the passions.

> In what does man's pre-eminence over the brute creation consist? The answer is as clear as that a half is less than the whole, in Reason. What acquirement exalts one being above another? Virtue, we spontaneously reply. For what purpose were the passions implanted? That man by struggling with them might attain a degree of knowledge denied to the brutes, whispers Experience. (*VRW*, 12)

It is interesting to notice that reason is the fundamental trait of human beings, not the passions. Passions are "implanted" so that reason can do its work. In some sense the passions are secondary. This is an important contrast to Rousseau, who tells us that human beings are born with minimal physical (animal) passions. As the species develops or becomes more social, the passions increase and human beings develop reason. The apparent perfection of the individual occurs in tandem with the "decrepitude" of the species (*Discourses*, 167).

Given her conception of the human condition, Wollstonecraft tells her readers that human being's happiness is determined by noble pursuits, rather than by physical pleasure (or absence of pain). The political community should be measured by whether or not it promotes human beings' noble pursuit. "Consequently the perfection of our nature and capability of happiness, must be estimated by the degree of reason, virtue, and knowledge, that distinguish the individual, and direct laws which bind society" (*VRW*, 12). In contrast to state of nature theorists, Wollstonecraft does not consider freedom or liberty to be the end of the political community. For Wollstonecraft, the political community exists so that human beings may perfect their natures.

With this understanding of the human condition and the political community, the specific "prevailing prejudice" with which Wollstonecraft finds it necessary to dispute is Rousseau's conception of the state of nature.

> Impressed by this view of the misery and disorder which pervaded society, and fatigued with jostling against artificial fools, Rousseau became enamored of solitude, and, being at the same time an optimist, he labours with uncommon eloquence to prove that man was naturally a solitary animal. (*VRW*, 13)

Although Wollstonecraft admires Rousseau for educating Emile to be free from the corrupt social prejudices of the eighteenth century, she clearly rejects the view that it is natural for human beings to live outside of a political community. Rousseau's view, she argues, is based on a mistaken conception of "the Author of things." Wollstonecraft notices that Rousseau emphasizes God's benevolence, but does so to the detriment of God's omniscience.

> Reared on a false hypothesis his [Rousseau's] arguments in favor of a state of nature are plausible, but unsound. I say unsound; for to assert that a state of nature is preferable to civilization, in all its possible perfection, is, in other words, to arraign supreme wisdom; and the paradoxical exclamation, that God has made all things right, and that error has been introduced by the creature, whom he formed, knowing what he formed, is as unphilosophical as impious. (*VRW*, 14)

By describing man as a naturally solitary animal, Rousseau suggests that man is capable of corrupting God's design. The movement from the state of nature into civil society and human reason, which developed along with this movement, is contrary to the Author's plan and an abuse of his benevolence.[3] Rather, Wollstonecraft argues, God intended that man cultivate his rational attributes and He meant for man to do it in a civil society.

> Had mankind remained for ever in the brutal state of nature, which even his [Rousseau's] magic pen cannot paint as a state in which a single virtue took root, it would have been clear, though not to the sensitive unreflecting wanderer, that man was born to run the circle of life and death, and adorn God's garden for some purpose which could not easily be reconciled with his attributes. (*VRW*, 14)

Given that God intended for human beings to cultivate their reason and strive toward virtue, Wollstonecraft rejects Rousseau's state of nature in favor of civil society, albeit a greatly improved society than either Wollstonecraft or Rousseau experiences.

> But the nature of the poison points out the antidote; and had Rousseau
> mounted one step higher in his investigation, or could his eye have
> pierced through the foggy atmosphere, which he almost disdained to
> breathe, his active mind would have darted forward to contemplate
> the perfection of man in the establishment of true civilization, instead
> of taking his ferocious flight back to the night of sensual ignorance.
> (*VRW*, 19)

Though Rousseau does not stray very far from Paris during his lifetime, a
common theme of his writings is the restoration of man's natural condition.

Having laid out "the first principles" or "the most simple truths" to
which Wollstonecraft adheres, we can turn our attention to Wollstonecraft's
critique of Sophie in Book V of the *Emile*.[4] The contradiction between Emile
and Sophie that Wollstonecraft notices and condemns reflects a contradiction between the male and the female Savage in the state of nature. Thus, the
criticism that Wollstonecraft levels against Sophie points to a deeper critique
of Rousseau's natural rights theory. Judging by "the most simple truths" put
forth by Wollstonecraft, Sophie and the woman in the state of nature are
half-beings, chimeras in the mythological sense.

II. THE LITTLE GLUTTON

Sprinkled throughout *A Vindication of the Rights of Woman* are direct and
indirect criticisms of Rousseau's ideal woman, Sophie. However, it is not
until the chapter five, "Animadversions of Some Writers Who Have Rendered Women Objects of Pity, Bordering on Contempt," that Wollstonecraft
systematically critiques Sophie.[5] Wollstonecraft selects lengthy quotes from
Book V of the *Emile* to illustrate Rousseau's understanding of the female
character. Interspersed between these quotes is Wollstonecraft's reaction to
Rousseau's treatment of the female. After a brief look at the ambiguities of
Rousseau's discussion of the female sex, I will turn my attention to the passages quoted by Wollstonecraft and her objections. These objections elaborate Wollstonecraft's critique of Rousseau's state of nature.

Recall that Rousseau tells us that little girls and little boys are equal.
He suggests they are the same, "girls are children, boys are children; the same
name suffices for beings so much alike" (*Emile*, 211). Emile, the little boy,
is able to satisfy his relatively few desires. He does not seem to be dependent
on anyone. As a result, Emile is considered natural; he enjoys numerical
unity. We would expect then that the little girl, a being so much like the
little boy, would also enjoy numerical unity or the wholeness of natural man.

However, we should not jump to this conclusion. Rousseau has presented us with two impressions of children in the *Emile*. Rousseau has also told us that the first condition of a child is one of "want and weakness, his first voices are complaints and tears. The child feels his needs and cannot satisfy them. He implores another's help by screams" (*Emile*, 65). It is not long before the child recognizes the effect of his tears and his tears become orders. "Thus, from their own weakness, which is in the first place the source of the feeling of their dependence, is subsequently born the idea of empire and domination" (*Emile*, 65). Rousseau carefully plans Emile's education to minimize Emile's sense of weakness. Consequently, Emile feels independent and he has no inclination to tyranny. A child may be a strong, independent creature like Emile or he may be a tyrant, a fractional creature dependent on others to satisfy his many wants. Due to man's initial weakness as an infant, both possibilities seem to be natural. As we will see by considering Rousseau's introduction of Sophie in Book V of the *Emile*, little girls are acutely aware of their dependence and prone from the first to "the idea of empire and domination."

At the outset of Book V of the *Emile*, Rousseau announces that "In everything not connected with sex, woman is man" (*Emile*, 357). This proclamation seems to be consistent with Rousseau's earlier claim that human beings are born twice, once for our species and once for our sex. Because our sex is our second birth, it would seem that males and females are first and foremost human beings and secondly, men and women. The difficulty Rousseau encounters is determining what in women's constitution is due to sex.

Though Rousseau has prepared his readers to understand girls and boys to be the same, he soon reveals that the differences between boys and girls are rather great. "There is no parity between the sexes. The male is male only at certain moments. The female is female her whole life or at least during her whole youth" (*Emile*, 361). Rousseau goes on to tell us that this disparity is due to the female's physical capacity to bear children. The woman needs special consideration beginning with her pregnancy. "She needs care during her pregnancy; she needs rest at the time of childbirth; she needs a soft sedentary life to suckle her children; she needs patience and gentleness, a zeal and an affection that nothing can rebuff in order to raise her children" (*Emile*, 361). If a woman is most obviously a female at the time of bearing and caring for children, it seems unnecessary to expect her to be a "female her whole life or at least during her youth." Contrary to this claim, it would seem that youth or childhood would be the time when a female would be the least influenced by her sex.

Rousseau anticipates this puzzle and goes on to explain why a female is a female her whole life, even as a little girl. "She [the mother] serves as the link between them [her children] and their father; she alone makes him love them and gives him the confidence to call them his own. How much tenderness and care is required to maintain the union of the whole family!" (*Emile*, 361). If a woman is to instill this confidence in the father of her children, it must be done prior to the birth of her children. In a rather lengthy note to the *Second Discourse*, Rousseau refutes Locke's claim that children are the reason for attachment between men and women in the state of nature. "If a given woman is of no interest to a man for these nine months, if he ceases even to know her, why will he help her after the birth?. . For it is not a matter of knowing why a man remains attached to a woman after birth, but why he gets attached to her after the conception" (*Discourses*, 215). Rousseau's correction of Locke is relevant for men and women living in the civil society, as well as the state of nature. Because the man's attachment to the woman must be secured prior to the birth of the children in order to ensure that the man will help provide for the offspring, public opinion is especially important to the female. "It is important, then, not only that a woman be faithful, but that she be judged faithful by her husband, by those near her, by everyone . . . If it is important that a father love his children, it is important that he esteem their mother" (*Emile*, 361). The cultivation of this esteem must begin at a young age. The importance of public opinion to women is not simply conventional. Rather, the female's concern for public opinion has its foundation in nature.

> For them [women] to have what is necessary to their station, they depend on us [men] to give it to them, to want to give it to them, to esteem them worthy of it. They depend on our sentiments, on the value we set on their merit, on the importance we attach to their charms and their virtues. By the very law of nature women are at the mercy of men's judgments, as much for their own sake as for that of their children. (*Emile*, 364)

We should note that women's dependence on men's judgment for the sake of their children means that women bear the responsibility of ensuring the survival of the species. Once children have been born, it is up to the woman to make sure they are properly fed and protected. This will be true of the female Savage as well as the eighteenth-century woman. Because of the woman's dependence, or the species' dependence, on the man's esteem for the woman, woman is rendered a fractional creature. "When a man acts well, he depends only on himself and can brave public judgment; but when a woman acts well, she has accomplished only *half* of her task, and what is thought of her is no less important to her than what she actually is" (*Emile*, 364, emphasis added).

Having promised to "attack the principles on which [Sophie's] education was built, Wollstonecraft harvests her greatest evidence that Rousseau understands the female to be a "half-being" from these passages in the *Emile*. In her chapter, "Animadversions of Some of the Writers Who Have Rendered Women Objects of Pity, Bordering on Contempt," Wollstonecraft begins by challenging Rousseau's fundamental premise that due to her relative physical weakness, woman ought to make herself pleasing to men. In doing so, woman gains power over them. Wollstonecraft quotes the *Emile* at length:

> Hence we deduce a third consequence from the different constitutions of the sexes; which is, that the strongest should be master in appearance, and be dependent in fact on the weakest; and that not from any frivolous practice of gallantry or vanity of protectorship, but from an invariable law of nature, which when furnishing woman with a greater facility to excite desires than she has given man to satisfy them, makes the latter dependent on the good pleasure of the former, and compels him to endeavor to please in his turn, *in order to obtain her consent that he should be the strongest*. (*VRW*, 78, Wollstonecraft's emphasis, *Emile*, 359–360)

Some commentators, most notably Joel Schwartz, have suggested that this courtship establishes a certain interdependence between men and women, making "political rule" possible. Schwartz describes the relationship in Aristotelian terms. "It is in some sense a political relationship because the interdependence of the partners is expressed in each partner's experience of ruling and being ruled through it."[6] Wollstonecraft does not see it this way. She cannot help adding an exasperated footnote to Rousseau's words, "What nonsense!" (*VRW*, 78).

However, Wollstonecraft's opposition to Rousseau's account of the relationship between the sexes is not simply reactionary. She provides philosophical grounds for her disagreement with Rousseau. Wollstonecraft's begins her objection with an argument that she has made throughout the *Vindication*. "I have already asserted that in educating women these fundamental principles lead to a system of cunning and lasciviousness" (*VRW*, 78). Over and over again, Wollstonecraft has argued against the notion that human dignity can be achieved by gaining power over others. It is a lesson she learns from

Rousseau. This remains true for Wollstonecraft when women gain power or mastery over men by taking advantage of both sexes' weaknesses. Rather than creating a balance of power, it creates a potential for tyranny. Both tyranny and slavery are grossly unnatural to the human condition. It is important to remind ourselves that Wollstonecraft and Rousseau, for that matter, charge their contemporaries with cunning and lasciviousness, not human beings who are thought to embody natural qualities. From Wollstonecraft's perspective, the "woman who suits this [natural] man" *(Emile,* 363) seems no different than the fractional creature, who suits the corrupt eighteenth-century man.

In other words, Wollstonecraft also understands Rousseau's characterization of the "natural" relationship between men and women to be "political," though not in an Aristotelian sense as Schwarz suggests. The relationship between men and women that Rousseau presents in the *Emile* is "political" in another sense. The "political" for Rousseau results from the degeneration of man's natural condition. He is no longer independent and able to provide for his relatively few desires. Instead his desires are multiplied and he "must constantly try to interest [others] in his fate and to make them really or apparently find their own profit in working for his" *(Discourses,* 170). For Rousseau, the "political" is freighted with the desire of human beings to dominate one another. This is what Wollstonecraft, unlike Schwartz, notices in Rousseau's description of the "natural" relations between the sexes. The implication that I am drawing from Wollstonecraft's interpretation of Rousseau is that Rousseau fails to fulfill his promise to describe human beings' natural independence and goodness. (Wollstonecraft will make this implication explicit in her discussion of Rousseau's education of little girls.) In pursuing her utopian dream, Wollstonecraft has followed Rousseau into the land of chimeras only to find out that it is, at least in part, inhabited by fractional creatures, monsters.

Wollstonecraft continues to object to Rousseau's characterization of the relationship between the sexes. As Rousseau presents it the relationship between man and woman is determined by the woman's need to feed herself and her children. Now, Wollstonecraft challenges a fundamental premise of natural rights theories more generally: the notion that human beings are motivated by self-preservation.

> Supposing woman to have been formed only to please, and be subject to man, the conclusion is just, she ought to sacrifice every other consideration to render herself agreeable to him: and let this brutal desire of self-preservation be the grand spring of all her actions, when it is

proved to be the iron bed of fate, to fit which her character should be stretched or contracted regardless of all moral or physical distinctions. (*VRW*, 78–79)[7]

Given her philosophical commitments to reason and virtue, Wollstonecraft does not believe that self-preservation can explain human beings' actions, and particularly, the relationship between man and woman. On the contrary, Wollstonecraft maintains that they have nobler motivations.

In her "animadversions," Wollstonecraft continues her assault on Rousseau, turning her attention to the little girl he presents to his readers. Having explained why it is that "the female is female her whole life or at least during her whole youth" (*Emile*, 361), Rousseau begins his discussion of educating little girls. "Since the body is born, so to speak, before the soul, the body ought to be cultivated first" (*Emile*, 365). Earlier in the treatise Rousseau had given the impression that all human beings are born first for the species and secondly for their sex (*Emile*, 211). Rousseau now clarifies, if not reverses, this initial claim. It now seems that the sex, which is at the very minimum defined by the body is born first. "The order is common to the two sexes, but the aim of the cultivation is different. For man this aim is the development of strength; for woman it is the development of attractiveness" (*Emile*, 365). Because woman's first cultivation is attractiveness, her first education is that of pleasing others. The soul, which is to be born after the female body is thus necessarily fractional.

Again, Wollstonecraft plucks the most provocative passages from these pages of the *Emile* to demonstrate the fractional character of Rousseau's little girl. She tirelessly quotes Rousseau:

> Girls are from their earliest infancy fond of dress. Not content with being pretty, they are desirous of being thought so; we see, by all their little airs, that this thought engages their attention; and they are hardly capable of understanding what is said to them, before they are to be governed by talking to them of what people will think of their behavior. The same motive, however, indiscreetly made use of with boys, has not the same effect: provided they are let pursue their amusements at pleasure, they care very little what people think of them. (*VRW*, 80, *Emile*, 365)

Wollstonecraft follows her lengthy quotations with two objections. First of all, Rousseau's education of little girls is simply an education of the body. "Rousseau is not the only man who has indirectly said that merely the person of a *young* woman, without any mind, unless animal spirits come under that description, is very pleasing" (*VW*, 81). For Wollstonecraft, the body is associated with the animal. It is the mind that is distinctive of human beings. In forming the female body to be attractive and neglecting the mind, Rousseau renders little girls brutes, rather than human beings.

Wollstonecraft makes a second objection to Rousseau's description of what is natural to the little girl. In claiming to describe what is natural to the little girl, Rousseau presents his readers with the conventional. "To render it weak, and what some call beautiful, the understanding is neglected, and girls forced to sit still, play with dolls and listen to foolish conversations;—the effect of habit is insisted upon as an undoubted indication of nature" (*VRW*, 81). This criticism of Rousseau sounds familiar to readers of the *Second Discourse*. After all, Rousseau also accuses his predecessors, most notably Hobbes and Locke, of never reaching the state of nature that their philosophical inquiries sought (*Discourses*, 132). Rousseau promises to distinguish himself from earlier state of nature theorists by describing man's truly natural condition, rather than describing his social vices and attributing them to man's natural temper. Wollstonecraft declares that Rousseau commits the same theoretical mistake as his predecessors. As evidence that Rousseau has not arrived at the nature of little girls, Wollstonecraft points to Rousseau's France.[8]

> Rousseau's observations, it is proper to remark were made in a country where the art of pleasing was refined only to extract the grossness of vice. *He did not go back to nature*, or his ruling appetite disturbed the operations of reason, else he would not have drawn these crude inferences. (*VRW*, 81,my emphasis)

Rather than describing what is natural, a wholeness or independence from the opinion of others, it seems to Wollstonecraft that Rousseau attributes to the little girl what is conventional, a slavish dependence on public opinion.

Wollstonecraft raises a further objection to Rousseau's education of little girls. Not only does Rousseau attribute their conventional qualities to nature, but he treats little girls like grown up women instead of children. "In short, they are treated like women, almost from their very birth, and compliments were listened to instead of instruction" (*VRW*, 81). To suggest little girls, in particular the little girl considered by Rousseau in Book V of the *Emile*, are treated like adult women is a harsher criticism than it may seem at first glance. It reveals an inconsistency in Rousseau's pedagogy, which underlines the difficulty of arriving at Rousseau's egalitarian state of nature. Just as Rousseau accuses those who have written political treatises of not arriving at the state of nature, so he accuses those who have written educational treatises of not describing childhood. "They are always seeking the man in the child without thinking of what he is before being a man" or in this case, woman (*Emile*, 34). The natural wholeness afforded to Emile in his childhood, which most approximates the condition of man in the state of nature, is possible, Rousseau claims, because Emile's childhood is not determined by what is expected of him as an adult.[9] A similar education, in which questions of the adult female's place in civil society are put off, is denied to the little girl. Instead, she is educated to be a civil, fractional creature. The result of these apparent inconsistencies is a suspicion that the female has no place in Rousseau's the pure state of nature, in which human beings are independent and good.

The education of little girls prescribed by Rousseau results in woman, who is in "perpetual conflict with herself" (*VW*, 82, *Emile*, 369). Rousseau declares "It is just that this sex share the pain of the evils it has caused us" (*Emile*, 369). From the context, the reader cannot be sure what evils Rousseau attribute to the female sex. I will suggest that Rousseau holds woman responsible for the birth of *amour-propre* in man, which then gives way to the moral sentiment of love (*Discourses*, 155). It is the female, who is fractional in nature, and sets in motion that "chain of wonders" that explains how "the strong could resolve to serve the weak, and the People to purchase an idea of repose at the price of real felicity" (*Discourses*, 131). The moral sentiment of love, the factious sentiment is responsible for luring the Savage from the pure state of nature and its peaceful solitude. This argument will be more fully developed when I turn my attention to the female Savage in the state of nature. For now, it is instructive to consider Wollstonecraft's objection to Rousseau. Wollstonecraft does not see that the perpetual conflict women endure is natural to them. Instead, Wollstonecraft attributes this perpetual conflict to a negligent educational system.

> Modesty, temperance, and self-denial, are the sober offspring of reason; but when sensibility is nurtured at the expense of understanding, such weak beings must be restrained by arbitrary means, and be subjected to continual conflicts; but give their activity of mind a wider range, and nobler passions and motives will govern their appetites and sentiments. (*VRW*, 82)[10]

Although Rousseau and Wollstonecraft are both critical of the fractional character of eighteenth-century Europeans, they disagree on the fractional character of all little girls and Sophie (*Emile*, 357). For Wollstonecraft, a more natural treatment of little girls would encourage the use of the reason and would enhance their "nobler passions." Wollstonecraft does not attempt to restore the wholeness of woman by approximating the conditions of the Savage in the state of nature. Quite the contrary, Wollstonecraft advocates nurturing the qualities that Rousseau considers civil, reason and virtue, in order to restore the corrupted fractional character of woman to its natural wholeness. Wollstonecraft's implication seems to be that reason and virtue are natural not only to woman, but to human beings as such; a belief made explicit in Wollstonecraft's criticism of Rousseau's neglect of little girls' minds.

Unlike the case of Emile, Rousseau does not suggest that little girls be encouraged to minimize their passions. Nor are they taught to satisfy their passions by their own efforts. Instead, like weak and dependent infants, they soon "consider the people who surround them as instruments depending on them to be set in motion, they make use of those people to follow their inclination and to supplement their own weakness" (*Emile*, 67). Although Rousseau may not intend to make women tyrants, he appreciates the pernicious effects of weakness and dependency on infants. "That is how they become difficult, tyrannical, imperious, wicked, unmanageable—a development which does not come from natural spirit of domination but which rather gives one to them, for it does not require long experience to sense how pleasant it is to act with the hands of others and to need only to stir one's tongue and make the universe move" (*Emile*, 67–68).

We should, as Wollstonecraft does, expect that weakness and dependency will have the same effect on the female child. As an example of the tyrannical propensity of little girls, I would point to Rousseau's own comparison of a little boy and little girl. Rousseau asks his readers to consider the attempts made by a little boy and girl to satisfy their hunger. According to common practice, both are forbidden to ask for anything at meals. Rather than simply stating his hunger, the boy tries to obtain meat by asking for salt. Rousseau thinks it no wonder that he is punished. He also tells us that this would not have been the case if the boy had acted in a more straightforward manner. In other words, the boy is expected to satisfy his hunger by direct means. By contrast, Rousseau tells his readers in an approving manner, the little girl is successful in obtaining food by indirect means. She relies on her charms. She points to all the foods she has tasted, conspicuously silent when passing the food she desires. Someone notices and asks, "'Didn't you eat some of that one?' 'Oh, no' replied the little glutton, sweetly lowering her eyes." We can guess what happens next. Rousseau simply ends his story by stating, "I shall add nothing" (*Emile*, 371).[11] The charms by which the little glutton obtains her food are just according to Rousseau. "What is, is good, and no general law is bad. This peculiar cleverness given to the fair sex is equitable compensation for their lesser share of strength, a compensation without which women would not be man's companion but his slave" (*Emile*, 371). As we will see, the female Savage, just like the little glutton must employ her charms in order to obtain food.

Wollstonecraft's objections to Rousseau's so called "natural" education of little girls are consistent with the first principles that she lays out for her readers at the beginning of her treatise. Wollstonecraft's condemnation of the "system of cunning and lasciviousness" suggests that Wollstonecraft understands human beings to be naturally benevolent. Furthermore, she objects to Rousseau's identification of "the brutal desire for self-preservation as the grand spring of all her actions." On the surface, Wollstonecraft's conception of human beings seems to be consistent with Rousseau's own understanding of natural man. The Savage in the pure state of nature is not marked by these qualities. Indeed, Rousseau criticizes Hobbes and Locke for attributing these aggressive, vicious qualities to natural man, telling his readers that they describe civil or fractional man (*Discourses*, 132). However, Wollstonecraft notices that Rousseau's characterization of the natural relationship between the sexes is marked by the desire to dominate others, it smacks of the political. Wollstonecraft's criticisms suggest that Rousseau cannot describe what is truly natural to man, a wholeness and goodness. This leads to an important distinction between Wollstonecraft and Rousseau. Wollstonecraft goes beyond Rousseau's understanding of natural man's goodness. According to Rousseau, man is naturally good because the state of nature is lush and he is strong. The simple pleasures of the solitary animal are easily satisfied. He does not become vicious until he is no longer able to satisfy his desires. Wollstonecraft, on the other hand, faults the neglect of reason and the nobler passions for the "system of cunning and lasciviousness." Wollstonecraft's emphasis on reason and the nobler passions suggest that she understands man's natural benevolence to be rooted in the soul, not the body. By taking note of Wollstonecraft's objections to the little girl presented by Rousseau, we gain a better understanding of what Wollstonecraft considers natural and we can see how it diverges from Rousseau. We can also see how the "natural" education of the little girl fosters a temper quite different from Emile and the Savage. Some scholars have suggested, on the surface, there appears to be an inconsistency between the *Emile* and Rousseau's most egalitarian writing, the *Second Discourse*. In the next section of this chapter I shall argue that the objections that Wollstonecraft raises against the little girl may also be leveled against the female Savage in the state of nature. Therefore, Wollstonecraft's objection to Sophie point to a deeper critique of Rousseau's natural rights theory. Wollstonecraft must reject Sophie, not because she is inconsistent with Rousseau's natural rights theory, but because Rousseau's natural rights theory is contrary to Wollstonecraft's "first principles."

III. THE FEMALE SAVAGE

As we have already seen in the first chapter, there is a comparison between the Savage in the state of nature and childhood and, in particular, the natural child, Emile. Rousseau identifies his account of the Savage's gradual movement toward civil society as "the life of your species" (*Discourses*, 132). Similarly, he tells his readers that Emile's story, and, in particular, Emile's courtship with Sophie, is "the history of my species" (*Emile*, 416). The Savage, on the level of the species, and Emile, on the level of the individual, experience similar development. Rousseau's natural education is an attempt to arrest or regulate Emile's development in order to preserve the natural wholeness that characterizes human beings, but was lost to the Savage as he became increasingly more social. The same parallel may be drawn between Sophie and the female Savage in the state of nature. After all, "Sophie ought to be a woman as Emile is a man—that is to say, she ought to have everything which suits the constitution of her species and her sex in order to fill her place in the physical and moral order" (*Emile*, 357). Just as nature served as a guide to Emile's education, so Rousseau suggests that nature guide Sophie's upbringing. "Do you wish to be well guided? Then always follow nature's indications. Everything that characterizes the fair sex should be respected as established by nature" (*Emile*, 363). If we are able to see a comparison between Emile as a child and the Savage, it is worthwhile to compare the little girl Rousseau presents to us in Book V of *Emile* and the female Savage.[12]

Rousseau's first words on the difference between the sexes in the *Emile* is that there is none in childhood. "Everything is equal: girls are children, boys are children; the same name suffices for beings so much alike" (*Emile*, 211). This seems to be Rousseau's opinion on the sexes in the state of nature as well. Rousseau begins his *Second Discourse* by identifying two sorts of inequality among human beings, the physical and the moral. Rousseau calls one "natural or Physical, because it is established by Nature, and which consists in the differences in age, health, strengths of Body, and qualities of the Mind, or Soul; The other, which may be called moral, or political inequality, because it depends on a sort of convention, and is established, or at least authorized by Men's consent" (*Discourses*, 131).

Given that women are generally weaker than men, natural or physical inequality between the sexes would seem immediately apparent. In addition to their lesser physical strength, women's biological capacity to bear children and the necessity of caring for children, at least in infancy, would seem to render women weaker still. However, this is not the impression of the female Savage that we are given by Rousseau in the *Second Discourse*. Quite the contrary, the particular traits of female human beings tends to protect the child, not only fortifying the species, but also strengthening the mother. Penny Weiss has argued that the male and female are equal and virtually the same in the state of nature. The ability to bear offspring barely disrupts this sameness (Weiss, 46–48). Weiss relies on Rousseau's account of the earliest stages of nature to defend her claim. Rousseau suggests further there is no natural maternal instinct. The female Savage will breastfeed the new baby, but only in an effort to relieve her discomfort, not out of concern for the infant. Only habit makes a child dear to his mother and this habit has no time to form in the state of nature. As soon as the child has strength to forage on his own, he wanders off, leaving even his mother (*Discourses*, 145).

However minimal the period of breastfeeding may be, it implies some challenges to the radical independence and sameness of the male and female in the state of nature. In his treatment of the *Second Discourse*, Roger Masters notes that Rousseau's first challenge in describing the Savage is to explain how the species could survive in a purely animal condition, given the Savage's radical autonomy. The Savage, and as a result the species, seems especially vulnerable in infancy (Masters, 120). Rousseau mentions two particular threats to the baby Savage. The first difficulty the female Savage and the baby Savage face is how the mother can provide for her own nourishment and still be available to feed the infant. This concern is easily addressed by Rousseau.

> As regards Childhood, I even note that, since the Mother carries her child with her everywhere, she can feed it much more readily than can the female of a number of animals, forced as they are to wear themselves out going back and forth, one way to find food, the other to suckle or feed their young. (*Discourses*, 137)

By always carrying her child with her, the female Savage is able to ensure that the baby Savage is well nourished. In this way, Masters points out, the infant, and also the species, are protected from danger. I would suggest an additional benefit to the female Savage. Constantly carrying a baby is a fairly good upper body work out and is sure to compensate the female Savage for her relative weakness.

The second threat to the baby Savage (and, therefore, the species) that Rousseau points out comes from other animals. Because human beings learn to walk later than other animals, there is a danger that they would be helpless prey to other animals.[13] Again, Rousseau dismisses this concern with the assurance that the female Savage is able to flea from dangerous animals with her now rather large baby in her arms. "Their Children may walk late and with difficulty, but Mothers carry them with ease: an advantage not enjoyed by other species where the mother, when pursued, finds herself compelled to abandon her young or to adjust her pace to theirs" (*Discourses*, 139). Again, the implication is that in protecting the child and ensuring the continuation of the species, the female Savage is made stronger.

It is worth stopping to consider the relative strength of the male Savage. Though Rousseau tells us that savages in the pure state of nature acquire "all the vigor of which the human species is capable" (*Discourses*, 135), it is not clear how the male Savage enhances his natural strength. Rousseau tells us that the Savage is timid and avoids confrontation with other animals (*Discourses*, 135). We also learn from Rousseau that men in the state of nature are rather lazy. They have a "mortal hatred of all sustained work" (*Discourses*, 144). In contrast to civil man, the Savage "wants only to live and to remain idle, and even a Stoic's ataraxia does not approximate his profound indifference to everything else" (*Discourses*, 187). The seemingly obvious difference between the male and female Savage in physical strength is mitigated by the female's necessity to constantly carry her child and the male's inclination to remain idle. The result is the male and female Savage are very nearly the same in the state of nature.

> The simplicity and the uniformity of animal and savage life, where all eat the same foods, live in the same fashion, and do exactly the same things, it will be evident how much smaller the difference between man and man must be in the state of Nature than in the state of society. (*Discourses*, 158)

It is not until, what Rousseau calls, the first revolution that "the first difference was established in the ways of living of the two sexes, which until then had but one" (*Discourses*, 164). The one difference looks to be the female's capacity to bear children, not her relative weakness. On the surface, this one difference is likely to make the female stronger, and, therefore, more equal to the male Savage.

Yet, this one physical difference between male and female, which Rousseau goes a long way to minimize, has profound moral consequences for the

male and the female Savage. As a result of this one difference, the female
Savage has more in common with Sophie, "a fanciful kind of *half* being,
one of Rousseau's wild chimeras" (*VRW*, 39) than she has with natural man.
It is necessary to take a second look at Rousseau's treatment of the sexes in
the *Second Discourse*. Following his preface to the *Second Discourse*, Rousseau
offers a "Notice about the Notes," explaining his decision to put them at the
end of the treatise. Rousseau admits the notes seem to stray from the topic
at hand and may distract the reader from "the straightest road" to the end of
the discourse. Rousseau throws down his gauntlet to his more careful readers
and challenges them to read his discourse a second time. "Those who will
have the courage to start over again can amuse themselves the second time
with beating the bushes, and trying to peruse the notes; there will be little
harm in the others' not reading them at all" (*Discourse*, 129). It is in these
notes that we recognize Rousseau's inability to sustain nature's perfection and
we see the fractional, "unnatural" character of the female Savage in the state
of nature.

The first things Rousseau tells us about the state of nature, in reading the *Second Discourse*, are nature's abundance and generosity. "The Earth,
abandoned to its natural fertility, and covered by immense forests which no
Axe ever mutilated, at every step offers Storage and shelter to the animals of
every species" (*Discourses*, 134). The state of nature is particularly kind to
human beings, who are not limited by instinct to eat only certain food. They
enjoy a variety of nature's bounty (*Discourses*, 134). Man and beast differ in
that "Nature alone does everything in the operations of the Beast, whereas
man contributes to his operations by his capacity as a free agent" (*Discourse*,
140). As an example of man's free agency, Rousseau contrasts human beings'
eating habits to other animals' diet. "Thus a Pigeon would starve to death
next to a Bowl filled with the choicest meats, and a Cat atop heaps of fruit or
of grain, although each could very well have found nourishment in the food
it disdains if it had occurred to it to try some" (*Discourses*, 140). In addition
to the mother's ability to always carry her child, thus making it easier to
feed and protect her offspring, Rousseau distinguishes the Savage from other
beasts by this ability to enjoy a variety of food. It contributes to the species
survival.

However, courageously reading the *Second Discourse* for a second time,
"beating the bushes and trying to peruse the notes," we learn that eating
anything and everything is contrary to man's best interest and contrary to
nature.[14] Although the Savage, as a free agent, could choose to eat meat,
unlike the Pigeon, Rousseau tells his more careful readers that it is not natural for him to do so. Rousseau offers both physical and moral evidence for

this claim. In one of his notes, Rousseau considers the number of teats various species, including the human, have to suckle their young. Some of the animals have only a few, such as the Mare, the Cow, the Doe, and the female human being. Others, such as the Cat, the she-Wolf, and the Tigress, have many teats. Rousseau concludes that animals living off of vegetation require more time to feed themselves and, therefore, nature only provides them with two teats, as they do not have time to suckle many offspring. Animals living off of meat, however, are able to eat much more quickly and have more time to feed their young. So, nature provides these animals with several teats (*Discourses*, 196, 214). Because the female Savage has only two teats, Rousseau compares her to other animals with only two teats and concludes she must be a vegetarian.

Rousseau also provides his readers with moral evidence that human beings were not meant to eat meat. As we have already noted, the characteristic of natural man (whether the Savage, Emile or the Solitary Walker) is his numerical unity or his wholeness. Natural man is not a fraction. He does not compare himself to others. In his treatment of the Savage's diet, Roger Masters notes that man only begins to eat meat after he begins to imitate other animals (Masters, 122). Imitating animals requires a certain degree of comparison. The Savage must measure himself against the brute and determine that he was strong enough or quick enough to imitate the animal. To be sure, comparing oneself to an animal in the state of nature is not as destructive to the human soul as comparing oneself to other civil men in eighteenth-century France, but the act of comparison is unnatural. Therefore, eating meat is unnatural.

> Man's free agency, his ability to choose meat instead of vegetation, comes
> at a high cost. For since prey is almost the only object which Carnivores
> fight, and Frugivorous live in constant peace with one another, it is clear
> that if the human species were of the latter kind, it could have subsisted
> much more easily in the state of Nature, and would have much less need
> and many fewer occasions to leave it. (*Discourses*, 194)

In discussing Emile's diet, Rousseau's words are even harsher. Meat eaters are generally "more cruel and ferocious" than other men.

> This is observed in all places and all times. English barbarism is known;
> the Zoroastrians, on the contrary, are the gentlest of men. All savages are
> cruel, and it is not their morals which cause them to be so. This cruelty
> comes from their food. They go to war as to hunt and treat men like
> bears. (*Emile*, 153)

By choosing meat over vegetation, the Savage brings himself not only into greater contact with others, but greater conflict with his fellow creatures. The natural disposition of the Savage is corrupted. He is no longer timid and lazy, but gentle and good. Rather, he is fierce and cruel.

Rousseau presents his readers with two options: the life of the vegetarian and that of the carnivore. The former enjoys the tranquility and the lush abundance of the state of nature. He is able to "live and remain idle" (*Discourses*, 187). The latter, the carnivore, sacrifices his wholeness. In comparing himself to animals he becomes fractional. He is vicious and at war with others. Given these choices, the reader must wonder what would prompt man to employ his comparative faculties and choose to eat meat. Nature is in some respect flawed. Perhaps the state of nature is not as lush as Rousseau initially imagines. Or, perhaps the abundance that is found in the state of nature is in some respect incompatible with the needs of human beings.

As we have noted by considering Wollstonecraft's first principles, Wollstonecraft warns us of this difficulty in *A Vindication of the Rights of Woman*. In an effort to preserve the perfection of the state of nature, Rousseau makes "the paradoxical exclamation, that God has made all things right, and that error has been introduced by the creature, whom he formed, knowing what he formed" (*VRW*, 14). Knowing both the state of nature and the creatures he formed to live in it, we would expect a benevolent and omniscient God to provide for the naturally solitary and good human beings in the state of nature. By further considering the female Savage and noticing her similarities to Rousseau's ideal woman in Book V of the *Emile*, we recognize the imperfection of the state of nature and the fractional character of human beings in their natural condition.

Roger Masters instructs his readers to consider Rousseau's claims about the female Savage's capacity to feed and protect both herself and her offspring. Though Rousseau notices that her ability to carry her child makes it easier for the female Savage to keep her child with her at all times, doing so makes it rather difficult to gather the necessary amount of vegetation needed to sustain her and her child. Yet, leaving the child alone in order to gather food renders the offspring vulnerable to other animals. In order to effectively nourish herself and her child, the female Savage deviates from the practice of eating vegetables and begins to eat meat. Masters points out that eating meat maintains the independence of men and women in the state of nature (Masters, 125). However, the female Savage's independence from the male Savage is at the expense of her numerical unity and her naturally humane temper. The female Savage is less than human. She is a ferocious brute.

The female Savage does not necessarily have to choose to eat meat. She does have another option. The female Savage, like the Little Glutton, may employ her charms in order to obtain food. She can seek the assistance of the male Savage in gathering food. Because the Savage harbors a "mortal hatred of all sustained work," this may be easier said than done. Much like man as Rousseau describes him in the last perilous stage of the state of nature or the civil man of the eighteenth century, the female Savage "must constantly try to interest [the male Savage] in [her] fate and to make [him] really or apparently find [his] own Interest in working for [hers]" (*Discourses*, 170).

This begs the question of how the female interests the male in her fate. Rousseau does not explicitly tell us in the *Second Discourse*, but he does offer some clues for those readers who have the courage to read his notes. Rousseau takes up Locke's suggestion that the male Savage assists the female Savage for the sake of caring for his children. Rousseau rejects this notion. If the male Savage is not interested in the female Savage prior to conception, he will simply wander away and has no reason to assist the female nine months after their union. "If a given woman is of no interest to a man for these nine months, if he ceases even to know her, why will he help her after the birth?" (*Discourses*, 215). Rather than wonder why a man remains attached to a woman, Rousseau tells us the more interesting question is why the male becomes attached to the female in the first place.

Rousseau considers a second possibility, the female Savage uses the promise of the satisfaction of physical desire to convince the male Savage to work for her benefit (and the benefit of the offspring). "Now it is easy to see that the moral aspect of love is a factitious sentiment; born of social practice in order to establish their rule and to make dominant the sex that should obey" (*Discourses*, 155). Just how the female Savage establishes her rule is not explained in the *Second Discourse*. Before we know it, Rousseau reports that the first revolution occurs, the result of which is the family (*Discourses*, 164). In order to understand how the female Savage interests the male Savage in her fate, as well as the fate of her children, it is necessary to recall the explanation Rousseau gives to readers of the *Emile*. At the outset of Rousseau's introduction to Sophie, Rousseau impresses upon us the importance of public opinion to women.

> For them to have what is necessary to their station, they depend on us to give it to them, to want to give it to them, to esteem them worthy of it. They depend on our sentiments, on the value we set on their merit, on the importance we attach to their charms and virtues. (*Emile*, 364)

The importance of others' judgment may seem to be conventional (as it certainly is in the case of Emile), but, for the female, the importance of others' opinion has its foundations in nature. "By the very law of nature women are at the mercy of men's judgments, as much for their own sake as for that of their children" (*Emile*, 364). Regardless if a woman's "station" is the eighteenth-century aristocracy or the state of nature she must render herself pleasing to the judgment of a man in order to obtain "what is necessary to her station."[15]

While the female Savage is able to retain her gentle and humane character, it is at the expense of her independence. In order to provide for herself and her offspring, thereby ensuring the survival of the species, the female Savage sacrifices the natural vigor of her species. Throughout the *Vindications*, Wollstonecraft regrets that women sacrifice their strength to please men. "But should it be proved that woman is naturally weaker than man, whence does it follow that it is natural for her to labour to become still weaker than nature intended her to be?" (*VRW*, 41).[16] The female Savage is a half being. As we have already seen in the works of both Rousseau and Wollstonecraft, this type of weakness seeks to be compensated and tends toward tyranny. The female Savage is no exception to this rule.

> But the moment one man needs the help of another; as soon as it was found to be useful for one to have provisions for two, equality disappeared, property appeared, work became necessary, and the vast forests changed into smiling Fields that had to be watered with the sweat of men, and where slavery and misery were soon seen to sprout and grow together with the harvests. (*Discourses*, 167)

From the very earliest stages of the state of nature, if the species were to survive, the female Savage had to convince the male Savage to do something contrary to his natural inclinations, work for the benefit of another. [17] In other words, the female Savage makes use of the male Savage to follow her inclination and to supplement her own weakness (*Emile*, 67–68). Just like the Little Glutton, the female Savage obtains her food by "this particular cleverness given to the fair sex" as "equitable compensation for their lesser share in strength." By nature the female Savage is motivated by the desire for preservation, not only her own, but that of her children and, consequently, the species. As a result, the relationship between men and women, even in the state of nature, is characterized by "cunning and lasciviousness." These are the objections Wollstonecraft makes in protest to Rousseau's introduction of Sophie and which run contrary to her "first principles."

By considering Rousseau's treatment of female nature in both the *Emile* and the *Second Discourse*, and by remarking on the similarities between the two treatments, rather than the differences, we are able to see Rousseau's inability to arrive at a pure state of nature. In contrast to his predecessors, Rousseau tells his readers that the state of nature is lush and bountiful. As a consequence, human beings enjoy complete independence from others and, therefore, are naturally good. The female Savage's inability to feed and protect the offspring (that is, ensure the survival of the species) without the assistance of the male belies the perfection of the state of nature. It would seem that human beings' needs for survival are incompatible with nature's abundance. Human beings are not solitary creatures. Furthermore, as Rousseau insists throughout his corpus, contact with other human beings is the occasion for vice. In order to obtain help from the male, the female Savage manipulates the desires of the male. From the earliest stages of the state of nature, human beings are concerned with the body, the female with food and the male with sex. It seems that human beings, and most particularly women, are naturally motivated by self-preservation. Despite Rousseau's promise to prove other-wise, human beings as Rousseau presents them are marked by "cunning and lasciviousness." For Wollstonecraft, who holds that human beings are meant to develop their rational capacity and expects that virtue will prevail, this is surely a disappointment. Rousseau's egalitarian political theory does not provide a framework for the independence and freedom from public opinion for woman as Wollstonecraft had hoped.

Chapter Three

Navigating the Land of Chimeras with Our Only Star & Compass

Lured by the promise of fulfilling her utopian dream, Mary Wollstonecraft follows Rousseau into his land of chimeras. Rousseau teaches us, "We are so to speak, born twice . . . once for our species and once for our sex" (*Emile*, 211). The equality and independence of human beings is to be achieved by properly combining these two parts, the human and the sex. Contrary to his critics' claim that Rousseau pursues a chimera or fanciful vision, he insists that human beings' nature ought to be whole and unfractured by the vicious passions, which emerge in civil society. Rousseau promises the readers of the *Emile* that he will educate his young pupil to be whole and independent. By following Rousseau into the land of chimeras, Wollstonecraft hopes that Roussseau will introduce her to woman who is also whole, free from public opinion, and despite her physical differences, equal to man. As we have seen in the first chapter, Wollstonecraft learns from reading Rousseau's *Emile* that the female sex can have salutary effects on the individual woman and the family, as well as the political community. From the outset of her most famous treatise, *A Vindication of the Rights of Woman*, Wollstonecraft follows Rousseau by urging women to eschew their corrupt, selfish pleasures. In the dedicatory letter, Wollstonecraft urges women to foster natural inclinations, which make them tender, dutiful wives and mothers. As a consequence, Wollstonecraft hopes that women will become virtuous and important members of the political community. The happiness of women and the political reform Wollstonecraft advocates depends largely on the differences between men and women.

Although Rousseau imparts to Wollstonecraft the importance of the female sex, he disappoints her in educating the other half of woman, the human half, that part of her which she shares with the species. Rousseau assures the readers of the *Emile* that in childhood, "Everything is equal: girls are children, boys are children; the same name suffices for beings so much alike" (*Emile*, 211). Unfortunately, Rousseau fails to respect this equality between boys and girls in his pedagogy. As we have seen in the second chapter, the little girl whom Rousseau presents to us by way of introducing his ideal woman, Sophie, is female even at this very early age. "The female is female her whole life or at least during her whole youth. Everything recalls her sex to her" (*Emile*, 361). Because she must court the attention and the assistance of a man to ensure that she and her children are well cared for, the female begins to cultivate her reputation at a young age. She is always concerned with others' good opinion of her. The concern with the opinion of others awakens the passions and fosters what Wollstonecraft calls "cunning and lasciviousness." This is true of the Little Glutton and it is true of the female Savage in the State of Nature. Woman, as Rousseau presents her in both the *Emile* and the *Second Discourse*, is a fractured and dependent half-being, who lacks the qualities of the whole, independent human being. Having followed Rousseau into the land of chimeras Wollstonecraft does not fulfill her utopian dream, but finds instead monsters.

Although Rousseau lures Wollstonecraft into the land of chimeras and then disappoints her, he does not abandon her. Throughout his writings, Rousseau presents himself as an alternative to other thinkers, most notably his predecessor John Locke.[1] Perhaps, Locke is to be Wollstonecraft's guide through the land of chimeras in search of woman who is whole, comprised of *both* the female *and* the human.

Scholars of Wollstonecraft are unable to ignore the intellectual relationship between John Locke and Mary Wollstonecraft. Wollstonecraft's professional association with the well known Dissenters of her time, such as Richard Price, Joseph Johnson, and Thomas Paine, connects her to Locke's intellectual descendents. Susan Khin Zaw writes, "Mainstream academia has tended to view Wollstonecraft as of interest (if at all) solely to political and cultural history, by virtue of extending to women liberal conceptions of rights and freedoms picked up from Locke and her more radical acquaintances" (Zaw, 84).

Opening *A Vindication of the Rights of Woman* to the dedicatory letter, we see some evidence that Wollstonecraft subscribes to Lockean principles. Alongside her appeal for the restoration of men's and women's virtues, Wollstonecraft implores her readers to recognize the equality of all human beings. In no other part of the treatise (including the chapter entitled "The Rights and Involved Duties of Mankind Considered") does Wollstonecraft use so forcefully the rhetoric of natural rights doctrine in order to articulate her hopes for women and for the political community. The *Vindication* is dedicated to Charles Maurice de Talleyrand-Péigord, a well known politician in revolutionary France. Wollstonecraft announces her belief that rights and the social contract should be extended to women. Repeating his words back to him, Wollstonecraft challenges Talleyrand to include women in France's new political regime.

> Consider, Sir, dispassionately . . ."that to see one half of the human race excluded from all participation of government, was a political phænomenon that, according to abstract principles, it was impossible to explain." If so, on what does your constitution rest"? If the abstract rights of man will bear discussion and explanation, those of women, by parity of reasoning will not shrink from the test. (*VRW*, 4–5)

Echoing Locke, Wollstonecraft goes on to justify women's political equality by women's capacity for reason.[2] Wollstonecraft wonders "whether, when men contend for their freedom, and be allowed to judge for themselves respecting their own happiness, it be not inconsistent and unjust to subjugate women . . . Who made man the exclusive judge, if woman partake with him the gift of reason?" (*VRW*, 5). John Locke's political thought provides, in this instance, a framework by which Wollstonecraft can argue that women are equal to men. By virtue of their capacity to reason, women consist of the human, as well as the sex. However, Wollstonecraft's commitment to a liberal conception of rights is questionable.

Virginia Muller also considers Wollstonecraft's relationship to the Dissenters, but points to her critical confrontation with liberalism. Wollstonecraft, for example, rejects property as the basis for democracy. Nonetheless, Muller argues, "Along with the other liberal theorists of her time, her [Wollstonecraft's] roots are Lockean" (Muller, 48). The tenets of Wollstonecraft's thought, which link her to Locke, are her belief in reason, the possibility for change, her hope that education will be the catalyst for change, and her commitment to individual liberty (Muller, 48).

In this section of the book I shall explore the influence of John Locke on Mary Wollstonecraft. However, I plan to proceed cautiously. Ralph Wardle tells us in his biography of Wollstonecraft that it is unlikely that she read Locke's explicitly political works, though there is evidence that Wollstonecraft read Locke's educational treatise, *Some Thoughts Concerning Education* (Wardle, 118). In this chapter, I will consider the lessons Wollstonecraft may have learned by reading *Some Thoughts* and how she may have put these lessons to use in the *Vindication*.[3] Recall Rousseau's criticism of Locke's educational treatise: Locke concludes the education of his young pupil prior to the birth of the sex and the social passions associated with it. In other words,

Locke simply educates the human half of the child. Although Rousseau condemns Locke's education as incomplete, Wollstonecraft appreciates the relative equality it affords male and female children. The little girl presented in *Some Thoughts* is strong and active. Locke preserves her natural vigor, which, in turn, prepares her for reason and virtue. Certainly, Wollstonecraft would consider Locke's presentation of the female preferable to the Rousseau's Sophie. In contrast to Rousseau's "half-being," his "wild chimera" (*VRW*, 39), Locke promises to educate the female to share what is common to all human beings, reason and virtue. And, so Wollstonecraft adopts the basic tents of Locke's education and role for females, believing that the chimera or the utopian dream that she pursues is best found by following "our only star and compass," reason.

I. BEINGS SO MUCH ALIKE

John Locke begins his treatise, *Some Thoughts Concerning Education*, by indicating to his readers the importance that education has for political life. *Some Thoughts* comprises educational prescriptions that Locke had originally made in letters written to Edward Clarke, concerning Clarke's young son. Locke explains that he consents to have this private correspondence made public only after much prompting from friends and only out of a sense of civic responsibility.

> For I think it every man's indispensable duty to do all the service he
> can for his country; and I see not what difference he puts between
> himself and his cattle, who lives without that thought. This subject is
> of so great concernment, and a right way of education is of so general
> advantage, that did I find my abilities answered my wishes, I should
> not have needed exhortations or importunities from others.[4]

From the start of his treatise, Locke suggests to his readers that educating the young, even children who are not our own, is the concern of all citizens. The private has real bearing on the public. The strict separation between the public and the private, which generally characterizes liberalism, is relaxed.

In his treatment of *Some Thoughts Concerning Education*, Nathan Tarcov considers its relationship to Locke's political writings. He draws a contrast between Locke's writings and ancient works of political philosophy. Plato's *Republic*, for example, considers the best regime *and* treats the education of citizens. "But Locke's politics are liberal politics, after all; they entail a limited government, and it is limited above all by being freed from the effort of trying to make men good except insofar as that is required to render secure their lives liberty, liberty, and property."[5] Relying on Locke's minor educational writings, Tarcov tells readers of *Some Thoughts* that politics consists of two parts. The first part we may find in the *Two Treatises*. It consists of the origin and extent of political power—those elements that we would generally attribute to liberal politics. The second part consists of the art of governing men and is concerned with determining men's characters. Locke does not recommend books on this latter part of politics (Tarcov, 5). Tarcov suggests that "one can conclude that Locke's account of the art of governing children aids in the task of understanding what he might have written on the second part of politics" (Tarcov, 7). By reading Locke's educational treatise we can begin to understand how the citizens of a liberal political regime, who are free and equal by nature, are educated to preserve their rights and fulfill their duties in a liberal political order.

Scholars of western political thought have noted that the identification of women with the private sphere has precluded their participation in political life.[6] By drawing a relationship between the public and the private in his educational treatise, Locke also blurs the distinction between male and female. Locke does so by educating children of both sexes in a similar manner, fostering in them all of the virtues, which are generally associated with either the male or the female.

Before beginning his prescriptions for the proper education, Locke considers the end of education and offers a definition of happiness. "A sound mind in a sound body is a short but full description of a happy state in this world: he that has these two has little more to wish for, and he that wants either of them will be but little the better for anything else" (*STCE*, 10). Lest we leave our chances for happiness to luck or nature, Locke quickly tells us, "I think I may say that all the men we meet with, nine parts of ten are what they are, good or evil, useful or not, by their education. 'Tis that which makes the great difference in mankind" (*STCE*, 10). After offering his readers the end of education, Locke then turns his attention to the means by which we are to attain happiness. Locke begins with the health of the body because "how requisite a strong constitution, able to endure hardships and fatigue, is to one that will make a figure in the world, is too obvious to need any proof" (*STCE*, 10). *Sotto voce*, Locke criticizes his contemporaries for being weak or, at least, for promoting weakness. He suggests one rule as a correction: gentlemen should use their children as honest farmers do (*STCE*, 10). Insisting "that most children's constitutions are either spoiled, or at least, harmed, by *cockering* and *tenderness*" of mothers, Locke prescribes several ways of fortifying children. He suggests that parents take care not to dress their children too warmly and that they wash their feet in cold water. In addition, Locke suggests that children be allowed to play outdoors. By following Locke's advice, children will become immune to the elements and strong, "able to endure hardships" and "make a figure in the world" (STCE, 10).

After discussing the proper care of a child's body, Locke turns to the education of the mind. The two are not unrelated. "Due care being had to keep the body in strength and vigor so that it may be able to obey and execute the orders of the *mind*, the next and principal business is to set the *mind* right, that on all occasions it may be disposed to consent to nothing but what may be suitable to the dignity and the excellency of a rational creature" (*STCE*, 25). For Locke, the "dignity and excellency of a rational creature" is a certain freedom from our passions. In this respect, Locke has something in common with Rousseau and Wollstonecraft. Like these later thinkers, Locke discourages awakening of passions in children.[7] However, unlike Rousseau, Locke does not depend on the minimalization of our passions to preserve human independence and dignity. Instead, Locke teaches us that reason controls the passions. As we have seen in chapter two, Wollstonecraft departs from Rousseau on this principle as well.

Locke understands a strong mind in the same way that he understands a strong body. "As the strength of the body lies in being able to endure hardships, so does that of the mind" (*STCE*, 25). Just as parents must begin to form good physical habits in their children at a young age (eating only when they are hungry, for example) so they must encourage good mental habits in their children. "And the great principle and foundation of all virtue and worth is placed in this, that a man is able to *deny himself* his desires, cross his own inclinations, and purely follow what reason directs as best though the appetite lean the other way" (*STCE*, 25). If a child is indulged at an early age, Locke holds little hope that he will eventually deny himself his desires. Quite, the contrary, Locke warns

> For he that has been used to have his will in everything as long as he was in [petti]coats, why should we think it strange that he should desire it and contend for it still when he is in breeches? . . . He had the will of his maid before he could speak or go; he had the mastery of his parents ever since he could prattle; and why, now that he is grown up, is stronger and wiser than he was then, why now of a sudden must he be restrained or curbed? (*STCE*, 26)

Locke suggests that, in order to ensure that children will enjoy freedom and equality as adults, children must be subject to parents' strict authority when they are young.

Locke imagines that the proper education of children will culminate in affection and friendship between father and son. The young gentleman will become the equal to his father. In order to achieve this equality, a parent must recognize the child's inferiority. "Children, I confess are not born in full state of this *Equality*, though they are born to it. Their Parents have a sort of Rule and Jurisdiction over them when they come into the World, and for some time after, but 'tis a temporary one" (*TT*, 304). The authority of the parents extends only until the child gains use of his own reason. "The Bonds of this Subjection are like the Swaddling Cloths they are wrapt up in, and supported by in the weakness of their Infancy. Age and Reason as they grow up, loosen them till at length they drop quite off, and leave a Man at his own free Disposal" (*TT*, 304). A failure to support the child in his infancy so that he may come to rely on his own reason as an adult is the responsibility of parents. "The *Power*, then *that Parents have* over their Children, arises from that Duty which is incumbent on them, to take care of their Off-Spring, during the imperfect state of Childhood. To inform the Mind, and govern the Actions of their yet ignorant Nonage, till Reason shall take its place, and ease them from that Trouble, is what the Children want, and the Parents are bound to" (*TT*, 306). It is in this way that father and son eventually become equal to one another. "But after that, the Father and Son are equally *free* as much as Tutor and Pupil after Nonage; equally Subjects of the same Law together, without any Dominion left in the Father over the Life, Liberty, or Estate of his Son, whether they be only in the State and under the Law of Nature, or under the positive Laws of an Establish'd Government" (*TT*, 307).

Parents, Locke tells us, should expect honor from their children only to the extent that they fulfill their obligation to them. "The *honour due from a Child*, places in the Parents a perpetual right to respect, reverence, support and compliance too, more or less, as the Father's care, cost, and kindness in his Education, has been more or less" (*TT*, 312). In other words, parents should only expect honor from their children, if they have properly educated their children, if they have brought them to the use of their own reason. [8]

Locke makes a similar argument in *Some Thoughts Concerning Education*. He warns parents not to undermine the natural equality to which their children are born by allowing them too much freedom. "Be sure then to establish authority of a father *as soon* as he is capable of submission and can understand in whose power he is. If you would have him stand in awe of you, imprint it in his infancy, and as he approaches more to a man admit him nearer to your familiarity; so shall you have him your obedient subject (as is fit) whilst he is a child, and your affectionate friend when he is a man" (*STCE*, 30). Most parents, too eager for the affection of their children, are too indulgent with them when they are little and desire their submission later. "For liberty and indulgence can do no good to *children*: their want of judgment makes them stand in need of restraint and discipline. And, on the contrary, imperiousness and severity is but an ill way of treating men, who have reason of their own to guide them" (*STCE*, 31). Locke suggests that children are best educated if they are under the strict discipline of his parents. Gradually, the discipline is to be abated as the child becomes more able to defer to his own reason.

Before turning our attention to the ways in which Wollstonecraft may have followed Locke's *Some Thoughts* in making her own recommendations for female education in the *Vindication*, it is worth stopping to consider whether Locke considers his educational plan appropriate for girls. Wendy Gunther-Canada argues, no. Gunther-Canada acknowledges the important contributions that Locke and Rousseau make to educational writings. However, Gunther-Canada goes on to suggest, Wollstonecraft's "voice from the void" remained necessary because neither Locke nor Rousseau were able to overcome their presuppositions about gender. "Although both of these works moved past the politics of generation to focus on childhood neither Locke nor Rousseau could get beyond the politics of gender to educate the girl" (Gunther-Canada, 56). After all, Locke's educational treatise is comprised of the letters he had previously written to Edward Clarke concerning the education of his son (*STCE*, 7–8, 12). *Some Thoughts*, then, is explicitly concerned with the education of a young gentleman. We would expect Wollstonecraft to object to an education, which preserves hereditary honors bestowed to those of a certain class and sex. However, despite the young gentleman for whom Locke's prescriptions were made, his educational plan is rather egalitarian and, I would suggest, may be easily extended to girls.

Given the socially dynamic era during which Locke writes *Some Thoughts*, Locke advises parents who educate their children simply for a position of privilege that they do their children a disservice. "He that . . . breeds his son so as if he designed him to sleep over his life in the plenty and ease of a full fortune he intends to leave him, little considers the examples he has seen or the age he lives in" (*STCE*, 18). On the contrary, education should prepare the child for any social position. "The great cordial of nature is sleep . . . he is very unfortunate who can take his cordial only in his mother's fine gilt cup, and not in a wooden dish" (*STCE*, 22). Robert Horowitz warns the readers of *Some Thoughts* not to jump to the conclusion that Locke means to perpetuate a titled nobility. "While the gentry consisted largely of families of varying degrees of wealth, within its ranks were always to be found men of modest means but of exceptional intelligence, industry, and foresight who possessed the capacity for improving their circumstances."[9]

Locke does not protect the hereditary privilege of wealth, nor does he protect the hereditary privilege of sex. While Locke's immediate task is to edu-cate a young gentleman, his prescriptions may easily be adopted to educate girls in a manner that is similar or equal to boys. Locke minimizes the differences between the sexes in two ways: By implicitly extending his educational prin-ciples to girls and by suggesting boys be educated in a manner generally reserved for girls. In this way, Locke fosters qualities traditionally associated with boys and those generally ascribed to girls in children of both sexes. Locke admits that he writes for the benefit of a young gentleman and his prescriptions "will not so perfectly suit the education of *daughters*" (*STCE*, 12). However, the distinctions Locke would make are not so great that he feels he must elaborate. Instead, he leaves it to his readers to judge. "Where the difference of sex requires different treatment, it will be no hard matter to distinguish" (*STCE*, 12). As it turns out, it is difficult to distinguish which of Locke's prescriptions are inappropriate for daughters. The question of how little girls are to be educated differently from boys comes up almost immediately. One of the first suggestions Locke makes for children is outdoor activity (*STCE*, 14). By exposing a child to the sun and wind, the body will be made strong and healthy, "brought to bear almost any-thing" (*STCE*, 14). Certainly, this seems appropriate for boys. Our conceptions of manliness include bodily strength. Locke knows that, for girls, the concern is not that the body should be made strong, but that it should be made attrac-tive. Wollstonecraft never tires of pointing out female beauty is all too often perniciously identified with weakness.[10] It would seem that this would be one of those instances "where sex requires different treatment." Locke anticipates this concern, but does not give it a second thought.

> And although greater regard be had to beauty in the daughters, yet I will take the liberty to say that the more they are in the *air*, without preju-dice to their faces, the stronger and healthier they will be; and the nearer they come to the hardships of their brothers in their education, the greater advantage will they receive from it all the remaining parts of their lives. (*STCE*, 14)

Prohibiting girls from playing outdoors may make them conventionally beautiful, but it also makes them unnaturally weak. In addition to the immediate benefit to the health of the girl, Locke promises future benefit from outdoor activity. Locke does not pause to elaborate the "greater advantage" that girls will receive from their early exposure to the elements, but continues to inform parents on the proper care of the young pupil's body. We know, however, that Locke prepares for the education of the mind with the education of the body. We can infer then that Locke expects that the strength and health of the little girl's body will foster the strength of her mind. This expectation is met by considering the second way by which Locke minimizes the differences between little girls and boys.

Just as Locke has advised his readers to educate girls in a similar manner to boys, he tells us that boys should be educated more like girls. Locke considers the benefits of sending young gentlemen away to school. "Being abroad, it is true will make him bolder and better able to bustle and shift amongst boys his own age; and the emulation of schoolfellows often puts life and industry into young lads" (*STCE*, 46). The trouble is, schoolmasters are more concerned with teaching their pupils "languages of the ancient Greeks and Romans" (*STCE*, 46) than they are with "forming their minds to virtue" (*STCE*, 46). Locke decides against sending a young gentleman to school. Instead, Locke suggests he be educated at home. Tarcov attributes Locke's preference for educating the child at home to Locke's rejection of "the schoolboy code of manliness" (Tarcov, 112). To be sure, Locke rejects the accepted behavior of schoolboys, but to suggest that it is a "code of manliness" is a euphemism, to say the least.

> For, as that boldness and spirit which lads get amongst their playfellows at school, it has ordinarily such a mixture of rudeness and ill-turned confidence that those misbecoming and shifting in the world must be unlearned and all the tincture washed out again to make way for better principles and such manners as make a truly worthy man. (*STCE*, 46)

Schoolboys, according to Locke, are pranksters and cheats. Locke acknowledges that a private education may allow for a certain shyness in the child but prefers it nonetheless.

> He that considers how diametrically opposite the skill of living well and managing as a man should do his affairs in the world is to the malapertness, tricking, or violence learned amongst schoolboys will think the faults of a privater education infinitely to be preferred to such improvements and will take care to preserve his child's innocence and modesty at home, as being near of kin and more in the way of those qualities which make a useful and able man. (*STCE*, 46).

Modesty, which is generally associated with females, is now associated with manliness by Locke.

By educating a son at home, he will be educated more like his sister. In defense of the private education, Locke adds that no one finds or suspects "that retirement and bashfulness which their daughters are brought up in make them less knowing or less able women" (*STCE*, 46). "Knowing" and "able" women must achieve parity with "useful and able" men. For if the consequence of their education were so greatly different, Locke could not suggest to his readers that parents adopt the means to an inferior end. Locke goes on to defend his preference for a private education. "Virtue is harder to be got than knowledge of the world, and if lost in a young man is seldom recovered. Sheepishness and ignorance of the world, the faults imputed to a private education, are neither the necessary consequences of being bred at home nor, if they were, are they incurable evils" (*STCE*, 46). Locke condemns the parents who misunderstand the ends of education. He does not prescribe a strong body and a strong mind so that the young gentleman is "better able to bustle and shift" amongst his peers. He prescribes a strong body and mind for the sake of virtue. "It is preposterous therefore to sacrifice his innocency [sic] to the attaining of confidence and some little skill of bustling for himself amongst others by his conversation with ill-bred and vicious boys when the chief use of that sturdiness and standing upon his own legs is only for the preservation of his virtue" (*STCE*, 47). Virtue, though it requires attention and care, is more characteristic of a private education, the type of education that is usually afforded to little girls. Indeed, Locke tells his readers that modesty, a virtue fostered in female children, "better fits them for instruction; and therefore there needs not any great care to stock them with confidence beforehand. That which requires most time, pains, and assiduity is to work into them [boys] the principles and practice of virtue and good-breeding" (*STCE*, 47).

Still, Locke knows some will insist on the practical benefits of sending their sons to school. "But fathers, observing that fortune is often most successfully courted by bold and bustling men, are glad to see their sons pert and forward betimes, take it for a happy omen that they will be thriving men, and look on the tricks they play their schoolfellows or learn from them as proficiency in the art of living and making their way in the world" (*STCE*, 48). Locke is quick to correct this notion of knowing, able men. "And 'tis not the waggeries or cheats practiced amongst schoolboys . . . that make an able man, but the principles of justice, generosity and sobriety, joined with observation and industry, qualities which I judge schoolboys do not learn from one another" (*STCE*, 48). If Locke's proposed education is, in some respects, more feminine as Tarcov has suggested, it would seem that females have a greater propensity for these virtues of justice, generosity, and sobriety. We should note that for Locke justice, a virtue generally belonging to the public sphere and often associated with men, is made possible and encouraged by the presence of modesty, an attribute which is often associated with women. The education that Locke prescribes in *Some Thoughts* bridges the gap between the public and the private and, in so doing, Locke's education combines the masculine and the feminine virtues. A certain type of equality between boys and girls, "beings so much alike," is achieved by extending Locke's educational principles to girls, as well as boys. Using reason to navigate the land of chimeras, Locke offers Wollstonecraft an example of an education, which educates the human half of the female.

II. RATIONAL CREATURES RUN WILD

Commentators on Wollstonecraft's corpus have noticed the influence of Locke's *Some Thoughts* on Wollstonecraft's educational writings. Janet Todd and Moira Ferguson write, "Throughout these early works Wollstonecraft consistently treated education as the solution to women's mental and physical lack of development and as a sine qua non for independence, equality, and the virtuous life."[11] Not only does Wollstonecraft adopt Locke's educational principles for her early educational writings, but she also continues to adhere to them in her later political treatise, *A Vindication of the Rights of Woman*. Even Virginia Sapiro, who has warned us not to mistake Wollstonecraft's political thought as simply Lockean, must acknowledge Locke's influence on Wollstonecraft. "Wollstonecraft's goal was the development of habits of mind that would give the person the independent ability to reason toward virtue" (Sapiro, 240).

Like Locke, Wollstonecraft begins her treatise by indicating the important connection between a liberal political regime and the education afforded to its citizens. *A Vindication of the Rights of Woman* is dedicated to Charles Maurice de Talleyrand-Périgord, whose report on public education Wollstonecraft admired. As we have already noticed, Wollstonecraft's dedicatory letter is the place in the *Vindication* at which she relies most on the rhetoric of natural rights and social contract theory in order to understand political life. Wollstonecraft announces at the outset that she dedicates the volume to Talleyrand because education is so necessary to secure the rights of woman. "Having read with great pleasure a pamphlet which you have lately published, I dedicate this volume to you; to induce you to reconsider the subject, and maturely weigh what I have advanced respecting the rights of woman and national education" (*VRW*, 4). Ensuring the rights of woman and including her in a national education plan will promote woman's independence. "Independence I have long considered as the grand blessing of life, the basis of every virtue—and independence I will ever secure by contracting my wants, though I were to live on a barren heath" (*VRW*, 4). Education is necessary to promote equality and independence. In a manner similar to Locke, Wollstonecraft establishes a close link between the private and the public.

Wollstonecraft begins the introduction to *A Vindication of the Rights of Woman* by considering the inferiority of women as it exists in her time. "I have sighed when obliged to confess, that either nature has made a great difference between man and man, or that the civilization which has hitherto taken place in the world has been very partial" (*VRW*, 7). Given the choice of nature or civilization, Wollstonecraft, like Locke, attributes the great difference between man and man to civilization and, more particularly, to education.[12] Women, who are rendered especially "weak and wretched," suffer from "a false system of education, gathered from books written on this subject by men, who considering females rather as women than human creatures, have been more anxious to make them alluring mistresses than affectionate wives and rational mothers" (*VRW*, 7). As we have already seen by considering the similarities and differences between Rousseau and Wollstonecraft, she does not consider civilization to be a corrupting force, which necessarily degrades human beings' equality and independence. Quite the contrary, for Wollstonecraft, civilization has great potential to encourage reason and virtue in human beings and, thereby, allow them to be equal and independent. In this respect, Wollstonecraft seems to have more in common with Locke than she does with Rousseau.

The first obstacle Wollstonecraft must overcome in advocating the equality of women is the obvious difference between men and women in physical strength. "In the government of the physical world it is observable that the female in point of strength is, in general, inferior to the male. This is a law of nature; and it does not appear to be suspended or abrogated in favor of woman" (*VRW*, 8). That being said, Wollstonecraft condemns men for their (rather successful) attempt to render women weaker still. "But not content with this natural pre-eminence, men endeavour to sink us still lower, merely to render us alluring objects for a moment" (*VRW*, 8). Women are complicit in their degradation, for they take pleasure in the attention bestowed upon them for their feminine beauty and elegance, disregarding their human qualities. As a result, they mistake fleeting pleasure for happiness. Wollstonecraft echoes Locke in offering her own definition of happiness. "I earnestly wish to point out in what true dignity and human happiness consists— I wish to persuade women to endeavour to acquire strength, both of mind and body, and to convince them that the soft phrases, susceptibility of heart, delicacy of sentiment, and refinement of taste, are almost synonymous with epithets of weakness" (VRW, 9).

Wollstonecraft's correction of women's education has two components, which often seem difficult to distinguish. Wollstonecraft expects that reason and virtue are to be the basis for equality between men and women. The capacity for reason and virtue are similar in both men and women, they are attributes common to all human beings. Encouraging reason and virtue in females educates the human half and not simply the sex. Above all, Wollstonecraft wants women to be rational and virtuous creatures. She argues that, afforded the proper education, women as well as men, would have rational capacity. However, in order to promote reason and virtue in women, Wollstonecraft must correct false notions of beauty, which are often associated with physical weakness. The education of girls that Wollstonecraft witnesses, which renders females "alluring objects for the moment," corrupts them in two ways. Because frailty is considered alluring, it encourages physical weakness. Women are thought to be incapable of any hardship. The ability to endure hardship, as we have seen by considering Locke's treatise on education, is so often associated with virtue. Furthermore, the excessive attention to the body deprives the mind of attention. As an antidote to the misguided education of women, which treats the female sex simply as woman, but not as human, Wollstonecraft advocates a restoration of woman's natural physical strength (though it may remain relatively less than man's), along with the cultivation of her reason.

> The most perfect education . . . is such an exercise of the understanding as is best calculated to strengthen the body and form the heart. Or, in other words, to enable the individual to attain such habits of virtue as will render it independent. In fact, it is a farce to call any being virtuous whose virtues do not result from the exercise of its own reason. (VRW, 21)

Wollstonecraft had understood Rousseau to be of the same mind (VRW, 21). She was disappointed that he did not put forth such an education for Sophie in order to foster her independence. The education Wollstonecraft prescribes in the *Vindication* does echo the educational principles put forth by Locke in *Some Thoughts Concerning Education.*

Throughout the *Vindication*, Wollstonecraft returns to the commonly held belief that man's greater physical strength gives him superiority over woman. "I will allow that bodily strength seems to give man a natural superiority over woman; and this is the only solid basis on which the superiority of the sex can be built" (*VRW*, 39). If Wollstonecraft is to contend for the equality between men and women, she will have to do so on metaphysical grounds. She does so by arguing that men and women have similar capacity for reason and virtue. "But I still insist, that not only virtue, but the knowledge of the two sexes should be the same in nature, if not degree, and that women considered not only as moral, but rational creatures, ought to endeavour to acquire human virtue (perfections) by the same means as men" (*VRW*, 39). That being said, Wollstonecraft still has not resolved the difficulty of women's inferior physical strength and she must return to it immediately. "But, if strength of body be, with some shew [sic] of reason, the boast of men, why are women so infatuated as to be proud of a defect?" (*VRW*, 39). Therefore, Wollstonecraft's first concern in educating women to be rational and virtuous human beings is the improvement of the female body. "The first step of those mothers and fathers, who really attend to the education of females, should be, if not to strengthen the body, at least, not to destroy the constitution by mistaken notions of beauty and female excellence" (*VRW*, 40). In order to at least preserve, if not improve upon, women's natural physical strength, Wollstonecraft suggests parents follow a plan contrary to Rousseau's educational prescriptions. "The mother, who wishes to give true dignity of character to her daughter, must, regardless of sneers of ignorance, proceed on a plan diametrically opposite to that which Rousseau has recommended with all the deluding charms of eloquence and philosophical sophistry" (*VRW*, 41).

In denigrating Rousseau's principles for educating girls, Wollstonecraft puts forth principles of education similar to those suggested by John Locke in *Some Thoughts Concerning Education.* One of the first prescriptions Locke makes for a young child (male or female) is outdoor activity. Wollstonecraft also advocates exercise. "Throughout the whole animal kingdom every young creature requires almost continual exercise, and the infancy of children, conformable to this intimation should be passed in harmless gambols, that exercise the feet and hands, without requiring very minute direction from the head, or the constant attention of a nurse" (*VRW*, 41). Indeed, the restraint placed on young girls is particularly damaging. Wollstonecraft draws an analogy to Chinese bands. "To preserve personal beauty, woman's glory! The limbs and faculties are cramped with worse than Chinese bands, and the sedentary life which they are condemned to live, whilst boys frolic in the open air, weakens the muscles and relaxes the nerves" (*VRW*, 41). Wollstonecraft's editor notes that Wollstonecraft may have learned about Chinese bands by reading Locke's *Some Thoughts*. And, Locke does, in fact, give a fairly lengthy and alarming account of the damage Chinese bands (and by implication, other restrictive clothing) can have on the human body (*STCE*, 15–16).

Wollstonecraft follows Locke in recognizing the benefit of physical activity for children. In this respect, boys and girls are the same. Beginning from this Lockean premise, Wollstonecraft goes on to further minimize the differences between boys and girls. Rousseau attributes girls' inactivity and interest in their lifeless dolls to their nature. For Wollstonecraft, it is simply the likely consequence of prohibiting any choice of activity to girls. Wollstonecraft makes an argument heard by many feminists today: If allowed a choice, girls would not choose their traditional pastimes, such as playing with dolls.

> I have probably had an opportunity of observing more girls in their infancy than J.J. Rousseau—I can recollect my own feelings, and I have looked steadily around me; yet, so far from coinciding with him in opinion respecting the first dawn of the female character, I will venture to affirm, that a girl, whose spirits have not been damped by inactivity, or innocence tainted by false shame, will always be a romp, and the doll will never excite attention unless confinement allows her no alternative. (*VRW*, 43)

Convention, not nature, determines the interest of little girls.[13] Wollstonecraft continues. Not only is there no natural distinction in the type of play girls and boys enjoy, but there is also no natural distinction in their choice of playmates. "Girls and boys, in short, would play harmlessly together, if distinction of sex was not inculcated long before nature makes any difference" (*VRW*, 43). In other words, in childhood, "everything is equal" (*Emile,* 211). By allowing young girls their natural vigor, Wollstonecraft begins to educate the human half of woman.

Having established the relative physical equality of girls and boys, Wollstonecraft can then argue for their relative metaphyiscal equality. "I will go further, and affirm, as an indisputable fact, that most of the women, in the circle of my observation, who have acted like rational creatures, or shewn [sic] any vigour of intellect, have accidentally been allowed to run wild—as some of the elegant formers of the fair sex would insinuate" (*VRW*, 43). For Wollstonecraft, like Locke, there is a direct relationship between the strength and health of the body and the strength of the mind.

Wollstonecraft argues that for a child to grow up to be rational and virtuous, she needs the fortitude that comes with a strong body. Virtue entails enduring hardship, which is difficult for a weak creature. In addition to a strong body, Wollstonecraft knows that the mind must be fortified so that reason may control the passions. Just as Locke has recommended that children depend on the reason of their parents until their own reason gains its strength, so too does Wollstonecraft.

In her discussion of the child's duty to her parents, Wollstonecraft tells her readers the respect a child owes to his or her parents depends on the extent to which a parent fulfills his or her responsibility to the child. The responsibility of the parent is to foster the reason of the child, gradually teaching the child to depend on his or her own reason to control his passions. This is the duty of parents, according to Locke as well. And, like Locke, Wollstonecraft worries that parents do not fulfill their responsibility. Too often parents are concerned with making their children simply obey them without teaching them to consult reason and to obey it, be it their parents' reason or their own. "For the absurd duty, too often inculcated, of obeying a parent only on account of his being a parent, shackles the mind, and prepares it for a slavish submission to any power but reason" (*VRW*, 153). This propensity in parents is greater when raising daughters. Wollstonecraft's suggestions for encouraging reason in daughters echoes Locke's recommendations for cultivating reason in the young gentleman. "Females, it is true, are too much under the dominion of their parents; and few parents think of addressing their children in the following manner . . . It is your interest to obey me till you can judge yourself . . . but when your mind arrives at maturity, you must only obey me, or rather respect my opinions, so far as they coincide with the light that is breaking in you own mind" (*VRW*, 154). Locke goes on to advise parents that they do not go too far in gaining control over their children's passions, bending the will of their children to their own. Wollstonecraft adopts Locke's prescription. "A slavish bondage to parents cramps every faculty of mind; and Mr. Locke very judiciously observes, that 'if the mind be curbed and humbled too much in children; if their spirits be abased and broken too much by too strict an hand over them; they lose all vigour and industry'" (*VRW*, 155). By yielding only to the reason (and not the authority) of her parents, a young girl allows her own reason to develop and becomes accustomed to obeying it. When the child gains the use of her own reason, she becomes her parents' equal, no longer subject to their authority. She respects and seeks her parents' opinion, perhaps in the manner of friendship, as Locke imagines the relationship between father and son, but she, like the gentleman, is not obliged to obey. Reason, along with virtue, allows the female independence.

As the young girl gradually learns to depend on her own strengthening reason, Wollstonecraft hopes that she will also practice virtue. As is the case for Locke, Wollstonecraft considers modesty an important foundation for educating girls to be virtuous. Writing in the wake of Rousseau's *Emile* Wollstonecraft, much more so than Locke, is sensitive to the way in which modesty has been considered particularly feminine and used as a means to perpetuate women's physical and rational weaknesses. As a result, Wollstonecraft's treatment of modesty is more complicated than Locke's discussion of this virtue. Wollstonecraft diverges from Rousseau's understanding of modesty. Rousseau suggests that modesty, the real or feigned aversion to a man's sexual advances, is the means by which the female counters the male's greater physical strength. The ambivalent character of modesty excites the male sexually, allowing the female to manipulate his passions to her own safety and advantage. Wollstonecraft's understanding of modesty is more compatible with the strong body and mind, rather than a weak body, that she hopes for in educating the human half of the female. Wollstonecraft offers two conceptions of modesty. In the first instance, Wollstonecraft follows the tradition that associates it with chastity. Chastity, as opposed to the pretension to chastity that often veils the manipulation of men's sexual desires, results in purity of mind. In the second instance, modesty is a type of self-knowledge.

> I have noticed two distinct modes; and in defining modesty, it appears to me equally proper to discriminate that purity of mind, which is the effect of chastity, from a simplicity of character that leads us to form a just opinion of ourselves, equally distant from vanity or presumption, though by no means incompatible with a lofty consciousness of our own dignity. Modesty, in the latter signification of the term, that soberness of mind which teaches a man not to think more highly of himself than he ought to think, and should be distinguished from humility, because humility is a kind of self-abasement. (*VRW*, 121–122)

In a rhetorical flourish so typical of Wollstonecraft, she continues to refute the notion that modesty is compatible with sexual attraction and, instead identifies it with human reason and knowledge.

> Purity of mind, or that genuine delicacy, which is the only virtuous support of chastity, is near akin to the refinement of humanity, which never resides in any but cultivated minds. It is something nobler than

innocence, it is the delicacy of reflections, and not the coyness of ignorance. The reserve of reason . . . is seldom seen in any degree, unless the soul is active, [and] may easily be distinguished from rustic shyness or wanton skittishness; and so far from being incompatible with knowledge, it is its fairest fruit. (*VRW*, 122–123)

By asserting modesty's connection with reason and the human soul, modesty becomes a virtue, which is common to all human beings, rather than the preserve of the female sex. Wollstonecraft demonstrates modesty's human, rather than feminine quality, by arguing that it is to be expected in men, more so than women.

Wollstonecraft allows for the possibility that virtue may differ in the degree to which it is present in male and female, though she insists the virtue and knowledge of both sexes must be the same in nature (*VRW*, 39). Unlike Locke, Wollstonecraft struggles to promote the virtue of modesty with a concern for what is common to all human beings *and* a concern for what is particular to the sex. In this instance, Wollstonecraft admits that modesty, perhaps, should be attributed to women more so than men—but only insofar as women may be considered more chaste. "As a sex, women are more chaste than men, and as modesty is the effect of chastity, they may deserve to have this virtue ascribed to them in rather an appropriate sense" (*VRW*, 124). Due to the perverted conception of modesty popular in Wollstonecraft's day, she is reluctant to attribute modesty—purity or soberness of mind—to women. "Yet, I must be allowed to add an hesitating if:—for I doubt whether chastity will produce modesty, though it may propriety of conduct, when it is merely a respect for the opinion of the world, and when coquetry and the lovelorn tales of novelists employ thoughts" (*VRW*, 124–125). Given her understanding of modesty, Wollstonecraft finds modesty more common in men than women. "Nay, from experience, and reason, I should be led to expect to meet with more modesty amongst men than women, simply because men exercise their understandings more than women" (*VRW*, 125).

Throughout the *Vindication*, Wollstonecraft asserts that virtue must be the same in male and female. She makes this claim in order to assert women's capacity for reason. In other words, she makes the claim to extend traditionally male virtues to women. In this instance, however, Wollstonecraft does just the opposite: she extends this traditionally feminine virtue to men. "Modesty must be cultivated by both sexes, or it will ever remain a sickly hothouse plant, whilst the affection of it, the fig leaf borrowed by wantonness, may give zest to voluptuous enjoyments"

(*VRW*, 126). Modesty must be common to all. If not, the lack of it in one sex will discourage it in the other and result in vice. Recall that Locke also minimizes the differences between male and female by extending this virtue, so often associated with the female sex, to males. Locke does so because he appreciates the benefit modesty has to instruction and argues that it encourages other virtues, such as justice. Wollstonecraft also sees modesty as the foundation to other virtues, in particular the exercise of one's duties. Wollstonecraft pleads with her readers to adopt her understanding of modesty and to acquire it.

> Would ye, O my sisters, really possess modesty, ye must remember that the possession of virtue . . . is incompatible with ignorance and vanity! Ye must acquire that soberness of mind, which the exercise of duties, and the pursuit of knowledge, alone must inspire, or ye will remain in a doubtful dependent situation, and only be loved whilst ye are fair! The downcast eye, the rosy blush, the retiring grace, are all proper in their season; but modesty, being the child of reason, cannot long exist with the sensibility that is not tempered by reflection. (*VRW*, 130–131)

Modesty, which Wollstonecraft associates with soberness of mind, is a virtue that may serve as the foundation for other virtues. In this respect, Wollstonecraft's understanding is more similar to Locke's than Rousseau's conception of modesty. Rousseau's notion of modesty leads to cunning and lasciviousness, creating vicious monsters.

Wollstonecraft follows Locke in emphasizing to parents the importance of educating both male and female children to be strong in both body and mind. Both authors further minimize the difference between boys and girls by fostering similar virtues in them, in particular, modesty. For these reasons, Locke would seem to be a better guide to Wollstonecraft as she makes her way through the land of chimeras in pursuit of her utopian dream. We now turn our attention to the expectations Locke and Wollstonecraft have for the robust and rational young lady in her adult role.

III. GOOD BREEDING

As we have seen both Locke and Wollstonecraft begin their treatises by indicating the important connection between a liberal political regime and the education afforded to its citizens. For both Locke and Wollstonecraft, the adult female retains her relative equality to her husband and contributes to the political community by educating her children. It remains to be seen how girls, educated according to Locke's prescriptions will participate in the community, and if Locke can provide an example of rational motherhood in a similar manner as he offered an example of girls strong in mind and body.

Rousseau criticizes Locke for concluding the little gentleman's education just before the sexual passions have been awakened and before the young man must choose a wife (*Emile*, 357). The implication is that Locke gives us no indication of the woman suitable for this young man or the character of their relationship. I would suggest the contrary. To be sure, Locke does not treat the education of girls separately in the way that Rousseau does. As I have already argued, Locke's expectations for female children may be inferred from his expectations for male children. In a similar manner, Locke alerts us to the importance of choosing a wife with certain qualities by comparing the choice of a wife to the choice of a tutor. When instructing parents in the selection of a tutor for their sons, Locke warns his readers to take this task seriously. "In this choice be as curious as you would be in that of a wife for him, for you must not think of trial or changing afterwards; that would cause great inconvenience to you, and greater to your son" (*STCE*, 64). Locke's comparison invites his readers to wonder what qualities the tutor and the wife have in common.

Locke cites a handful of important qualities a tutor must possess and his readers will readily appreciate these qualities apply to a good wife and mother, as well. Foremost among these qualities, Locke recommends the tutor be well bred. "Good breeding" is a fairly ambiguous phrase and smacks of the aristocratic. It is worthwhile to determine how Locke understands it. After insisting on "good breeding" in the choice of a tutor, Locke tells his readers, "Breeding is that which sets a gloss upon all his other good qualities and renders them useful to him in procuring the esteem and good will of all that he come near" (*STCE*, 65). It is the "first and most taking of all social virtues" (*STCE*, 107). He later tells us there is but one rule to follow in order to avoid ill breeding: "not to think meanly of ourselves and not to think meanly of others" (*STCE*, 106). To be sure there is a superficial element to good breeding and Locke does acknowledge the outward expression of it. However, he also appreciates that this outward expression emanates from a "general good will and regard for all people" and "a disposition of the mind" (*STCE*, 107). For the author of the *Second Treatise*, the challenge of education is to make human beings, who are free and equal in the state of nature, able to preserve their rights and fulfill their duties in civil society. This requires a certain deference and regard for others, which is demonstrated by good breeding and by virtue.[14] Given the importance education has to civil society, Locke advises parents to expect more than is commonly looked for in tutors. "The character of a sober man and a scholar is . . . what everyone expects in a tutor. This generally is thought enough and is all that parents commonly look for. But when such a one has emptied out into his pupil all the Latin and logic he has brought from the university, will that furniture make him a fine gentleman?" Recall that Locke recommends educating children at home for the sake of virtue. Again, Locke warns us that virtue should not be sacrificed for knowledge of ancient languages. Locke quickly challenges parents to consider how it would be possible for their children to become better bred than the man, who instructed them. "Or can it be expected that he should be better bred, better skilled in the world, better principled in the grounds and foundations of virtue and generosity than his young *tutor* is?" (*STCE*, 64–65).

Locke's question concerning the tutor may also be raised with respect to the child's mother. Can it be expected that a child will be "better principled in the grounds and foundations of virtue and generosity" than his mother"? We have only to remember the importance Locke places on parents' good example to their children. "I must here take the liberty to mind *parents* of this one thing, viz. that he that will have his son have a respect for him and his orders must himself have a great reverence for his son . . . You must do nothing before him which you would not have him imitate. If anything escape you which you would have pass for a fault in him, he will be sure to shelter himself under your example" (*STCE*, 50, my emphasis). We may take Locke's point further still. And, of course, it is not only children, in Locke's view, but all of us who are "prone to imitation" (*STCE*, 50). The company we keep can have a positive or negative influence on adults as well as children. A man can be expected to be principled and reasonable only if his wife, with whom constantly associates, is so as well.

Moreover, Locke recommends that the mother take on the role of the tutor, in at least one subject, in a way that demonstrates the woman's capacity for reason and knowledge. Although Locke suggest the usual subjects for study, such as Latin, geography, and astronomy, he considers "Latin and language" the "least part of education" and "scholarly" credentials the least qualities to be sought in a tutor. Locke argues instead, "one who, knowing how much virtue and a well-tempered soul is to be preferred to any sort of *learning* or *language*, makes it his chief business to form the mind of his scholars and give that a right disposition" (*STCE*, 135). Locke anticipates those who would protest, insisting on the difficulty of Latin. "And, indeed, whatever stir there is made about getting of Latin as the great and difficult business, his mother may teach it him herself" (*STCE*, 135). Before we take this as an insult to mothers, we should consider Locke's description of a mother taking on this task. Though Locke may consider a tutor's scholarly credentials overrated, he appreciates that learning Latin takes some effort. If a mother wished to teach her child Latin, she must first teach herself to read Latin, beginning with a Latin Testament.[15] "And when she understands the Evangelists in Latin, let her in the same manner read Aesop's *Fables*, and so proceed on to Europius, Justin, and other such books" (*STCE*, 135). The mother who gains knowledge of Latin by following Locke's advice appears to acquire on her own something of a classical education—something which would have surely appealed to Wollstonecraft, an autodidact herself.

Finally, Locke insists the father respect the tutor. "You must be sure to use him with great respect and cause all of your family to do so too. For you cannot expect your son should have any regard for one whom he sees you or his mother or others slight. If you think him worthy of contempt, you have chosen amiss" (*STCE*, 62). Only if the tutor is chosen correctly, however, will he be deserving of respect. By comparing the choice of a wife to the choice of a tutor, Locke has indicated the seriousness and importance of the matter. If the wife is chosen correctly, perhaps on the basis for her capacity for reason and virtue, she too will be deserving of respect.

Locke allows us to observe a mother educating her children and preparing them for civil society. Potentially sharing many of the traits of a good tutor, Locke's rational mother instructs her children in various academic subjects and serves as an example of good breeding and virtue. Locke's rational mother achieves intellectual equality with the tutor, who is able to assume the responsibilities of the father and serves a substitute for him in some ways. In this respect, the rational mother, who instructs her children, seems to be independent of her husband and able to perform the duties generally associated with fatherhood. Although Wollstonecraft articulates the hope that mothers will be able to follow this example, Wollstonecraft's discussion of rational motherhood seems to be ambivalent. As we have seen Wollstonecraft is confident in her assertion that female children should be educated in to be rational, virtuous creatures and confident in the benefit that rational mothers will have to the political community.[16]

Nonetheless, Wollstonecraft recognizes the allure of Rousseau's Sophie to her contemporary readers and she poses two alternatives to them, hoping to convince them of the superiority of rational motherhood. Consider the possibilities for a woman who is suddenly widowed or, in other words, a woman who suddenly left completely independent of her husband. "A double duty devolves on her; to educate them in the character of both father and mother; to form their principles and secure their property" (*VRW*, 48). Indeed, this seems to be the task of a good Lockean mother and father. Wollstonecraft imagines that the future of this woman and these children could be quite bleak or it could be filled with contentment, depending on the education of the unfortunate woman has had. "But supposing, no very improbable conjecture, that a being only taught to please must still find her happiness in pleasing—what an example of folly, not to say vice, will she be to her daughters!" (*VRW*, 49). Rather than being an affectionate and reliable mother, this woman will seek the satisfaction of her vanity from other men. It won't be long, Wollstonecraft supposes, before such a woman makes rivals of her daughters, "rivals more cruel than any other, because they invite comparison, and drive her from the throne of beauty, who has never thought of a seat on the bench of reason" (*VRW*, 49). Wollstonecraft stops herself from any further elaboration on this vicious mother. "It does not require a lively pencil, or the discriminating outline of a caricature, to sketch the domestic miseries and petty vices which such a mistress of a family diffuses" (*VRW*, 49). Yet, Wollstonecraft is quick to point out to her readers, this woman acts in accordance with the education that has been afforded to her. "Still she only acts as a woman ought to act, brought up according to Rousseau's system. She can never be reproached for being masculine, or turning out of her sphere; nay, she may observe another of his grand rules, and cautiously preserving her reputation free from spot, be reckoned a good kind of woman. Yet in what respect can she be termed good?" (*VRW*, 49).

Wollstonecraft suggests an alternative to this vicious creature, widowed and so ill-prepared to discharge her duties as a mother. "I must relieve myself by drawing another picture. Let fancy now present a woman with a tolerable understanding" (*VRW*, 50). Wollstonecraft quickly adds a reminder to her reader that she is not concerned with exceptional women, "a woman with a tolerable understanding" may be found without straying from "the line of mediocrity" (*VRW*, 50). The education allowed to Wollstonecraft's second example is similar to the education that she and Locke have prescribed for little girls. Her "constitution, strengthened by exercise, has allowed her body to acquire its full vigor; her mind, at the same time, gradually expanding itself to comprehend the moral duties of life, and in what human virtue and dignity consist" (*VRW*, 50). Wollstonecraft imagines this woman is also suddenly widowed, "perhaps without a sufficient provision; but she is not desolate!" (*VRW*, 50). Being strong in body and in mind, she is well-prepared to discharge her duties. In the flourishing rhetoric that is typical of Wollstonecraft (though not of Locke), Wollstonecraft gives an account of the peace and contentment this woman finds in the wake of her husband's death.

She subdues every wayward passion to fulfil [sic] the double duty of being the father as well as the mother of her children. Raised to heroism by misfortunes, she represses the first faint dawning of a natural inclination, before it ripens into love, and in the bloom of life forgets her sex . . . She no longer thinks of pleasing, and conscious dignity prevents her from priding herself on account of the praise her conduct demands. (*VRW*, 50–51)

In contrast to the woman, who has been educated according to Rousseau's principles, the mother who has been educated according to Locke's principles, is not the enemy of her children. Quite the contrary, they adore her and they are grateful to her for fulfilling her responsibility to them.

I think I see her surrounded by her children, reaping the reward of her care. The intelligent eye meets hers, whilst health and innocence smile on their chubby cheeks, and as they grow up the care of life are lessened by their grateful attention. She lives to see the virtues which she endeavoured to plant on principles, fixed into habits, to see her children attain a strength of character sufficient to enable them to endure adversity with forgetting their mother's example. (*VRW*, 51)

All too familiar with the women of her day, Wollstonecraft's experience has been that women, encouraged to be pleasing, rather than rational, are vicious mothers. Nonetheless, Wollstoencraft can imagine a woman, educated according to Locke's principles. This woman discharges her duties and, by educating her children to be rational and virtuous, she ensures that her children will be able to discharge their duties. Wollstonecraft allows for the possibility that father and mother have different responsibilities to their children. However, the differences between father and mother are not so great as to render a mother dependent on her children's father, as Rousseau would have us believe. Rather, in taking for an example a widowed mother, Wollstonecraft is ale to show her readers the differences between father and mother may be overcome. Just as Locke's rational mother takes the place of the tutor, who takes the place of the father, Wollstonecraft's rational mother is able to perform the duties required to educate children. "Woman, I allow, may have different duties to fulfil [sic]; but they are *human* duties, and the principles that should regulate the discharge of them, I sturdily maintain, must be the same" (*VRW*, 51, Wollstonecraft's emphasis).

In offering us the example of a widow, Wollstonecraft seems to add to Locke's example of a woman independent of her husband. Locke demonstrates that a wife achieves independence from her husband by exercising her faculties and educating her children. In some respects, this makes the rational and virtuous mother equal to or superior to a tutor. The tutor is hired to fulfill part of the responsibilities of the father. Therefore, Locke's rational mother and father are both capable of educating their children and, in comparable in reason and virtue. However, Wollstonecraft mentions that the parents must "form their principles and secure their property." Although she does not give any attention to the woman's ability to do the latter, we can infer that she does an acceptable job. The "cares of life" are not so great that they cannot be "lessened by their [the children's] grateful attention" (*VRW*, 51). Locke does not give us any indication of this mother's ability to discharge the duty of securing property.

Returning to the land of chimeras, with Locke as her guide, Wollstonecraft has found human beings who have been born "once for our species." Childhood as it is presented by Locke is a condition in which "everything is equal: girls are children, boys are children; the same name suffices for beings so much alike" (*Emile*, 211). Locke shows Wollstonecraft little girls who are strong in body and in mind. As adults, these women are rational mothers and they educate their children to be rational and virtuous citizens. However, we should be reminded of Virginia Sapiro's warning. Wollstonecraft is not "a late eighteenth century John Locke in drag" (Sapiro, xx). In the next chapter, I will demonstrate Wollstonecraft's departure from Locke. By considering the differences in the education prescribed by Locke and Wollstonecraft, it becomes clear that Locke and Wollstonecraft have different conceptions of human reason. Their different conceptions of human reason point to different understandings of human nature and, consequently, the political community. Locke, like Rousseau, presents to Wollstonecraft a wild chimera, a "half-being" (*VRW*, 39), albeit the other, human half.

Chapter Four

John Locke's Other Half Being

At first glance, the influence of John Locke on Mary Wollstonecraft seems rather clear. It is especially clear when considering Wollstonecraft's early career. The title of her first published work, *Thoughts on the Education of Our Daughters*, implies Wollstonecraft's intention to imitate Locke. Wollstonecraft's intention is made explicit in the first pages of her educational treatise. She writes, "To be able to follow Mr. Locke's system (and this may be said of almost all treatises on education) the parents must have subdued their own passions."[1] Locke's influence seems to persist in Wollstonecraft's most well known political treatise, *A Vindication of the Rights of Woman*. As we have seen in the previous chapter, in prescribing an education that would foster independence and virtue in women, Wollstonecraft does follow Locke's teaching in some important respects. For example, like Locke, she encourages young girls to play outside in order to form healthier, robust bodies. Both authors consider a strong body important to the subsequent formation of a strong mind. However, upon closer examination of both Locke's and Wollstonecraft's treatment of human reason, it becomes clear that Wollstonecraft understands human reason very differently from Locke. In this chapter, I will consider Locke's conception of the human mind: the limits of human reason and the end of human reason. I will then turn my attention to Wollstonecraft's conception of the human soul and her understanding of reason. In contrast to Locke, Wollstonecraft argues there are innate principles of truth. Not only does she encourage her readers to contemplate God, but she argues that human beings can attain divine wisdom. Furthermore, Wollstonecraft departs from her predecessor by suggesting that the end of reason is not simply liberty in civil society, but the perfection of our nature. Finally, I will consider the implications their different conceptions of human reason have for the relationship between husband and wife. Not only does Wollstonecraft want to see reason and virtue restored to women, but she would like to see the relationship between man and woman improved. In the end, Locke disappoints our hopes that he is able to be Wollstonecraft's guide through the land of chimeras. We are disappointed, not so much by Locke's understanding of the female half of woman, but by his understanding of the *human* half of both man and woman. To be sure, Locke offers to Wollstonecraft an example of a woman who is, to a certain degree, rational and virtuous and, in some important respects, enjoys equality with man. However, Locke's human being, male or female, is a fraction of the creature Wollstonecraft sees as human. Neither male nor female exhibit the great potential for human reason, nor do they exhibit affection for their "fellow creatures." Like Rousseau, Locke presents to Wollstonecraft a woman, who is "wild chimera," a "half-being."

I. INNATE PRINCIPLES

Perhaps one of Locke's most well known pronouncements about human reason and knowledge comes, not from his educational treatise, but his epistemological work, *An Essay Concerning Human Understanding*. Locke begins this treatise by reminding his readers of established opinion. "It is established opinion amongst some men, that there are in the understanding certain *innate principles*; some primary notions . . . characters, as it were stamped upon the mind of man; which the soul receives in its first being, and brings into the world with it."[2] In an effort to challenge premodern claims about knowledge, Locke argues there are no innate principles, neither practical nor speculative. "It would be sufficient to convince unprejudiced readers of the falseness of this supposition, if I should only show (as I hope I shall in the following parts of this Discourse) how men, barely by the use of their natural faculties, may attain to all the knowledge they have, without the help of any innate impressions; and may arrive at certainty, without any such original notions of principles" (*ECHU*, 38). In order to support his claim that human beings are able to attain knowledge without the benefit of innate principles, Locke points to children and idiots.

> If therefore children and idiots have souls, have minds, with those impressions upon them, *they* must unavoidably perceive them, and necessarily know and assent to these truths; which since they do not, it is evident that there are no such impressions . . . To say a notion is imprinted on the mind, and yet at the same time to say, that the mind is ignorant of it, and never yet took notice of it, is to make this impression nothing. (*ECHU*, 40)

To those who would argue that the innate principles become known to a person when he or she comes to the use of reason, Locke is quick to reply, arguing there is an implied contradiction. "So that to make reason discover those truths thus imprinted, is to say that the use of reason discovers to a man what he knew before: and if men have those innate impressed truths originally, and before the use of reason, and yet are always ignorant of them till they come to the use of reason, it is in effect to say, that men know and know them not at the same time" (*ECHU*, 43). Innate principles are prior to reason and, therefore, Locke explains they are not discoverable by reason. Quite the contrary, principles of knowledge, which are presumed to be innate, would guide reason in human beings' in their search for knowledge. "For all reasoning is search, and casting about, and requires pains and application. And how can it with any tolerable sense be supposed, that what was imprinted by nature, as the foundation and guide of our reason, should need use of reason to discover it?" (*ECHU*, 44).

Book I of the *Essay* is devoted to refuting established opinion, demonstrating the errors of those who claim the existence of innate principles. In the second book of the *Essay*, Locke offers his explanation of how human beings come by the principles, which are presumed to be innate. He begins this book by discussing "ideas in general, and their original." Locke seems to use "ideas" in a similar manner as he used "principles." "Native ideas," like innate principles are considered "original characters, stamped upon their minds in their first being" (*ECHU*, 121). Locke tells his readers that he has already refuted the arguments in the previous book, the book dedicated to demonstrating there are no innate principles of knowledge. Rather than conceiving of our souls stamped with innate principles, Locke suggests instead that we "suppose the mind to be, as we say, white paper, void of all characters, without any ideas" (*ECHU*, 121). The immediate question is raised, "How comes it [the mind] to be furnished? Whence comes it by that vast store which the busy and boundless fancy of man has painted on it with an almost endless variety?" (*ECHU*, 121). Locke is prepared with his explanation. "To this I answer, in one word, from EXPERIENCE. In that all our knowledge is founded; and from that it ultimately derives itself" (*ECHU*, 122). Again, Locke supports his claim by pointing to the example of children.

> He that attentively considers the state of a child, at his first coming into the world, will have little reason to think him stored with plenty of ideas, that are to be the matter of his future knowledge. It is *by degrees* he comes to be furnished with them. And though the ideas of obvious and familiar qualities imprint themselves before the memory begins to keep a register of time or order. (*ECHU*, 125)

From simple ideas, human beings build more complicated ideas and eventually are able to discover through reason, abstract truths, which are thought to be innate principles.

Locke maintains there are no innate practical principles of knowledge. He simply points out the lack of agreement on moral principles. In order for such moral principles of knowledge to be innate, Locke insists, the principles would be readily acknowledged by all mankind. "Whether there be any such moral principles, wherein all men do agree, I appeal to any who have been but moderately conversant in the history of mankind, and looked abroad beyond the smoke of their own chimneys. Where is that practical truth that is universally received, without doubt or question, as it must be if innate?" (*ECHU*, 66). To say that human beings do not come into the world with "innate principles of knowledge," "primary notions," or "characters stamped upon the mind of man" is not to say that human beings are completely lacking in any innate attributes. In his discussion of the practical principles of knowledge, Locke reveals "natural tendencies" of man. "Nature, I must confess, has put into man a desire of happiness and an aversion to misery: these indeed are innate practical principles which (as practical principles ought) *do* continue constantly to operate and influence all our actions without ceasing: these may be observed in all persons and all ages, steady and universal" (*ECHU*, 67). However, Locke is careful to distinguish these natural tendencies, which he also refers to as practical principles, from principles of knowledge.[3] "But these are *inclinations of the appetite* to good, not impression of truth on the understanding" (*ECHU*, 67). These natural tendencies are passions, not principles of knowledge, even practical principles of knowledge.

> I deny not that there are natural tendencies imprinted on the minds of men; and that from the very first instances of sense and perception, there are some things that are grateful and other unwelcome to them; some things that they incline to and other that they fly: but this makes nothing for innate characters on the mind, which are to be the principles of knowledge regulating our practice. (*ECHU*, 67)

Our natural tendencies, by this initial account, may be characterized by our simplest passions, the desire for pleasure and the desire to avoid pain. Locke seeks to refute claims that speculative and practical principles of knowledge are innate, not that human beings are simply lacking inherent attributes.

As we have seen, Locke tells his readers that it is by the use of our natural faculties that we attain knowledge. In his discussion of the origin of our ideas, Locke gives us further indication of the natural faculties of human beings. Knowledge, Locke never tires of reminding his readers, is not "stamped upon their [human beings'] minds in their very first being" (*ECHU*, 121). Instead, knowledge is gained by the cooperation of our senses and our "operations of the mind" (*ECHU*, 122). Our senses convey perceptions of the external world to the mind. Knowledge is further acquired by the operations of our own minds: "perception, thinking, doubting, believing, reasoning, knowing, willing," for example (*ECHU*, 123). "Secondly, the other fountain from which experience furnishes the understanding with ideas is,—the perception of the operations of our own mind within us, as it is employed about the ideas it has got;—which operations, when the soul comes to reflect on and consider, do furnish the understanding with another set of ideas, which could not be had from things without" (*ECHU*, 123). Locke calls this perception of the operations of the mind, reflection (*ECHU*, 124). While principles of knowledge are not innate, the operations of the mind, the activities by which all human beings acquire knowledge, do seem to be inherent. "This source of ideas," Locke tells us, "every man had wholly in himself" (*ECHU*, 123). The natural tendencies of human beings, by this account, include the operations of the mind. Principles of knowledge will be formed by combining our passions with the operations of the mind.

In his treatment of Locke's *Essay*, Thomas Pangle observes that "Locke begins the *Essay* seeming almost to take perverse delight in showing the lack of fidelity or agreement which mankind exhibits as regards even the most basic moral principles."[4] Pangle goes on to say "he also eventually, and more quietly, points to some modest success or consensus men have achieved in moral reflection" (Pangle, 184). Pangle offers an example of Locke's epistemology in order to explain how a natural tendency is combined with perceptions or observations so that "by degrees" a principle of knowledge is established. Pangle chooses as his example the fundamental principle of Lockean political thought, "natural right." Drawing on Locke's *Two Treatises of Government*, Pangle begins with human beings' propensity to avoid suffering. "The desire for preservation is not only 'planted' in men, as it is in other animals; it is a 'natural Inclination,' 'wrought into the very Principles of their Nature.'" Pangle goes on to explain, "The full strength of this inclination is indeed somewhat shrouded in most men, to begin with; the passion needs the assistance of reason to become the explicit core of the natural inclination to the pursuit of happiness" (Pangle, 187).[5] With the use of his reason, man recognizes the need of assistance from other human beings, who also desire their own preservation. "The human animal, in its desire for preservation, can readily come to see that it needs the aid of other similarly insecure and farsighted humans: the rational desire for comfortable self-preservation constitutes all men, or all men insofar as they are rational, as 'one Community of Nature,' 'one Society distinct from all other Creatures'" (Pangle, 187). From the simple idea of an aversion to suffering, human beings construct a more complicated idea of their relationship to others. On the basis of their rationality and the ways in which it is used to secure preservation, human beings distinguish themselves from other animals. From this point, it is just a short distance to "some modest success . . . in moral reflection." "A human may be said to belong to this 'community—to be, in the moral sense, a human being—inasmuch as he makes it manifest to other humans that he regards his strong desire for comfortable preservation (property) as something more than a mere personal desire: that is to say, inasmuch as he uses his powers to abstract and combine ideas to express his desires in terms of the mixed mode that is a right, a 'natural' right" (Pangle, 187). While the desire for self preservation may be innate in human beings, the practical principle of knowledge, natural right, which instructs human beings to recognize and respect their fellow creatures, is not. It is established by the combination of natural tendencies, our passions and the operations of our mind.

Locke's epistemology is echoed in *Some Thoughts*. Locke begins his educational treatise by telling his readers that "all the men we meet with, nine parts of ten are what they are, good or evil, useful or not, by their education. 'Tis that which makes a great difference in mankind" (*STCE*, 10). Again, Locke relies on children to make his point. He immediately turns his attention from men to infants.

> The little almost insensible impressions on our tender infancies have very important and lasting consequences: and there is as in the fountains of some rivers, where a gentle application of the hand turns the flexible waters into channels that make them take quite contrary courses, and by this little direction given them at first in the source, they receive different tendencies and arrive at last at very remote and distant places. (*STCE*, 10)

Consistent with Locke's argument in his *Essay*, Locke suggests to his readers that education, acquiring knowledge begins with perception at our youngest age. Given that we are not born with any innate ideas, the minds of human beings may take on a variety of characters based on the earliest impressions and subsequent experiences. "We are all sort of chameleons that still take a tincture from things near us" (*STCE*, 44–45).

These are not Locke's last words on the innate qualities of the human mind in *Some Thoughts Concerning Education*. Locke returns to the topic of "the particular constitution of his mind" in his prescriptions for a treating a child's temper. To the extent that Locke notices natural qualities of the mind, Locke identifies them with temper, which have more in common with the passions than it does with reason or knowledge. This suggestion, as we have seen, is explicit in Locke's earlier epistemological treatise. Indeed, in *Some Thoughts,* Locke cautions parents that the natural qualities of the mind or temper may be a propensity for vice. "Stubbornness, lying, and ill-natured actions are not (as has been said) to be permitted in him from the beginning, whatever his temper may be; those seeds of vices are not to be suffered to take any root, but must be carefully weeded out as soon as ever they begin to show themselves in him" (*STCE*, 75).

As we have seen by following Pangle's example of the principle of natural right, moral principles are constructed by joining natural inclinations or passions to reason. Because reason is not developed in children, parents must intervene. In order that "the seeds of vice are not suffered to take any root," Locke recommends that parents quickly and effectively establish their authority over their children. Lacking a "natural principle" and the cultivated capacity to reason as a means by which to control their passions, the authority of the parents must curb the child's natural inclination to "stubbornness" or "ill-natured actions." "[Y]our authority is to take place and influence his mind from the dawning of any knowledge in him that it may operate as a natural principle, whereof he never perceived the beginning, never knew that it could be otherwise." (*STCE*, 75). If parents' authority is established early the child will be accustomed to it and the authority of the parents will have the force of nature. "By this, if the *reverence* he owes you be established early, it will always be sacred to him, and it will be as hard for him to resist it as the principles of his nature" (*STCE*, 75). The "principles of nature" are not reason or innate knowledge, but temper or passions.

Furthermore, not only does Locke suggest there are no innate ideas, which are consistent among all human beings, but he tells his readers that the tempers of the mind vary as well. "Some men by the unalterable frame of their constitutions are *stout*, others *timorous*, some *confident*, others *modest*, *tractable* or *obstinate, curious* or *careless, quick* or *slow.* There are not more differences in men's faces and the outward lineaments of their bodies than there are in the makes and tempers of their minds" (*STCE*, 76). Unlike the differences of the body, the differences of the mind become harder to discern over time. Children learn to deceive others about their natural qualities. "Only there is this difference, that the distinguished characters of the face and the lineaments of the body grow more plain and visible with time and age, but the peculiar *physiognomy of the mind* is most discernible in children, before art and cunning has taught them to hide their deformities and conceal their ill inclinations under a dissembled outside" (*STCE*, 76). The reader may infer from Locke that there is not a natural trajectory toward improvement in human beings or a fulfillment of a nobler end. If not carefully guarded by parents, children will deceive them and cultivate vice, becoming worse than their original, natural inclinations. Locke's implication is typical of the modern conception of nature in two respects: first, human beings' nature is to be understood from its beginnings rather than the ends and, secondly, human nature is to be overcome, rather than fulfilled.

Consistent with Locke's explicit claim in *An Essay Concerning Human Understanding* that neither practical nor speculative principles of knowledge are innate, Locke tells readers of *Some Thoughts Concerning Education* that parents must implant both practical and speculative principles of knowledge in their children. Foremost among the practical principles of knowledge put forth in Locke's political work, the so-called *Second Treatise,* is natural right. As we have seen by following Pangle's explanation of Locke's epistemology, by combining our desire for self-preservation and the operation of the mind, human beings come to recognize a responsibility for their own preservation and the preservation of other living things. "Though Man in that State have an uncontroleable Liberty to dispose of his Person or Possessions, yet he has not the Liberty to destroy himself, or so much as any Creature in his Possession but where some nobler use, than its bare Preservation call for it."[6] The former responsibility is easily met. Human beings naturally avoid their own suffering. The latter is more difficult to establish and requires the operations of the mind (perception, thinking, reasoning, etc.). In *Some Thoughts*, Locke notices that children are often cruel to other living creatures. "One thing I have frequently observed in children, that when they have got possession of any poor creature they are apt to use it ill: they often *torment* and treat very roughly young birds, butterflies, and such other poor animals which fall into their hands, and that with a seeming kind of pleasure" (*STCE*, 90). Locke is reluctant to say that cruelty is natural to human beings. In fact, he goes on to suggest that benignity is a "*more* natural temper" (*STCE*, 91, my emphasis). Given that cruelty and benignity are two possible tempers—more or less natural—the duty to preserve other living things requires the combination of natural tendencies, in the manner that Pangle describes. Until the reason of children is sufficiently developed to form these principles of knowledge, Locke depends on parents to insist upon a proper disposition toward living creatures in their children. "Children should from the beginning be bred up in an abhorrence of *killing* or tormenting any living creature and be taught not to spoil or destroy anything, unless it be for the preservation or advantage of some other that is nobler" (*STCE*, 91). As Pangle reminds us, the desire for preservation "reaches its full mastery only in partnership with reason—and that partnership is by nature tenuous, reason by nature the frail junior partner" (Pangle, 189). However tenuous the partnership between the desire for self-preservation and reason may be, the partnership allows for a self-mastery. "And truly, if the preservation of all mankind, as much as in him lies, were everyone's persuasion, as indeed it is everyone's duty and the true principle to regulate our religion, politics, and morality, by the world would be much quieter and better natured than it is" (*STCE*, 91).

Though Locke does not explicitly rehearse the argument from the *Essay* in *Some Thoughts*, he does instruct parents that they must implant some speculative principles into their children's minds, suggesting that such principles are not innate. A notion of God, for example must be implanted into their minds. "As the foundation of this [virtue], there ought very early to be imprinted on his mind a true notion of *God*, as the independent Supreme Being, Author and Maker of all things, from whom we receive our good, who loves us and gives us all things. And, consequent to this, instill into him a love and reverence of this Supreme Being" (*STCE*, 103). However, Locke is quick to tell parents that they should not "explain the matter any farther; for fear, lest by talking too early to him of spirits, and being unseasonably forward to make him understand the incomprehensible nature of the infinite Being, his head be either filled with false or perplexed with unintelligible notions of him" (*STCE*, 102 -103). It is better, Locke instructs us, to implant into children's minds only a general and benevolent notion of God.

Locke's instruction of parents in *Some Thoughts* concerning the proper notion of God suggests a further characteristic of human understanding. For Locke, human understanding has its limits. In the introduction to *An Essay Concerning Human Understanding*, Locke tells his readers that one of the tasks that are set before him is to determine the proper objects of thought. In other words, Locke wants to be sure that reason is not called upon to contemplate those things that are beyond its capacity to understand. "We should not then perhaps be so forward, out of an affection of an universal knowledge, to raise questions, and perplex ourselves and others with disputes about things to which our understandings are not suited; and of which we cannot frame in our minds any clear or distinct perceptions, or where of (as it has perhaps too often happened) we have not any notions at all" (*ECHU*, 28–29). Discouraging human beings from contemplating what is beyond their capacity is an effort Locke continues in *Some Thoughts*. Locke suggests that parents implant a notion of God, which is both general and benevolent, in children's minds. The implication is that as they grow older and their reasoning faculties develop they will be more capable of contemplating a more complicated notion of God. However, Locke soon reveals that this fairly simple conception of God is good enough for grown men and women too. "And I think it would be better if men generally rested in such an idea of *God* without being too curious in their notions about a Being which all must acknowledge incomprehensible" (*STCE*, 103).

True to his suggestion of the limits of human capacity to contemplate the divine, Locke disagrees with the common practice of teaching children to read by reading the Bible. The Bible, Locke argues, is incompatible with the understanding of children. "And what an odd jumble of thoughts must a child have in his head, if he has any at all, such as he should have concerning religion, who in his tender age reads all the parts of the *Bible* indifferently as the Word of God without any other distinction. I am apt to think that this in some men has been the very reason why they never had clear and distinct thoughts of it all their lifetime" (*STCE*, 118). The expectation is that as human beings get older and their understandings become more sophisticated, they will eventually be able to understand and appreciate God by reading the Bible. Again, we are disappointed in this expectation, for Locke discourages, not only children, but adults from reading the Bible. (Recall Locke's hope that the rational mother, who teaches herself and her children Latin by reading the Gospels, will not trouble herself to understand them.)

The question of reading the Bible comes up again in Locke's discussion of the subjects of an older child's study. Locke considers whether a pupil should engage in natural philosophy. Locke defines natural philosophy as "the knowledge of the principles, properties, and operations of things as they are in themselves, I imagine there are two parts of it, one comprehending spirits with their nature and qualities, and the other *bodies*" (*STCE*, 144). Locke suspects that natural philosophy is beyond the capacity of human reason. "The works of nature are contrived by a wisdom and operate in ways too far surpassing our faculties to discover or capacities to conceive for us ever to be able to reduce them into a science" (*STCE*, 144). Despite the challenge that natural philosophy presents to our faculties, Locke does not immediately rule it out. The study of natural philosophy may be allowed, provided we have a proper conception of spirits. However, implanting the proper notion of spirits is a difficulty Locke does not seem able to overcome to his satisfaction. Perhaps, Locke proposes, "a good history of the Bible" will provide them with sufficient understanding without leaving their imaginations prey to "goblins, specter, and apparitions" (*STCE*, 144–145). Yet, as we have already seen, children's capacities do not allow for anything more than a simple notion of a benevolent God. The study of natural philosophy is made still more difficult "because matter being a thing that all our senses are constantly conversant with, it is so apt to possess the mind and exclude all other beings but matter, that prejudice, grounded on such principles, often leaves no room for the admittance of spirits or the allowing any such things as *immaterial beings in rerum natura*" (*STCE*, 145).

Finally, Locke acknowledges that natural philosophy does not contribute to human knowledge. "Though the world be full of systems of it [natural philosophy] I cannot say I know any one which can be taught a young man as science, wherein he may be sure to find truth and certainty, which is what all sciences give an expectation of" (*STCE*, 146). Locke is quick to add that this does not mean that the study of natural philosophy is totally without use to a young gentleman. If nothing else, it makes him a good conversationalist. "I do not hence conclude that none of them are to be read: it is necessary for a gentleman in this learned age to look into some of them to fit himself for conversation" (*STCE*, 146). Rather than "let loose our thoughts into the vast ocean of Being" (*ECUH*, 31), Locke would rather the young gentleman use his rational faculties in a more practical fashion. "There are very many things in it [the study of natural philosophy] that are convenient and necessary to be known to a gentleman, and a great many others that will abundantly reward the pains of the curious with delight and advantage. But these, I think are, rather to be found amongst such writers as have employed themselves in making rational experiments and observations than in starting barely speculative systems" (*STCE*, 146–147). Those studies that are more properly suited to human capacities and more beneficial to human beings are husbandry, planting, and gardening, for example. We should also notice that the knowledge gained from these studies may be employed to satisfy our desire for comfortable preservation, "the true principle by which to regulate our religion, politics, and morality" (*STCE*, 91).

Having determined the decidedly worldly limits of human understanding, we can then consider to what end a child is to be educated and to what end a human being is to employ his reason. Nathan Tarcov begins his study of Locke's *Some Thoughts Concerning Education* with an explanation for its relevance to the study of political theory. He reminds his readers that in ancient political theory "Both politics and education were supposed to serve ultimately the same end, the formation of good men" (Tarcov, 2). However, in contrast to Aristotle, Locke's politics are liberal. As a result, the political order need be considered with respect to the education of men only insofar as that education promotes the security of lives, liberty and property. Given the separation of politics and education, Locke's educational treatise is seemingly unrelated to his political writings and often overlooked. It is in Locke's educational treatise that he promotes reason and virtue. Tarcov notes Locke's insight in *Some Thoughts* that human beings love freedom and they want above all to be considered free and rational beings.[7] So, Locke's seemingly unrelated educational work has important implications of the political community. "The factual or prudential justification for liberty is not rationality but the pretension to rationality. There is a grave difficulty implicit in this insight because, according to Locke, this fundamental human desire for liberty is also primordially a desire for mastery, not only over oneself but also over others" (Tarcov, 8). Indeed, Locke is very firm with his readers. As much as children love liberty, "I now tell you they love something more: and that is *dominion*; and this is the first origin of the most vicious habits that are ordinary and *natural*" (*STCE*, 76; my emphasis). Tarcov then concerns himself, not so much with the rational foundation of morality, but with the task that Locke assigns himself: encouraging men to *practice* morality. Tarcov argues that the educational prescriptions proposed by Locke in *Some Thoughts* foster "a respect for others that makes liberty practicable" (Tarcov, 78). The end of reason, for Locke, is liberty, which may be enjoyed in civil society.[8]

After an initial discussion of the physical education of young children, Locke turns his attention to the mind. "The next principle of business is to set the *mind* right, that on all occasions it may be disposed to consent to nothing but what may be suitable to the dignity and the excellency of a rational creature" (*STCE*, 25). We soon learn that controlling our passions is what Locke considers suitable to the dignity of a rational creature and constitutes virtue. "He that has not mastery over his inclinations, he that knows not how to *resist* the importunity of *present pleasure or pain* for the sake of what reason tells him is fit to be done, wants the true principle of virtue and industry and is in danger never to be good for anything" (*STCE*, 32). Locke offers two means by which a person's virtue may be measured: "the knowledge of man's duty and the satisfaction it is to obey his Maker in following the dictates of that light God has given him with the hopes of acception and reward" or reputation (*STCE*, 38). Locke acknowledges that the former is the "true principle and measure of virtue." Nonetheless, he puts his stock in reputation. "[Reputation] is that which comes nearest to it; and being the testimony and applause that other people's reason, as it were by common consent, gives to virtuous and well ordered actions, it is the proper guide and encouragement of children, till they grow able to judge for themselves and to find what is right by their own reason" (*STCE*, 38). Again, we see that, given a choice between aspiring to the divine and resting content with the human, Locke chooses the latter.

Virtue, Locke insists, is the most important element of a child's education and is much more difficult to acquire than knowledge of the world (*STCE*, 46). Nonetheless, Locke continues to subtly overshadow virtue in favor of other, more worldly traits. Not only does Locke finds one's reputation a better guide than virtue, but, Locke consistently couples virtue with "good breeding" (*STCE*, 47 and 48, for example). Indeed, virtue and good breeding are compatible. Both are concerned with the well-tempered soul, the former by the way of reason and the latter by the way of reputation. Good breeding, Locke notes, may be displayed by observing just one simple rule: "not to think meanly of ourselves and not to think meanly of others" (*STCE*, 106). In order to avoid the qualities, which are contrary to good breeding, the young gentleman must cultivate "first, a disposition of the mind not to offend others; and secondly, the most acceptable and agreeable way of expressing that disposition" (*STCE*, 107). The concern for others, which signals good breeding, weeds out the seeds of vice, which Locke warns must not be allowed to take root. Good breeding makes it possible to live together harmoniously in civil society. "For the very end and business of *good breeding* is to supple the natural stiffness and so soften men's tempers that they may bend to compliance and accommodate themselves to those they have to do with" (*STCE*, 107). Good breeding is the means by which we establish our reputation, "that which comes the nearest" to virtue, a lesser but more dependable quality. "Children," Locke notices, "who live together often strive for mastery" (*STCE*, 80). This inclination must be thwarted and replaced by more "supple" qualities, which are among the virtues Locke identifies. "But not only that, but they should be taught to have all the *deference*, *complaisance*, and *civility* for one another imaginable. This, when they see it procures them respect, love, and esteem and that they lose no superiority by it, they will take more pleasure in than in insolent domineering; for so plainly is the other" (*STCE*, 81). Locke defines wisdom simply as "man's managing his business ably and with foresight in this world" (*STCE*, 105). By the time Locke offers advice for selecting a tutor, the concern for virtue is barely voiced by Locke. Tarcov notes that a tutor should have certain qualities: good breeding, knowledge of the world, virtue, and learning. "Of these parts, Locke discusses good breeding and knowledge of the world at length . . . but he treats learning only indirectly and, polemically, as subordinate to the others; more surprisingly, he treats virtue hardly at all" (Tarcov, 124). Tarcov further observes that "Locke treats at greatest length in his discussion of the tutor's qualities is knowledge of the world" (Tarcov, 125). Indeed, it is knowledge of the world and good breeding, which secure our comfort and our peace in civil society, making liberty possible.

Locke puts into practice the epistemological principles of *An Essay Concerning Human Understanding* in his educational treatise, *Some Thoughts Concerning Education*. Because, according to Locke, there are no innate principles of knowledge, both practical principles of knowledge, like natural right, and speculative principles of knowledge, like a notion of God, must be implanted in children. Just as Locke discouraged readers of the *Essay* from attempting to understand those ideas that are beyond the capacity of human rational faculties to comprehend, Locke advises parents against allowing children, and even themselves, from pursuing metaphysical studies. The result of Locke's teaching is that human reason is employed to curb and direct our natural tempers, rendering us industrious and more civil toward each other, preserving our lives and our liberty.

II. SOULS STAMPED WITH THE HEAVENLY IMAGE

In her biography of Wollstonecraft, Janet Todd does not question the extent to which Locke's educational treatise influences Wollstonecraft. Wollstonecraft's work, in particular her early educational treatise, *Thoughts Concerning the Education of Our Daughters,* according to Todd, "accepted the prevailing Lockean view of mind as a transparent entity which needed to be controlled and safeguarded from the passions for reason to function" (Todd, 76). However, while the Lockean view of mind as "a transparent entity" on which "the busy and boundless fancy of man has painted on it with an almost endless variety" (*ECHU*, 121), may have finally been the prevailing conception of the human mind, it is not the only view that would have been available to Wollstonecraft. Todd quickly gives away and informs her readers that a competing notion of mind was also available to Wollstonecraft. "The book [*Thoughts on the Education of Our Daughters*] proceeded in a robust censorious way, rather in the manner of [James] Burgh, who believed in moral absolutes and felt that education must fit people to pass this life decently, while helping them ennoble their nature for the next" (Todd, 76). Contrary to Todd, who argues that Wollstonecraft adopts Locke's epistemology, I shall show that Wollstonecraft argues that principles of truth are innate, reason connects human beings with the divine and, therefore, the end of human reason is the perfection of our nature. Wollstonecraft does not follow Locke down an as of yet unbeaten path into the land of chimeras.

Wollstonecraft begins her educational treatise with a brief discussion of caring for daughters in the nursery. She then turns her attention to moral discipline. And, like Locke, the moral discipline Wollstonecraft prescribes for children is based on their natural temper. Recall that Locke warns parents that their children may have a natural proclivity to "ill-natured actions" and cautions parents that "those seeds of vice are not to be suffered to take any root" (*STCE*, 75). Although Wollstonecraft is not so suspicious of children's natural tempers as Locke seems to be, she recognizes children's vulnerability to vice. Wollstonecraft warns parents, particularly mothers, not "to *sow* those seeds, which have produced such luxuriant weeds in her own mind" (*TED*, 9, my emphasis). To prevent the seeds of vice from being implanted into their children, Wollstonecraft suggests they be kept from servants. We should note the significant difference between Locke and Wollstonecraft that Wollstonecraft's prescriptions imply. From Locke's perspective, children should be watched and protected from their own potentially vicious tempers. From Wollstonecraft's perspective, children should be watched and protected from the vicious character of adults. Keeping children from the company of servants, Wollstonecraft argues, provides an additional benefit: the already existing love of truth will not be effaced. "They [children] are taught cunning, the wisdom of that class of people [servants], and love of truth, the foundation of virtue, is soon obliterated from their minds" (*TED*, 9). Wollstonecraft's implication seems to be that the love of truth, if not truth itself, is innate in human beings. Wollstonecraft makes this implication explicit. "It is my opinion, a well-proved fact, that principles of truth are innate. Without reasoning we assent to many truths; we feel their force, and artful sophistry can only blunt those feelings which nature has implanted in us as instinctive guards to virtue" (*TED*, 9). Though Wollstonecraft begins her educational treatise with an intention to "follow Mr. Locke's system," she departs from it almost immediately. She distinguishes herself from Locke with the "fact" that principles of truth are innate. These innate principles of truth guard and protect virtue, suggesting that, for Wollstonecraft, virtue, not vice, is privileged by human nature.

Consistent with her prescriptions in her educational treatise, Wollstonecraft asserts in the *Vindication* that human beings have an inclination toward virtue. "It is, however, sufficient for my present purpose to assert, that, whatever effect circumstances have on the abilities, every being may become virtuous by the exercise of its own reason; for if but one being was created with vicious inclinations, that is positively bad, what can save us from atheism? Or if we worship a God, is not that God a devil?"(*VRW*, 21). Wollstonecraft notices that women's "vicious inclinations" are often encouraged by other educational writers on the assumption that females are created with the inclinations that Wollstonecraft finds so corrosive to the human soul. In *A Vindication of the Rights of Woman*, Wollstonecraft is at pains to demonstrate that those qualities, which are generally attributed to women and on which women generally rely in order to secure affection from men (a concern for their appearance, for example), are not inclinations with which females are created. Wollstonecraft refutes, among others, Dr. Gregory, author of a widely read treatise on the education of daughters, by insisting that a fondness for dress is not an innate principle of the soul.

> If they told us that in a pre-existent state the soul was fond of dress, and brought this inclination with it into a new body, I should listen to them with a half smile, as I often do when I hear a rant about innate elegance.—But if he only meant to say that the exercise of the faculties will produce this fondness—I deny it.—It is not natural; but arises, like false ambition in men, from a love of power. (*VRW*, 28)

Wollstonecraft suggests an alternative to the unnaturally weak and vain characters of women, which is thought to be so pleasing. She suspects that women, if properly educated, can attain strength of mind, perseverance, and, fortitude, and other virtues usually associated with men. The expectation that women will acquire these virtues and, as a consequence, relative equality with men, will certainly be viewed as utopian dreams, wild chimeras. Wollstonecraft is not daunted. For Wollstonecraft the notion that "every being may become virtuous by the exercise of its own reason" is an innate principle and it is from this principle that Wollstonecraft takes her bearings. "These may be termed Utopian dreams.—Thanks to that Being who impressed them on my soul, and gave me sufficient strength of mind to exert my own reason, till, becoming dependent only on him for the support of my virtues, I view, with indignation, the mistaken notions that enslave my sex" (*VRW*, 37). It follows from this that, for Wollstonecraft, reason or the discernment of truth is also an innate principle.

> Reason is, consequentially, the simple power of improvement; or, more properly speaking, of discerning truth . . . More or less may be conspicuous in one being than another; but the nature of reason must be the same in all, if it be an emanation of divinity, the tie that connects the creature with the Creator; for, can that soul be stamped with the heavenly image, that is not perfected by the exercise of its own reason? (*VRW*, 53)

Wollstonecraft's understanding of the soul, which is "stamped with the heavenly image," is a significant difference from Locke's understanding of the human mind, which is "white paper, void of all characters without any ideas"

(*ECHU*, 21). In further contrast to Locke, Wollstonecraft understands that innate principles are roughly the same—at least, the same in nature—among all human beings, suggesting that humans are able to achieve more than "modest success or consensus . . . on moral reflection" (Pangle, 184).

Given that Wollstonecraft understands principles of truth to be innate and reason to be a stamp from God, we can expect that she does not place worldly limits on human reason as does Locke. In her educational treatise, Wollstonecraft, like Locke, considers whether or not the Bible is appropriate reading material for children. However, Wollstonecraft's disposition to the Bible differs from Locke's. As we have already seen, Locke suggests a general and benevolent notion of God sufficient for both children and adults. He cautions his readers that reading the Bible may incite the reader to contemplate God, which will prove to be beyond the capacity of our faculties and result in superstition or frustration or both. Wollstonecraft also advises parents not to teach children to read by reading the Bible. However, in contrast to Locke, she does not mean to discourage us from contemplating God—quite the contrary. "The Bible should be read with particular respect, and they should not be taught reading by so sacred a book; lest they might consider as a task, which ought to be a source of the most exalted satisfaction" (*TED*, 21). Teaching children to read by some other means will prevent reading the Bible from becoming an onerous task. As a result, Wollstonecraft expects, reading the Bible will be both pleasurable and intellectually profitable for children and adults. This is rather different from Locke's suggestion that reading the Bible would be confusing and frustrating to both children and their parents.

Again, these differences between Locke and Wollstonecraft on the limits of human reason persist in Wollstonecraft's more famous political treatise, *A Vindication of the Rights of Woman*. She begins this work with a chapter entitled, "The Rights and Involved Duties of Mankind Considered." Wollstonecraft begins her chapter on the rights of mankind by returning to "first principles" (*VRW*, 11). Reason, Wollstonecraft tells us, separates us from the animals and varying degrees of virtue separate human beings from each other. "In what does man's pre-eminence over the brute creation consist? The answer is clear that half is less than a whole, in Reason. What acquirement exalts one being above another? Virtue; we spontaneously reply. For what purpose were the passions implanted? That man by struggling with them might attain a degree of knowledge denied to the brutes; whispers Experience" (*VRW*, 12). We should notice that, for Wollstonecraft, passion is in the service of reason. The struggle with our passions results in a certain knowledge.

This is different than Locke's conception of the relationship between reason and the passions. As Pangle demonstrates, reason must be wedded to the passions—in particular the desire for self preservation—in order to combine abstract ideas and to understand "natural right" (Pangle, 187). The proper relationship between reason and our desire for self preservation serves to guard and enlarge our freedom, a state in which human beings may "order their Actions, and dispose of their Possessions, and Persons as they think fit" (*TT*, 269). It may be said that, in this case, reason is the means by which we may satisfy our passions. In contrast to Wollstonecraft, Locke places reason in the service of the passions.

This chapter, "The Rights and Involved Duties of Mankind," is, in large part, Wollstonecraft's critique of Rousseau's state of nature. In considering Wollstonecraft's response to Rousseau, we may also infer some differences between Wollstonecraft's and Locke's understandings of human reason.[9] Above all, Wollstonecraft rejects Rousseau's argument that man in the pure state of nature lacks reason. Reason, Rousseau argues, is developed as man comes into greater and greater contact with other human beings. It is in the course of Wollstonecraft's objection to Rousseau that she tells her readers that human reason is divine. "But if, to crown the whole, there were to be rational creatures produced, allowed to rise in excellence by the exercise of powers implanted for that purpose; if benignity itself thought fit to call into existence a creature above the brutes, who could think and improve himself, why should that inestimable gift, for a gift it was, . . . be called, in direct terms, a curse?" (*VRW*, 14). Wollstonecraft rejects Rousseau's claim that human reason develops in the species over time, arguing instead that human reason is a gift, implanted in us by God. But she doesn't stop there. Wollstonecraft also tells her readers that reason makes us similar to God. "Why should he lead us from love of ourselves to the sublime emotions which the discovery of his wisdom and goodness excites, if these feelings were not set in motion to improve our nature, of which they make a part, and render us capable of enjoying a more godlike portion of happiness?" (*VRW*, 15).

Given this possibility of attaining divine wisdom and enjoying a "more godlike portion of happiness," Wollstonecraft finds contemplating God consistent with the rational faculties of human beings. Though Wollstonecraft does not specifically name Locke, she condemns those who are satisfied with certain, but limited understanding of God. "I disclaim that specious humility which, after investigating nature, stops at the author—The High and Lofty One, who inhabiteth eternity, doubtless possess many attributes of which we can form no conception; but reason tells me that they cannot clash with those I adore— and I am compelled to listen to her voice" (*VRW*, 46).

Wollstonecraft goes on to suggest that it is not only possible to contemplate and to understand God, but that it is natural. "It seems natural for man to search for excellence, and either to trace it in the object that he worships, or blindly to invest it with perfection, as a garment. But what good effect can the latter mode of worship have on the moral conduct of a rational being?" (*VRW*, 46)

Wollstonecraft distinguishes her understanding of human reason from Locke's conception in a final respect: the end of reason or education. Keeping in mind Wollstonecraft's political and intellectual association with Locke's descendents, we would expect Wollstonecraft to echo Locke's political principles. However, this expectation is disappointed. In contrast to Locke, liberty, for Wollstonecraft, is not the end of human reason, but only the beginning. Wollstonecraft argues for the rights of woman, liberty included, not for the sake of these rights themselves, but for the sake of a more noble purpose. "Contending for the rights of woman, my main argument is built on this simple principle, that if she be not prepared by education to become the companion of man, she will stop the progress of knowledge and virtue" (*VRW*, 4). Freedom, therefore, is necessary so that woman's reason will flourish and she will be able to understand her "good." "And how can woman be expected to co-operate unless she know why she ought to be virtuous? unless freedom strengthen her reason till she comprehend her duty, and see in what manner it is connected with her real good?" (*VRW*, 4). In a similar vein, Wollstonecraft also tells her readers that "Liberty is the mother of virtue, and if women be, by their very constitution, slaves and not allowed to breathe the sharp invigorating air of freedom, they must ever languish like exotics, and be reckoned beautiful flaws in nature" (*VRW*, 37). Liberty is the necessary condition for reason and virtue to flourish, to be sure, but it is not sufficient to prevent women from becoming like exotic plant, "beautiful flaws in nature." The end of reason, therefore, cannot be liberty, but rather the fulfillment of human nature.

Wollstonecraft attributes the condition of women to a mistaken notion of education. They have been educated simply with respect to their sex in order to become the pleasing companions of men. Wollstonecraft faults this education because it results in a fractured and dependent "half-being." The women are only prepared for a specific role as wife in this life. Considering Locke's educational teaching, Locke educates young gentleman and, in large measure, young ladies to be strong in mind and in body. As a consequence, both male and female children attain a degree of virtue and good breeding. Nonetheless, the end of Locke's education is practical. The end of virtue and good breeding is "a respect for others that makes liberty practicable" (Tarcov,

98). The education Locke affords girls (and boys) has as its end preparation for this life. Wollstonecraft has greater expectations for education. Human reason, which flourishes with liberty, is not limited to a simple, nearly utilitarian contemplation of God, nor is it limited in its end to worldly practical matters. For Wollstonecraft the end of human reason is not the enlargement of our liberty, but participation in the divine. While the education that Locke implicitly prescribes for young girls is a significant improvement from Rousseau's treatment of female education, it remains necessary to correct Locke's mistaken notion of education too. "Into this error [a disregard for the human character of women] men have, probably, been led by viewing education in a false light; not considering it as the first step to form a being advancing toward perfection; but only as preparation for life" (*VRW*, 53). Despite the prospect of equality between men and women, Locke's education is incomplete because it educates only part of the human being, ignoring that part which shares something of the divine and by which human beings perfect their nature.

III. CONJUGAL SOCIETY RECONSIDERED

In addition to correcting Rousseau's mistaken notions of the female sex, as we have seen, Wollstonecraft attempts to correct his mistaken notions about the relations between man and woman, which Wollstonecraft considers the consequence of woman's corrupted character. Wollstonecraft recounts Rousseau's understanding of marriage:

> The social relations of the sexes are indeed truly admirable: from their union there results a moral person, of which woman may be termed the eyes and man the hand, with this dependence on each other, that it is from the man that the woman is to learn what she is to see, and it is of the woman that man is to learn what he ought to do. If woman could recur to the first principles of things as well as man, and man was capacitated to enter into their *minutiæ* as well as woman, always independent of each other, they would live in perpetual discord, and their union could not subsist. (*VRW*, 86–87)

Wollstonecraft is not seduced by Rousseau's prose and recognizes woman as "an irrational monster," a fractional creature, who is unable to educate her children without her other half.

> A blind will, "eyes without hands," would go a very little way; and perchance his abstract reason, that should concentrate the scattered beams

of her practical reason, may be employed in judging the flavor of wine, descanting on the sauces most proper for turtle; or, more profoundly intent at a card table, he may be generalizing his ideas as he bets away his fortune, leaving all the *minutiæ* of education to his helpmate, or to chance. (*VRW*, 89)

Locke's rational mother differs significantly from Rousseau's Sophie. Locke's rational mother's concerns are not sensual—"judging the flavor of wine or descanting on the sauces most proper for turtle." It is not "from the man that the woman is to learn what she is to see" in Locke's educational treatise. Indeed, Locke's rational mother seems to be independent of her husband and quite capable of educating the young gentleman in the place of the tutor. Locke's rational mother serves her political community by educating her children, imparting to them "good breeding." To be sure, the education that Locke implicitly prescribes for young girls seems to significantly correct the mistaken notion of education to which Wollstonecraft so vehemently objects. Rather, Locke expects she will instill a sense of "justice, generosity, and sobriety" into her young pupil, even if her husband spends his time at the gaming table. Locke's rational mother seems capable of the abstract reasoning that Rousseau would preserve for the male.

Locke provides an example of husband and wife, who are independent of each other, yet do not seem to live in "perpetual discord." However, Rousseau's fear that the "union could not subsist" deserves some consideration. *Some Thoughts* give us virtually no indication of the relationship between man and woman as husband and wife, only as father and mother. Remember, Locke's only clue concerning the match between man and woman is to compare the choice of a wife to the choice of a tutor. In other words, the primary concern a man has in choosing his wife is the proper care of his children. Readers of Locke's *Second Treatise* will find this relationship between husband and wife consistent with his treatment of conjugal society in his more famous political work. In offering his explanation for political society, Locke tells us,

Conjugal Society is made by a voluntary Compact between Man and Woman: and tho' it consist chiefly in such a Communion and Right in one anothers Bodies, as is necessary to its chief end, Procreation; yet it draws with it mutual Support, and Assistance, and a Communion of Interest too, as necessary not only to unite their Care, and Affection, but also necessary to their common Off-spring, who have Right to be nourished and maintained by them, till they are able to provide for themselves. (*TT*, 319)

Similar to other animals, human beings' primary reason for coupling is procreation. They differ from other animals in that the female human is able to conceive of another child before the first (or second or third) is able to care for itself. "The Father, who is bound to take care of those he hath begot, is under the Obligation to continue in Conjugal Society with the same Woman longer than other Creatures" (*TT*, 320). Obligation, not affection binds man and woman. But, on the bright side, Locke recognizes the benefit to the obligations of conjugal society.

> Wherein one cannot but admire the Wisdom of the great Creatour, who having given Man foresight and an Ability to lay up for the future, as well as to supply the present necessity, hath made it necessary, that *Society of Man and Wife should be more lasting*, than of Male and Female amongst other Creatures; that so their Industry might be encouraged, and their interest better united, to make Provision, and lay up Goods for their common Issue, which uncertain mixture, or easie and frequent Solutions of Conjugal Society would mightily disturb. (*TT*, 320)

Not only do the off-spring benefit from conjugal society, but man and woman do too. Their material comforts are increased by their cooperation. Locke does not devote his attention to the emotional or intellectual benefits of man and woman in conjugal society. Finally, the conjugal bond is based on the care of the children. When at last those obligations are satisfied, there is nothing that requires them to continue in conjugal society, "there being no necessity in the nature of the thing [this voluntary compact], nor to the ends of it, that it should always be for Life" (*TT*, 321).[10]

Wollstonecraft has greater expectations for the relationship between man and woman than does Locke. We should not forget that, though Wollstonecraft condemns Rousseau's characterization of woman, she also learns a great deal from Rousseau. As we have seen in the first chapter, Wollstonecraft learns from Rousseau the importance of sincere affection between husband and wife to the individual, the family, and the political community. Not only does Wollstonecraft think it possible to establish affection between husband and wife without sacrificing the full range of human reason, but she considers it possible to build this affection *on* human reason. Wollstonecraft promises "the woman who strengthens her body and exercises her mind will, by managing her family and practicing various virtues, become the friend, and not the humble dependent of her husband; and if she by possessing such substantial qualities, merit his regard, she will not find it necessary to conceal her affection, nor to pretend to an unnatural coldness to constitution to excite her husband's passions" (*VRW*, 29). For man and wife, Wollstonecraft prefers friendship to love. In contrast to love, which Wollstonecraft considers to be "transitory" and "the common passion, in which chance and sensation take the place of choice and reason" (*VRW*, 30), friendship is "the most holy band of society" (*VRW*, 30). Romantic love is preferred to the friendship of marriage "only by those who have not sufficient intellect to substitute the calm tenderness of friendship, the confidence of respect" (*VRW*, 30). Wollstonecraft's hopes for encouraging friendship between husbands and wives depends on women's use of reason.

> Were women more rationally educated, could they take a more comprehensive view of things, they would be contented to love but once in their lives; and after marriage calmly let passion subside into friendship—into that tender intimacy, which is the best refuge from care; yet is built on such pure, still affections, that idle jealousies would not be allowed to disturb the discharge of sober duties of life, or to engross the thoughts that ought to be otherwise employed. (*VRW*, 119–120)

By relying on reason as the foundation for marriage, Wollstonecraft is able to articulate a hope for marriage that differs from the relations between the sexes put forth by both Rousseau and Locke. Wollstonecraft preserves the affection that she finds in Rousseau's sentimental treatment of the family. Because Wollstonecraft's expectations are based on reason, and not the passions, Wollstonecraft is also able to imagine marriage which is not riddled with insecurity, cunning, and lasciviousness.

Wollstonecraft's understanding of marriage also has something in common with Locke's notion of conjugal society and, yet, departs from it in important respects. Though Wollstonecraft appreciates that marriage benefits husband and wife by encouraging each to "discharge of sober duties of life," the pair are not compelled by obligation. Instead, they are motivated by their affection for each other. Further, Wollstonecraft goes beyond Locke's understanding of conjugal society in that she expects that this affection will last a lifetime.

Just as Rousseau does, Locke presents to Wollstonecraft a "wild chimera," a "half-being," who lacks the great potential of human reason, as well as affection for her husband. To be sure, the emphasis Locke places on reason, and the subsequent potential for virtue, in his educational treatise, *Some*

Thoughts Concerning Education, provides an example of the relative equality between men and women to Wollstonecraft. However, after closer consideration, it is evident that Wollstonecraft's conception of human reason departs significantly from Locke's notion. Unlike Locke, Wollstonecraft considers principles of truth to be innate. The proper object of contemplation is God and the end of human reason or education is the perfection of our nature. Given Wollstonecraft's understanding of human nature, her hopes for the relationship between husband and wife differ significantly from the example provided by Locke in either his educational or political treatise. Locke, as it turns out, is not a suitable guide for Wollstonecraft through the land of chimeras.

Chapter Five
Nature Does Nothing in Vain

Writing her best known treatise, *A Vindication of the Rights of Woman*, at the close of the eighteenth century, Mary Wollstonecraft regrets the inequality of human beings, which characterizes the decaying aristocracies of her time. "After considering the historic page, and viewing the living world with anxious solicitude, the most melancholy emotions of sorrowful indignation have depressed my spirits, and I have sighed when obliged to confess, that either nature has made a great difference between man and man, or that the civilization which has hitherto taken place in the world has been very partial" (*VRW*, 7). Wollstonecraft laments that women, in particular, are degraded by this inequality. "The conduct and manners of women . . . prove their minds are not in a healthy state; for like flowers planted in too rich soil, strength and usefulness are sacrificed to beauty" (*VRW*, 7). Wollstonecraft condemns their education as the reason for women's "weak and wretched" condition. "One cause of this barren blooming I attribute to a false sense of education, gathered from books written by men on this subject who, considering females rather as women than human, have been more anxious to make them alluring mistresses than affectionate wives and rational mothers" (*VRW*, 7). Preferring beauty to brains, these men have discouraged women from more noble pursuits. Aware of the power their beauty affords women, they are complicit in their own corruption. The women of her day, Wollstonecraft laments, are willing to neglect their human qualities in order to make themselves pleasing as females. Woman, is a "half-being" or "a wild chimera" (*VRW*, 39). Considering women as "human creatures," as well as females, would restore their dignity to them. In the *Vindication*, Wollstonecraft is seeking a way to combine the female and the human in order to fulfill her utopian dream: a woman who is both an "affectionate wife and a rational mother," a woman who enjoys independence and equality to her husband.

Considering the historic page on which Wollstonecraft writes and the intellectual and political circles in which she moves, we would expect Wollstonecraft's utopian dream to be fulfilled by the natural rights of human beings as they are articulated in state of nature theories. And, indeed, Wollstonecraft is often compared to two state of nature theorists: Rousseau and Locke. The equality of human beings in the state of nature is founded on their relative physical similarity and their equal vulnerability. Those thinkers, who subscribe to state of nature theories, must finally account for the physical differences between male and female, just as Wollstonecraft herself struggles to explain. Rousseau and Locke offer two different accounts of the physical differences between male and female. Yet, each one renders woman a wild chimera or a half being, albeit in different ways.

As we have seen in the first chapter, Wollstonecraft is lured into the land of chimeras by Rousseau, who teaches us that "We are so to speak, born twice: once to exist and once to live; once for our species and once for our sex" (*Emile*, 211). At the outset of Rousseau's prescription for female education, as well as his state of nature theory, male and female are equal and independent beings. It is only as the children grow, or as the species develops, that the difference in their sex threatens to fracture these whole, independent creatures. The education Rousseau designs for Emile in his educational treatise, the *Emile*, is meant to preserve the natural wholeness of man. Rousseau promises to combine the two parts of human beings, the species and the sex, in order to form a man, who is whole and unfractured by his passions. Sharing Rousseau's appreciation for the importance of the female sex to the woman, the family, and the political community, Wollstonecraft anticipates that Rousseau will introduce her to a woman who combines the human and the female sex in order to become an "affectionate wife and a rational mother" (*VRW*, 7). Unfortunately, Rousseau's natural woman, Sophie, is a great disappointment to Wollstonecraft. For Rousseau, the capacity to bear children has profound consequences for the female. Aware that she will someday bear children, which will render her vulnerable and in need the assistance of a man, she understands herself simply as female, rather than human. This is true both of Sophie and the female Savage in the state of nature. "The female is female her whole life or at least during her whole youth. Everything recalls her sex to her" (*Emile*, 361). The assistance, which the female requires of the male, is secured by making herself pleasing to him. She does so by feigning physical weakness in order to flatter the male's sense of his own strength. She turns her attention to her body, neglecting her mind. Courting the affection of the opposite sex in this manner fosters "cunning and lasciviousness." By her very nature, woman is a fractured and dependent half-being. Instead of realizing her utopian dream, Wollstonecraft finds monsters in Rousseau's land of chimeras.

Rousseau does not leave Wollstonecraft without a guide to help her to navigate the land of chimeras. He has offered his predecessor, John Locke, as an alternative to both his pedagogy and his state of nature theory. And, indeed, Locke's understanding of the part that sex has in forming a whole, independent human being differs from Rousseau's understanding in some very important respects. Locke implicitly affords to the young lady the same education he prescribes to the young gentleman in *Some Thoughts Concerning Education*. By encouraging little girls, as well as little boys to play outside, Locke's education preserves the child's natural strength. The vigor of the children prepares boys and girls for the education of the mind. As we have seen in a previous chapter, Locke encourages parents to educate their sons at home, just as they do their daughters, in order to foster virtue. Locke allows his readers to see how this vigorous, rational, and virtuous girl will conduct herself as an adult. The example Locke provides is a rational mother, who educates her children for liberal civil society. It is easy to see why Wollstonecraft may prefer the female of Locke's educational treatise to Rousseau's Sophie. However, like Rousseau, Locke presents a half-being. Upon closer examination, it turns out that neither Locke's understanding of the human nor the female lives up to Wollstonecraft's expectations for "affectionate wives and rational mothers." With respect to that part of woman, which is shared by all human beings, reason, Wollstonecraft and Locke have significantly different understandings. For Wollstonecraft, human reason connects us with the divine. For Locke, reason has decidedly worldly limits. As a result, the end of reason is different for these two thinkers. The end of reason for Locke is to quiet our passions so that we may live peaceably in civil society. Wollstonecraft, on the other hand, sees reason as the way by which we are to fulfill our nature as human beings. In addition to this difference on the role of human reason, Wollstonecraft must surely find the female portion of woman dissatisfying, as well. Though the mother of *Some Thoughts* quiets her passions and employs reason in order to fulfill her duty to her children, we have no indication of the relationship between husband and wife. Far from becoming the "affectionate wife," of whom Wollstonecraft dreams, the female (as well as the male, for that matter) seems to be indifferent to her spouse and completely independent of him. Though Locke's rational mother is fractured in a different manner than Rousseau's Sophie, she is also a half-being, a wild chimera or a monster, which does not fulfill Wollstonecraft's utopian dream.

The physical differences between male and female must be addressed by the state of nature theorists, who base the equality of human beings on the relative sameness of their physical needs and vulnerability. Rousseau, it seems to Wollstonecraft, chooses to exploit the physical differences, rendering the female weak and dependent, in order to cement our social bonds. Locke, on the other hand, has minimized the physical difference between male and female. The result is relative equality between husband and wife, but it is purchased at the price of their affection for each other. The independence of the rational mother from her husband seems to be accompanied by indifference. Neither the state of nature theories of Rousseau nor of Locke seem compatible with Wollstonecraft's pursuit of her utopian dream, a woman who is by nature whole, comprised of both the human and the female.

Still, Wollstonecraft is not left without a guide in the land of chimeras. Rousseau offers yet another alternative to his political philosophy: Aristotle. Rousseau begins his so-called *Second Discourse* by commenting on the difficulty of knowing the nature of human beings. He regrets, "every progress of the human Species removes it ever farther from its primitive state, the more new knowledge of it we accumulate, the more we deprive ourselves of the means of acquiring the most important knowledge of all, and that in a sense it is by dint of studying man that we have made it impossible for us to know him" (*Second Discourse*, 124). For Rousseau, and for modern thinkers more generally, the nature of human beings is determined by their origins. The original condition of human beings becomes harder to discern as the species adapts to progress. "What experiments would be needed in order to come to know natural man; and by what means can these experiments be performed within society?" The philosophical challenges are great and worthy of the greatest minds. "A good solution . . . does not seem to me unworthy of the Aristotles . . . of our century" (*Second Discourse*, 125). On that note, Rousseau begins his inquiry into the nature of man, offering his inquiry as a worthy alternative to Aristotle. Aristotle, I shall argue, turns out to be the proper guide to Wollstonecraft through the land of chimeras. Following Aristotle, Wollstonecraft may find her chimera or realize her utopian dream, a woman who is comprised by both the human and the female sex.

I do not suggest that Wollstonecraft made a rigorous study of Aristotle, as she seems to have done of Rousseau and, to some extent, Locke. Rather, I suggest that Aristotle provides a good theoretical grounding for Wollstonecraft's own inquiry into the nature of woman, without sacrificing one half of woman. I will begin this chapter by demonstrating the compatibility between Wollstonecraft and Aristotle. For both thinkers, the soul is central to their understanding of the human condition. Yet, as we have already seen, Wollstonecraft struggles with combining the human soul with the female body. Aristotle provides an explanation of how these two parts of the human being are compatible. I will then argue that Aristotle's treatment of the physical differences between male and female does not compromise woman's human character. In the following chapter, I will consider Aristotle's chimera, which resembles Wollstonecraft's utopian dream more than a monstrous half-being, in the context of the friendship between husband and wife. This friendship, I argue, very nearly fulfills Wollstonecraft's hopes for "affectionate wives," without sacrificing woman's relative equality or independence. In the last chapter I will turn my attention to Wollstonecraft's chimera in the context of political life. As a friend to her husband, woman fulfills her duty to herself, to her family, and to her political community. Wollstonecraft's chimera is a citizen.

I. BORN TO PROCREATE AND ROT?

To be sure, Aristotle's name does not pop up on the pages of *A Vindication of the Rights of Woman*, as does Rousseau's or Locke's name. And, yet, when reading her longest and most famous work, one may notice an affinity between Wollstonecraft, ensconced in the radical liberal intellectual circles of eighteenth-century Britain, and the ancient Athenian. Rather than base women's equality on human beings' original condition in the state of nature, Wollstonecraft's demand for women's equality is based on common aim of men and women: unfolding their faculties. In contrast to the modern conception of reason, which identifies reason as an instrument for gratifying desires, Wollstonecraft understands the passions in service to reason and instrumental in improving the quality of the soul. "In what does man's pre-eminence over the brute creation consists. The answer is clear as that a half is less than the whole; is Reason. What acquirement exalts one being above another? Virtue; we spontaneously reply. For what purpose were the passions implanted. That man by struggling with them might attain a degree of knowledge denied to the brutes; whispers Experience" (*VRW*, 12).

From the outset, Wollstonecraft is seeking to demonstrate to her readers that this conception of the soul is not gendered. We have noticed that Wollstonecraft begins her work by acknowledging women's apparent intellectual weakness. She condemns society, and in specific, education, for this great difference between man and man. Even those "men of genius" who claim to work for the improvement of women's faculties, do not understand their intellectual potential and needs. Instead, Wollstonecraft charges, these "men of genius" instruct females to be pleasing and encourage their constant attention to their body. In other words, that part of woman, which is human, the soul, is ignored. "In the true style of Mohametanism, they are treated as a kind of subordinate beings" (*VRW*, 8). Wollstonecraft's editor informs her readers that in the Mohammedan religion women were not permitted an afterlife, because they were not believed to have had souls. By comparing these thinkers to believers in the Mohammedan religion, Wollstonecraft quickly renders them foreign and incomprehensible. While the modern conception of mind as masculine may have been so pervasive that Wollstonecraft's defense of female's rational capacity would seem bizarre, Christianity had also become so influential that the suggestion that women do not have souls would also have seemed bizarre.[1] Teasing her audience, Wollstonecraft reminds it of Newton. "He was probably a being of superior order, accidentally trapped in a human body. Following the same train of thinking, I have been led to imagine that the few extraordinary women who have rushed in eccentrical directions out of the orbit prescribed to their sex, were *male* spirits, confined by mistake in female frames" (*VRW*, 34). Wollstonecraft immediately disciplines herself for her whimsical musings. "But if it be not philosophical to think of sex when the soul is mentioned, the inferiority must depend on the organs; or the heavenly fire, which is to ferment the clay, is not given in equal proportions" (*VRW*, 35).

Determined that soul is not gendered and that women have the same intellectual capacities as men, Wollstonecraft also asserts they share the same end, or to borrow from Aristotle's vocabulary, *telos*. Wollstonecraft's first task is "to consider women in the grand light of human creatures, who in common with men, are placed on this earth to unfold their faculties" (*VRW*, 8). Wollstonecraft reminds her readers that it is commonly believed that women are *inferior* to men, and she is quick to point out that this is a comparative term, which implies similarity. "If women are by nature inferior to men, their virtues must be the same in quality, if not in degree, founded on the principles, and have the same aim" (*VRW*, 26). The constant striving toward this aim marks the human with the divine. "Reason is, consequentially, the simple power of improvement; or more properly speaking, of discerning truth . . . More or less may be conspicuous in one being than another; but the nature of reason must be the same in all, if it be an emanation of divinity" (*VRW*, 53). Only after Wollstonecraft has completed her first task does she intend to "point out their [women's] peculiar designation" (*VRW*, 8). Wollstonecraft pursues a chimera—a utopian dream, in which the female soul unfolds its faculties and combines with female's "peculiar designation" to form a whole, unfractured by vicious passions.

Despite the certainty of her arguments for the character of women's souls, Wollstonecraft understands that women's claim to intellectual equality is threatened by the inescapable biological fact: women bear children. Because women are tethered to the body in a way that men are not, it is commonly believed they are more sensitive and less rational than men. After comparing Wollstonecraft's treatment of the family to Rousseau's, we know that Wollstonecraft herself appreciates a woman's sentiments for her husband and children. Wollstonecraft must confront her critics.

> Yet, that it is the condition for which woman was organized, has been insisted upon by the writers who have most vehemently argued in favour of the superiority of man; a superiority not in degree, but essence; though, to soften the argument, they have labored to prove, with chivalrous generousity, that the sexes ought not to be compared; man was made to reason, woman to feel: and that together, flesh and spirit, they make the most perfect whole, by blending happily reason and sensibility into one character. (*VRW*, 63)

Wollstonecraft seems at a loss for words and can only repeat what she has already said. "I come around to my old argument; if woman be allowed to have an immortal soul, she must have as the employment of life, an understanding to improve. And when, to render the present state more complete, though every thing proves it to be but a fraction of a mighty sum, she is incited by present gratification to forget her grand destination, nature is counteracted, or she was born only to procreate and rot" (*VRW*, 63). Certain that women must have a function other than "to procreate and rot," Wollstonecraft attempts to mitigate women's roles as mothers. Her attempt to establish the equal rational capacity of men and women eclipses the real, important biological differences between them. It is not until nearly the end of her work that Wollstonecraft takes up the question of whether or not the affections women have for their children is natural. Up until this point, Wollstonecraft has discussed motherhood as conventional and as a civic duty. It is as if a consideration of the natural bias for maternal affection would undermine her previous assertion that the character of the human soul extends to women as well as men.

Unable to avoid the fact that women do bear children, Wollstonecraft tells her readers that the care of infants is natural to women. "As the care of children in their infancy is one of the grand duties of the female character by nature, this duty would afford many forcible arguments for the strengthening the female understanding if it were properly considered" (*VRW*, 151). Though it may be a natural affection, Wollstonecraft insists it is not a strong affection and it must be fostered. "Natural affection, as it is termed, I believe to be a very faint tie, affections must grow out of the habitual exercise of a mutual sympathy; and what sympathy does a mother exercise who sends her babe to a nurse, and only takes it from a nurse to send it to a school?" (*VRW*, 152). Wollstonecraft does not discourage the proper affection between mother and child. In fact, she encourages it, believing that motherhood is rewarding to women and good for the community. Nonetheless, she wants to be clear: the affections mothers have for their children and the sensibility, in general, that seems to be common among women are not natural, biological necessity. This may serve as an example of Wollstonecraft's affinity with Aristotle. Wollstonecraft is not satisfied with the original or innate sentiment, but expects, through habit, to cultivate woman's nature. However, Wollstonecraft seems unable to explain how the real, important, biological differences between men and women are compatible with their shared human nature. Aristotle may well serve as a guide to Wollstonecraft through the land of chimeras, providing her with an example of woman, who fosters the rational, divine character of the human soul, while preserving the biological differences between male and female.

II. THE SOUL AND THE BODY

Aristotle begins his ethical and political work, *Nichomachean Ethics*, by suggesting "Every art and every investigation, and likewise every practical pursuit or undertaking, seems to aim at some good: hence it has been well said that the Good is That at which all things aim."[2] Aristotle assigns himself the task of determining the *telos* or the end of man.

> To say however that the Supreme Good is happiness will probably appear a truism; we still require a more explicit account of what constitutes happiness. Perhaps then we may arrive at this by ascertaining what is man's function . . . if this is so, and if we declare that the function of man is a certain form of life, and define that form of life as the exercise of the soul's faculties and activities in association with rational principle, and say that the function of a good man is to perform these activities well and rightly, and if the function is well performed in accordance with its own proper excellence—from these premises it follows that the good of man is the active exercise of his soul's faculties in conformity with excellence or virtue, or if there be several human excellences or virtues, in conformity with the best and most perfect among them. (*Ethics*, I, vii, 9–16)

Perhaps, one of Aristotle's most well known teachings is that human beings are rational and the function and *telos* of man is to live according to rational principles. Or, in the words of Mary Wollstonecraft, "human creatures . . . are placed on this earth to unfold their faculties" (*VRW*, 7).

Yet, these are not Aristotle's last words on the *telos* of man. Aristotle, like Wollstonecraft, also understands human beings to be creatures, who are made up of parts, the soul and the body. These parts are distinguishable by name, at least (*NE*, I, xiii, 10 and *DA* 413b 25–28). However, for Aristotle, unlike for Wollstonecraft, these parts are compatible, relieving us of making a choice between the human and the sex, between two half-beings. In his theoretical treatise on the soul, *De Anima*, Aristotle also considers the end toward which all living things strive. In this instance, Aristotle names generation as that end. "For any living thing that has reached its normal development and which is unmutilated, and whose mode of generation is not spontaneous, the most natural act is the production of another like itself, an animal producing an animal, a plant a plant, in that order that, as far as its nature allows, it may partake in the eternal and divine. That is the goal towards which all things strive, that for the sake of which they do whatever their nature renders possible."[3] Aristotle makes a similar claim throughout the *Generation of Animals*. He begins this treatise by noticing that offspring are of the same kind as their parents. "If, on the other hand, the products were dissimilar from their parents, and yet able to copulate, we should then get arising from them yet another different manner of creature, and out of their progeny yet another, and so it would go on *ad infinitum*. Nature, however, avoids what is infinite, because the infinite lacks completion and finality, whereas this is what Nature always seeks."[4] Generation, then, is part of Nature's ordered scheme.

Aristotle makes a stronger claim at the outset of Book II of *Generation of Animals*. Aristotle has already discussed male and female as principles of generation and he turns his attention to why the sexes, male and female, exist.

> As for the reason why one comes to be formed, and is, male, and another female, (a) in so far as this results from *necessity*, i.e. from the proximate motive cause and from what sort of matter, our argument as it proceeds must endeavor to explain; (b) in so far as this occurs on account of what is *better*, i.e., on account of the final cause (the Cause 'for the sake of which'), the principle is derived from the Upper Cosmos. (*GA*, 731b20–26)

Aristotle goes on to explain himself. "Of the things which are, some are eternal and divine, others admit alike of being and not-being, and the beautiful and the divine acts always, in virtue of its own nature, as a cause which produces that which is *better* in the things which admit of it" (*GA*, 731b26–28). Human beings share in the eternal by virtue of their soul. Yet, individual human beings cannot be said to be eternal.

> These are the causes on account of which generation of animals takes place, because since the nature of a class of this sort is unable to be eternal, that which comes into being is eternal in the manner that is open to it. Now it is impossible for it to be so numerically, since the 'being' of things is to be found in the particular, and if it really were so, then it would be eternal; it is *specifically*. That is why there is always a *class* of men, of animals, of plants; and since the principle of these is 'the male' and 'the female' it will surely be for the sake of generation that 'the male' and 'the female' are present in the individuals which are male and female. (*GA*, 731b32–732a3)

Although generation is the final cause, "for the sake of which" that human beings share with all living things, even plants, we should not minimize the importance it has for human beings according to Aristotle. In contrast to the modern conception of reproduction, generation is not simply associated with the brutes, but it is a means by which human beings share in the eternal.

Aristotle has offered two functions of human beings: "the exercise of the soul's faculties and activities in association with the rational principle" and generation, "the production of another like itself." Because modern thought has taught us to associate the former with the mind and the latter with the body, with the human and with the animal, it may seem counterintuitive to assign these two functions to one being.[5] And, yet, these two ends are consistent with Aristotle's more general understanding of the human condition, which occupies a place between the divine and the beastly. Because human beings have the nutritive and sensitive soul, they are properly considered animals. "This [power of self nutrition] is the originative power the possession of which leads us to speak of things as *living* at all, but it is the possession of sensation that leads us for the first time to speak of things as animals" (*DA*, 413b1–5). Yet, human beings also have the ability to think. Aristotle readily admits that he is unsure with respect to this part or type of soul. "We have no evidence yet about thought or the power of reflexion; it seems to be a different kind of soul, differing as what is eternal from what is perishable" (*DA*, 413b25–26). Possessing the power of reflection not only distinguishes human beings from animals, but human beings' capacity for reflection makes them similar to the divine in some way.

Having a place between beasts and gods, the human beings share something of both. Unlike modern thinkers, Aristotle has not assigned one of these final causes, "the exercise of the soul's faculties and activities in association with the rational principle" and generation, to each of the sexes. Rather all human beings, male and female, strive towards both of these ends. Nature, being so well ordered, makes it possible for human beings to exercise the rational faculties of the soul without impediment from generation. Aristotle makes his explanation by comparing plants to other animals. "In all her workmanship herein nature acts in every particular as reason would expect. A plant, in its essence, has no function or activity to perform other than the production of its seed; and since this is produced as the result of the union of male and female, Nature has mixed the two and placed them together, so that in plants male and female are not separate" (*GA*, 731a25–30). Male and female are joined in plants so as to facilitate their only function, generation. Animals, and particularly human beings, are distinguished from plants by their other functions or activities. The implication being that if male and female were joined in human beings as they are in plants, they would be completely occupied with the function of generation and, as a result, would be prevented from rational activity. Fortunately, Nature foresees such an obstacle and guards against it. "[G]eneration is not the only function which an animal has—that is a function common to all things living. All animals have, in addition, some measure of knowledge of a sort (some have more, some less, some very little indeed), because they have sense perception is, of course, a sort of knowledge" (*GA*, 731a31–35).[6] In order to allow for this activity, sense perception, nature has separated the male and the female sex into different living things. Both the male and female of the species enjoy "some measure of knowledge" in addition to the function of generation. "The value attach to this knowledge varies greatly according as we judge it by the standard of human intelligence or the class of lifeless objects. Compared with the intelligence possessed by man, it seems as nothing to possess the two senses of touch and taste only; but compared with entire absence of sensibility it seems a very fine thing indeed" (*GA*, 731b1–5). In this passage Aristotle is considering animals generally and does not pause to elaborate the particular character of human intelligence. We may further infer, compared to sense perception of animals, human intelligence "seems a very fine thing indeed," but compared to *nous* or the pure intelligence of the divine, "it seems as nothing to possess" human intelligence. There is nothing this passage to suggest that Nature is so ordered only to the benefit of the male. In fact,

Nature could not accommodate the male in such a way without rendering the female inactive. So too with human animals, there is an end that goes beyond generation. Human beings have "some measure of knowledge," which is not limited to sense perception. If Nature had separated the sexes in order to relieve the male of the function of generation and so that only the male may exercise the rational faculties of the soul, the female would not be able to perform her function of generation. But, we know this is not the case. Although the sexes have been separated to allow for another function, the male sex continues to play a part in generation. However, unlike the plant, which "has no function or activity to perform other than the production of its seed," the male animal is not continuously engaged in the function of generation. But then again, neither is the female. If she were deprived of "some measure of knowledge," it would mean that she is able to perform a single function only occasionally. She would be inactive as if "she was born only to procreate and rot" (*VRW*, 63). This notion is as offensive to Aristotle as it is to Wollstonecraft. It violates one of Aristotle's basic principles of Nature: Nature does nothing in vain.[7]

Aristotle, then, offers Wollstonecraft support by explaining that the end of all human beings, both male and female, is to exercise the soul's rational faculties. Nonetheless, he allows generation to be an important function of all human beings. Both are means by which they may share in the eternal. For Aristotle, these two ends are not irreconcilable. In no way does the capacity to bear children threaten to undermine the equality women may claim based on the character of the human soul. Rather than designate one of these functions to each of the sexes, as Rousseau has done, Aristotle expects that all human beings, male and female, will pursue these ends. Aristotle is able to avoid the half-beings, which populate Rousseau's land of chimeras, because he avoids the radical differences between men and women. We should also note how Wollstonecraft's understanding of human reason resonates more with Aristotle's explanation of the soul's rational faculties than it does with Locke's conception of human reason. For Wollstonecraft and Aristotle, it connects us with the divine. For Locke, reason has decidedly worldly limits, which render it incapable of contemplating the divine. Following Aristotle, rather than Rousseau or Locke, through the land of chimeras, we would not be asked to choose between two half-beings. It remains now to consider the important, necessary role in generation, which Aristotle offers both male and female.

III. THE PRODUCTION OF ANOTHER LIKE ITSELF

Like most of his works, Aristotle begins the *Generation of Animals* by surveying the prevailing opinions of generation. He devotes most of his attention to the theories of pangenesis and preformation. Pangenesis suggests that semen is taken from the whole body in order to provide all the body parts to the offspring.[8] Preformation suggests that the little human is already present in the semen and needs only to grow. These two theories are not necessarily in contradiction to one another. Both pangenesis and preformation suggest that the growth or the change in the offspring is simply alteration of the substance, rather than generation, the coming into being of a new substance. In her article on *Generation of Animals*, Daryl Tress reconstructs the title in Greek and offers the literal translation, "on the coming into being of living creatures."[9] The significance of this title, Tress tells us, is "that Aristotle raises his scientific questions regarding generation in a philosophical context; that is, his scientific questions are metaphysically informed and they are raised with a long lineage of attempts at understanding *genesis*, the transition from not-being to being" (Tress, 1992, 311). Recalling Aristotle's discussion of the soul in *De Anima*, "what has soul in it differs from what has not in that the former displays life" (*DA*, 413a21–23). We can expect, then, that the subject of generation must include a consideration of the soul. Tress notes Aristotle's dissatisfaction with both pangenesis and preformation on these grounds. "All of his reasons argue against what he regards as the real problem: the materialistic reduction and oversimplification that these two theories represent. Both theories fail to explain what principle organizes the many parts of the body" (Tress, 1992, 318).

   Aristotle finds fault with the prevailing theories of generation for a second reason. They allow for the possibility that the offspring could come entirely from one parent. "If semen is drawn from all parts of both parents alike, we shall have two animals formed, for the semen will contain all the parts of each" (*GA*, 722b5f). There must be a way to ensure that the parts from both parents are combined. Aristotle considers Empedocles suggestion. "Empedocles says that in the male and in the female there is as it might be a tally—a half of something—and that the whole is not drawn from either of the parents . . . Otherwise the question arises, why is it that the female animals do not generate out of themselves, if so be that the semen is drawn from the whole body and a receptacle for it is at hand?" (*GA*, 722b13–16). Tress corrects a common misunderstanding of Aristotle's critique of Empedocles. Aristotle's feminist critics have suggested that Aristotle rejects Empedocles theory because Aristotle would like to deny the female a significant role in generation. Though Empedocles' theory must finally be rejected, it is on the grounds that he cannot explain how the parts are assembled to create one organism (Tress, 1992, 321–322). I would add to Tress' discussion of this passage that Aristotle very explicitly states that he respects Empedocles' theory for its attempt to assure that both women and men have a role in generation. "No; so far as we can see, either the semen is not drawn from the whole body, or if it is, it happens in the way described by Empedocles—the two parents do not *both* supply the *same* proportions, and that is why they *need* intercourse with each other [emphasis mine]" (*GA*, 722b17–19).

Like Empedocles, Aristotle's explanation of generation will assign a significant and different role to both the male and the female. Consistent with his teaching that generation is the function of all living things, Aristotle asserts from the outset of his treatise that both the male and female are principles of generation (*GA*, 716a5). Yet, in contrast with Empedocles, Aristotle makes clear that within the function of generation, male and female differ.

> Now male and female differ in respect of their *logos*, in that the power or faculty possessed by the one differs from that possessed by the other; but they differ also in a bodily sense, in respect of certain physical parts. They differ in their *logos*, because the male is that which has the power to generate in another (as we have stated above), while the female is that which can generate in itself, i.e. it is that out of which the generated offspring, which is present in the generator, comes into being. (*GA*, 716a18–25)

Aristotle can explain the different contributions very concisely. "The male provides the 'form' and the 'principle of the movement' and the female provides the body, in other words, the material" (*GA*, 729a5f). Yet, an important aspect of the male's contribution may escape notice in what has come to be a "soundbite" of Aristotle's theory of generation. Often the "principle of movement" is overlooked in favor of the more provocative suggestion that the male contributes form.

> If we consider the matter on general grounds, we see that when some one thing is formed from the conjunction of an active partner with a passive one, the active partner is not situated with the thing being formed; and we may generalize this still further by substituting 'moving' and 'moved' for 'active' and 'passive.' Now of course the female, qua female, is passive, and the male, qua male, is active—it is that whence the principle of movement comes. (*GA*, 729b11–16)

This is what will prove to be an important difference between the contributions of the male and female. As we will see, the distinction between form and matter will be blurred by Aristotle's understanding of the relationship between the two. With such specific and unique contributions to make to generation, neither the female nor the male can generate offspring by itself. Rather, there must be cooperation between the two. "All blooded ones [animals], however, are formed from semen, so many as are formed as the result of copulation, that is to say, the male emits semen into the female, and upon the entry of the semen the young animals are 'set' and constituted and assume their proper shape" (*GA*, 733b20f).

Aristotle's explicit identification of the form with the male and the matter with the female may suggest to our modern ears the same radical distinction between male and female that Wollstonecraft faces. However, if we return to the text of *Generation of Animals*, as well as other treatises by Aristotle, we may better appreciate the relationship between form and matter, soul and body. It becomes clear that the contributions of male and female are remarkably similar though different in an important way.

For Aristotle, a substance is the unity of form and matter. Neither form nor matter can exist independently of the other. After completing his consideration of his predecessors teachings, Aristotle begins his own account of soul in book II of *De Anima*. "If then, we have to give a general formula applicable to all kinds of soul, we must describe it as an actuality of the first kind of a natural body. That is why we can dismiss as unnecessary the question whether soul and body are one: it is as though we were to ask whether the wax and its shape are one, or generally the matter of a thing and that of which it is the matter" (*DA*, 412b3–8). Aristotle believes this is a sufficient answer to the question, "What is soul?" He states a more concise, though no less difficult to understand, response to this question. "It is substance in the sense which corresponds to the account of a thing. That means that it is what it is to be for a body of the character just assigned" (*GA*, 412b10–12). In order to illustrate the relationship between soul and body, Aristotle takes the eye for an example. "Suppose that the eye were an animal—sight would have been its soul, for sight is the substance of the eye which corresponds to the account, the eye being merely the matter of seeing; when seeing is removed the eye is no longer an eye, except in name" (*DA*, 412b18–21). Aristotle then asks us to use this example as an analogy to human beings. "The soul is actuality in the sense corresponding to sight . . . the body corresponds to what is in potentiality, as the pupil *plus* the power of sight constitutes the eye, so the soul *plus* the body constitutes the animal. Aristotle concludes "that the soul is inseparable from its body" (*DA*, 413a4).

Not only does the soul require the body for its existence, but it requires a specific arrangement of the body.

Since then the complex here is the living thing, the body cannot be the actuality of the soul; it is the soul which is the actuality of a certain kind of body. Hence the rightness of the view that the soul cannot be without a body, while it cannot *be* a body of a definite kind. It was a mistake, therefore, to do as former thinkers did, merely fit it into a body without adding a definite specification of the kind or character of that body, although evidently one chance thing will not receive another. It comes about as reason requires that thing, the actuality of any given thing can only be realized in what is already potentially that thing, i.e. matter of its own appropriate to it. (*DA*, 414a16–27)

Though Aristotle does not offer any further comment on the "definite specification of the kind or character of that body" in *De Anima* (after all, it would be somewhat of a distraction from the task at hand), he does devote considerable attention to the union of form and matter in *Generation of Animals*. Again, Aristotle states that the matter is "already potentially that thing." The female's contribution to the offspring "contains all the parts of the body *potentially*, though none in actuality" (732a23). In addition to the very specific material, the union of soul and body, the coming to be of a substance requires particular circumstances. After the material is "set" by the motive cause, the semen, the parts of the offspring begin to form. Formation is the result of cooling and heat. For example, "the excessively earthy stuff," nails, horns, and hoofs, form when the heat belonging to this material has cooled (*GA*, 743a13). On the other hand, heat is needed to produce flesh and bones. It is in his explanation of the formation of flesh and bones that Aristotle repeats his principle that union of form and material is not accidental. "This heat, however, to produce flesh or bone, does not work on some causal material in some causal place at some causal time; material, place, time must be those ordained by Nature: that which is potentially will not be brought into being by a motive agent that lacks the appropriate actuality; so equally, that which possess the actuality will not produce the article out of any causal material" (*GA*, 743a20–26).

Keeping in mind Aristotle's understanding of the relationship between form and matter, soul and body, we are ready to consider in specific the female and male contributions to generation, matter and form. I would emphasize that Aristotle is discussing the *contributions* of male and female to generation. He does not suggest that these contributions are microcosms of the male and female. To say that the female contributes only matter is *not* to say that she has no soul. On the contrary, Aristotle states quite explicitly that male and female have the same soul. "Granted that the female possesses the same Soul [as the male] and that the residue provided by the female is the material [for fetation], why has the female any need of the male in addition? Why does not the female accomplish generation all by itself and from itself?"(*GA*, 741a5–10). This question continually reemerges throughout *Generation of Animals* and the difficulty with which Aristotle has in putting this question to rest is testimony to the value Aristotle places on the female.[10] Aristotle's continual confrontation with this question and his commitment to include both male and female should continually remind his readers that Aristotle does not simply delegate to the female the function of generation, while assigning to the male the exercise of the soul's rational faculties. In this respect, Aristotle distinguishes himself from Rousseau and offers Mary Wollstonecraft a way to form a chimera by combining these two parts of woman, that which belongs to the human and that which belongs to the female sex, in a manner that resembles a utopian dream, rather than a monster.

As Aristotle begins his consideration of the generative fluids, he is contemplating semen. "Now the aim of semen is to be, in its nature, the sort of stuff from which the things that take their rise in the realm of Nature are originally formed" (*GA*, 724a16–18). At this point, Aristotle has not made a distinction between the male and female generative fluids and is considering semen generally. Aristotle rules out the possibility that semen is part of the body. Nor is it a deformation of the body because it exists in "every single individual" (724b30f). He concludes that semen must be a residue. It "is derived from useful nourishment, and not only that, but from useful nourishment in its final form" (*GA*, 72625–30).

Having given a general account of semen, Aristotle seeks a more precise understanding of the generative fluids. Determined that Nature does nothing in vain, Aristotle distinguishes the role of the male and the female in generation. "Does the female discharge semen as the male does, which would mean that the object formed is a single mixture produced from two semens; or is there not discharge of semen from the female? And if there is none, then does the female contribute nothing whatever to generation, merely providing a place where generation may happen; or does it contribute something else, and if so, how and in what manner does it do so?" (*GA*, 733b31f). Aristotle must conclude that the female does not contribute semen in just the same way that the male does. Her contribution must be distinct. Aristotle calls the female's contribution menstrual fluid. It is a useful residue from nourishment, just as the semen is. However, because the female has a smaller share of heat, she is considered the weaker creature. The residue contributed to generation by the female, then, is "less thoroughly concocted" and is a bloodlike fluid (*GA*, 726b31f). Despite the differences in the menstrual fluid, Aristotle suggests that "the menstrual fluid is a residue and, it is the analogous thing in females to semen in males" (*GA*, 727a2–5). Just a few pages later, Aristotle makes a stronger case for the similarities between semen and menstrual fluid. "As we see, the menstrual fluid is semen, not indeed semen in a pure condition, but needing still to be acted upon" (728a26–28). This lends a complexity and richness to the offspring that may have been missed by insisting on the same contribution from male and female. Tress argues against those who believe Aristotle privileges the male's contribution to generation. "On, the contrary, Aristotle is here rejecting the identification of generative fluid with the male semen, and establishing instead a fuller conception of *sperma* [semen, in the general use] that includes both male and female contributions, contributions that do differ in kind. Each is unique; both are necessary" (Tress, 1992, 325).

Modern thought has conditioned us to understand the contributions of the male and female, form and matter, as radically different from each other. They are distinct, to be sure. They must be according to Aristotle's conception of Nature. However, Aristotle's understanding of the relationship between soul and body render the contributions much more similar than we might expect. Noticing the similarity requires, what modern thought would consider, an "elevation" of the material and a "corruption" of the form. The matter, the menstrual fluid, has already been described in comparison to semen. "For, as we see, the menstrual fluid is semen, not indeed semen in a pure condition, but needing still to be acted upon" (*GA*, 728a26–28). Wollstonecraft's own rationale about the character of the female soul may be appropriately adopted to explain the kinship between the male residue, semen, and the female residue, menstrual fluid. "If women are by nature inferior to men, their virtues must be the same in quality, if not in degree" (*VRW*, 27). The same may be said of menstrual fluid, if it is inferior to semen, it must be the same in quality, if not in degree. By considering Aristotle's comparison of the semen to blood, we are able to see that menstrual fluid is the same in quality, though different in degree.

Upon turning his attention to the female contribution to generation, Aristotle gives a general account of blood. Like semen, Aristotle tells his readers "blood is the final form of nourishment" (*GA*, 726b3). Aware that he has made the same claim for semen, Aristotle prevents us from thinking he has contradicted himself. "And since semen is also a residue from nourishment—from nourishment in its final form, surely it follows that semen will be either blood or the analogous substance, or something formed out of these" (*GA*, 7263–6). In his essay, "Aristotle's Psychology and Zoology," G.E.R. Lloyd points out the psychic functions of blood. "First the blood itself certainly serves a psychic end and a fundamental one: its final cause is nutrition, *PA* 650b2ff., 12f, and it is potentially, the body or the flesh, *PA*, 668a25ff."[11] Furthermore, the blood seems to be responsible for the organization of the organism in some manner. Recalling, Aristotle's critique of Empedocles, we know that this is an important metaphysical implications. "The network of blood-vessels serves other purposes as well, being compared to a framework for the rest of the body, *PA*, 668b24ff., binding together the front and the back, but their fundamental function is to nourish the body, and it is for this reason that they permeate every part of the body" (Lloyd, pp. 151–152).

Allowing that the blood performs the functions of the nutritive soul, we must wonder if the blood does not also have present in it the sensitive soul as well. Aristotle appreciates that dividing the soul is much easier said than done. "Whether these two parts [the rational and the irrational] are really distinct in the sense that the parts of the body or of any other divisible whole are distinct, or whether though distinguishable in [*logos*] as they are inseparable in [nature], like the convex and the concave sides of curves, is a question of no importance for the matter at hand" (*NE*, I, xiii, 10). While it may not be an important question to him in the context of the *Nichomachean Ethics*, a practical work, it is certainly a compelling question in his theoretical work on the soul, *De Anima*. The soul is characterized by the power of self-nutrition, sensation, and thinking. "Is each of these a soul or a part of a soul? And if a part, a part merely distinguishable by definition or a part distinct in local situation as well? In the case of certain of these powers, the answers to these questions are easy, in the case of others we are puzzled to say" (*DA*, 413b14–17). In this context, Aristotle arrives at much the same conclusion. Of the power of reflextion, Aristotle says it "seems to be a different kind of soul, differing as what is eternal from what is perishable; it alone is capable of separation. All other parts of the soul, it is evident from what we have said, are in spite of certain statements to the contrary, incapable of separate existence though, of course, distinguishable by definition" (*DA*, 413b25–28). Consistent with Aristotle's suggestion that the nutritive and sensitive souls are distinguishable only in speech, Lloyd suggests that blood performs functions of the sensitive soul as well. "The nature of the blood, he [Aristotle] says at *PA* 651a12ff., is responsible for many things both in respect of the *character* of animals and in respect of *perception,* in a chapter which has offered a variety of suggestions about how the intelligence, acuteness of perception, courage, and timidity of different species of animals are to be correlated with the quality of blood they posses, its heat, purity, thinness, whether it contains fibres, and so one" (Lloyd, 152). Lloyd's explanation of the psychic functions of blood are helpful in understanding the way in which

Aristotle differs from modern thinkers. Matter, according to Aristotle, cannot be stripped of its formal qualities. Aristotle, thus, provides the theoretical groundwork by which Wollstonecraft may refute "the men of genius,"who, considering females rather as women than human creatures" have sacrificed their souls to their beauty (*VRW*, 7).

Unfortunately, we are not able to rest with Lloyd's explanation. After all, menstrual fluid is a highly refined material and cannot simply be understood as blood. Aristotle refers to menstrual fluid as a "bloodlike" (*GA*, 726b31) fluid, unconcocted semen. Perhaps the best comparison that Aristotle offers is "semen emitted under strain due to excessively frequent intercourse" (726b10). This semen seems to occupy a quality between blood, as it is found throughout the body, and semen, which has been fully concocted. Menstrual fluid, then, has been highly refined and cannot be considered common blood. And, still, it is not thoroughly concocted and, therefore, differs from semen in its degree of purity. Aristotle characterizes menstrual fluid as "prime matter" (*GA*, 729a33). Our translator points us to Aristotle's definition of prime matter in *Metaphysics*. "But, as has been said, the proximate matter and the form are one and the same thing, the one potentially, the other actually. Therefore to ask the cause of their being one is like asking the cause of unity in general; for each thing is a unity and the potential and the actual are somehow one."[12] As Aristotle concludes his remarks on menstrual fluid and turns his attention to his theory of generation, it looks as if menstrual fluid, "prime matter," is *nearly* identical to form. In Wollstonecraft's words, they are the same in quality, if not in degree. Menstrual fluid, a form potentially, must be combined with semen, form actually, in order to become a substance.

The radical distinction between form and matter, male and female, is overcome by Aristotle by the inseparability of soul and matter. Just as matter cannot be stripped of formal qualities, so form cannot be stripped of its material qualities. In book II of *Generation of Animals*, Aristotle wonders about the nature of the male contribution to generation, which he also refers to as semen. Aristotle begins by describing the physical properties of semen. "Semen when it leaves the animal is thick and white, but when it cools it becomes fluid like water and is of the color of water"(*GA*, 735a30–33). Aristotle is puzzled by semen's likeness to water and to earth and considers the possibility that it is comprised of water or earth or both. He rejects this explanation of semen's material properties in favor of another explanation. According to Aristotle, the thickness and whiteness of the semen may be attributed to *pneuma*, a special type of hot air. "The reason is that *pneuma* gets mixed in with it, and this produces the increase of bulk and lets the whiteness show through, precisely as it does with foam, and also with snow (because snow too is a foam)" (*GA*, 735b20–23). Still, Aristotle cannot divorce semen from matter. He tells us "Semen, then, is a compound of *pneuma* and water (pneuma being hot air), and that is why it is fluid in its nature; it is made of water" (*GA*, 736a1–4). Noticing that semen of different animals varies, Aristotle must allow that the semen of some contain more earth than that of others. "It is, of course, true that one semen must of necessity be earthier than another, and the earthiest will be in those animals which, for their bodily bulk contain a large amount of earthy matter; but semen is thick and white because there is *pneuma* mixed with it. What is more, it is white in all cases" (*GA*, 736a8–11).

Throughout *Generation of Animals* Aristotle has been at pains to explain why the female does not generate alone and it now looks as if we may ask why the male does not generate alone. The semen, containing both form and matter, may seem capable of generation. Aristotle is steadfast to his theory that the female contributes the matter and the male contributes the form. In comparing the matter of semen to the matter of menstrual fluid, it becomes evident why it must be this way. The matter which constitutes semen is ordinary material, water and earth. On the other hand, the matter, which constitutes the menstrual fluid is rarified, prime matter, form potentially. The male contribution is unique in that it contains *pneuma* or the special heat, which creates movement. "Supposing it is true that the semen which is so introduced is not an ingredient in the fetation which is formed, but performs its function by means of dynamis which is contains (*GA*, 736a26–28). The material, which is unable to be used in generation, simply evaporates (*GA*, 737a15).

As an alternative to Rousseau or Locke, Aristotle proves to be a helpful guide in navigating the land of chimeras. Unlike the state of nature theorists, Aristotle is able to combine that part of woman, which is shared by all human beings, the soul's rational faculties, with that part of woman that belongs to the female sex. The chimera presented by Aristotle resembles Wollstonecraft's utopian dream more so than the monstrous half-beings presented by Rousseau and Locke. To be sure, the contribution that women make to generation differs in a significant way to the contribution the male makes. However, they are both necessary for generation. For Aristotle soul and body are not easily separated either physically or metaphysically. As a result, all human beings, male and female perform the functions of "the exercise of the soul's faculties and activities in association with the rational principle" and "the production of another like itself." In the next chapter, I will consider the chimera in the context of marriage. Again, Aristotle has much to impart to

Wollstonecraft. Aristotle's understanding of the friendship between husband and wife elaborates Wollstonecraft's hopes for affectionate wives.

Chapter Six

The Foundation of Almost Every Social Virtue

Traveling with Rousseau and then Locke into the land of chimeras, Wollstonecraft pursues her utopian dream, women who are considered "human creatures," as well as females. Wollstonecraft pursues "affectionate wives and rational mothers." Despite the promise of Rousseau's and Locke's egalitarian political theory and pedagogy, neither state of nature theorist is able to put together the two parts of woman, the human and the female sex, in a manner that creates a whole, independent woman. As a consequence of the fractured character of woman, the relationship between man and woman is also corrupted. For Rousseau, it is the sexual passions and the differences between the sexes, which unite otherwise independent beings. In an effort to restore our familial and social bonds, Rousseau encourages the differences between the sexes in his prescriptions for educating young girls. The human part of woman is sacrificed for the sake of the female, according to Wollstonecraft. Lacking reason, the female part of woman is also corrupted. Rousseau's "wild chimera" or "half-being" (VRW, 39), it seems to Wollstonecraft, is a dependent creature, who merely feigns affection for her husband in order to satisfy her own desires, which, at the close of the eighteenth century, are many and vicious. Furthermore, Wollstonecraft fears, the education Rousseau prescribes for the female does not prepare her to fulfill her duty to care for and to educate her children. Locke's "half-being," on the other hand, is educated to be strong in body and in mind. She is quite able to quiet her passions. And, as a result, she very competently performs her duty as mother and as citizen: she educates her children for liberal civil society. Although she is a rational mother, we can hardly say she is an affectionate wife. In his educational treatise, Locke does not allow us even a glimpse of this rational mother's interaction with her husband and we are left with the impression that husband and wife are indeed independent of each other, perhaps to the point of indifference. Traveling with Rousseau, and then Locke, through the land of chimeras, Wollstonecraft finds "half-beings," albeit different fractions of woman.

Although Rousseau does not provide a path by which Wollstonecraft may pursue her utopian dream through the land of chimeras, the Solitary Walker does not abandon the Hyena in Petticoats. At the start of his *Second Discourse*, Rousseau presents himself as an alternative to previous state of nature theorists, in particular John Locke. He also presents himself as and alternative to Aristotle and, in doing so, he suggests to us a third guide through the land of chimeras. As we have seen in the preceding chapter, Aristotle also understands human beings to be made up of parts, so to speak, soul and body. Human beings are characterized by souls and are distinguished from other living things by their soul's rational capacity. The end of human beings is "the active exercise of [a human being's] rational faculties in conformity with excellence or virtue" (*NE*, I, vii, 9–16). We have noticed a similar understanding of human nature in Wollstonecraft's *A Vindication of the Rights of Woman*. Aristotle also recognizes that part of the human being, which is specific to male or female, the sex. With respect to this part of the human being, the end is generation (*DA*, 415a26–415b1). Unlike Rousseau, one of the "Aristotles of our century" (*Second Discourse*, 125), Aristotle himself does not find these parts of the human being to be incompatible with each other, leading him to identify the former with the male and the latter with the female. Doing so would violate one of Aristotle's fundamental philosophic tenets: nature does nothing in vain. We have already seen how Aristotle affords both male and female necessary roles in generation. The different contributions made by the male and the female in generation preserves the need each has for the other. Yet, in contrast to Rousseau's understanding between the sexes, the female's capacity to bear children does not have such a profound influence on her that it renders her incapable of pursuing the end of all human beings, the exercise of the "soul's faculties in conformity with excellence or virtue."

In this chapter, I shall consider Aristotle's chimera in the context of marriage. Aristotle's discussion of friendship provides Wollstonecraft with the philosophical foundation for the further pursuit of her utopian dream of affectionate wives and rational mothers. Other commentators have noticed a certain compatibility between Wollstonecraft's hope for marriage and antiquity's understanding of friendship. Virginia Sapiro makes a passing comparison: "Like some of the Greeks she probably never read, Wollstonecraft defined the ideal relationship as friendship . . . Families should be based on friendship rather than patriarchy (and she hates both the subordinations of gender and age in the family), and a polity must be based on the same" (Sapiro, 1996, 36). Other scholars have been less hesitant to draw the connection between Wollstonecraft and ancient thinkers. Sylvana Tomaselli writes, "her ideal conception of the relationship between the sexes was one modeled on an idealized conception, which owed much to antiquity, of friendship between men" (Tomaselli, xxvi). Even in the face of radical feminism, Tomaselli argues that Wollstonecraft is relevant today, as long as we "conceive of reason as being genderless, to accept the pursuit of virtue is the good life for all human beings" (Tomaselli, xxix). Sapiro, perhaps, overstates Wollstonecraft's ignorance of classical philosophy. Though Wollstonecraft may not have made a rigorous study of it, she does make reference to both Plato and Aristotle in her writings (*VRM*, 19, 48). In contrast to these scholars, I will not consider Wollstonecraft's hope for marriage by making a broad comparison to ancient thinkers. Rather, I will turn my attention, in particular, to Aristotle's articulation of friendship. Tomaselli to the contrary, Aristotle does not limit his understanding of friendship to men. Indeed, Aristotle explicitly considers the friendship between husband and wife and offers it as a model for friendship generally. Aristotle, therefore, serves as a guide, I shall argue, for our understanding of what Wollstonecraft means by friendship between husband and wife.

The most sustained discussion of Wollstonecraft's conception of marriage in comparison to the ancient notion of friendship is by Ruth Abbey in her essay, "Back to the Future: Marriage as Friendship in the Thought of Mary Wollstonecraft." Abbey argues in order "for liberal theory to move forward it must take the political nature of the family seriously."[1] Wollstonecraft, Abbey suggests, does just that. And, what's more, Wollstonecraft applies liberal theories of justice to the family. To make her case, Abbey draws a comparison between Wollstonecraft's hope for marriage and the ancient understanding of friendship.[2]

> [S]he envisages a form of marriage that incorporates the major features of classical notion of higher friendship such as equality, free choice, reason, mutual esteem, and a profound concern for one another's moral character . . . Wollstonecraft uses the idea that marriage should emulate many features of higher friendship to criticize the practices and values of romance and family in eighteenth-century English society and to suggest a way in which marriage might be reconfigured to realize central liberal values. (Abbey, 79)

Abbey expresses the central tenets of Aristotle's notion of friendship in the vocabulary of liberalism in order to put ancient philosophy in the service of liberalism. In doing so, Abbey passes over distinctions between ancient philosophy and liberalism and she quickly moves over an important contribution that Wollstonecraft makes to political philosophy. Abbey is correct to suggest that Wollstonecraft understands marriage in much the same way as Aristotle understands friendship. However, as I have been arguing, Wollstonecraft's compatibility with Aristotle is due to her dissatisfaction with Rousseau's and Locke's understanding of the nature of woman and the character of the relations between the sexes; Wollstonecraft thus points to a fundamental dissatisfaction with state of nature theories and the civil society, which follows. Wollstonecraft does not offer a vision for marriage, which is comparable to Aristotle's conception of friendship in order to save liberalism, but to critique it.

I will begin this chapter by noticing a further comparison of Wollstonecraft to Aristotle. Not only does Wollstonecraft echo Aristotle's claim that the end or the *telos* of human beings is the exercise of our reason and the practice of virtue, but she also echoes his claim that human beings are political by nature. I will then consider Aristotle's conception of friendship, which Sapiro, Tomselli, and Abbey have noticed provides a model for Wollstonecraft's ideal relationship between husband and wife. Not only does Aristotle show us an example of Wollstonecraft's chimera or utopian dream, but Aristotle also offers Wollstonecraft a path through the land of chimeras. He gives us an indication of how it is possible for the vicious, "half-beings," which populate eighteenth-century Britain to fulfill Wollstonecraft's utopian dream of an affectionate and rational wife by practicing friendship to her husband. From a consideration of friendship in general, I will turn my attention to the friendship between husband and wife, in particular. For Aristotle and for Wollstonecraft, friendship between husband and wife is the occasion for "the active exercise of the soul's faculties in conformity with excellence or virtue." Instead of a "wild chimera," a "half-being," Aristotle offers his readers a glimpse of the chimera or the utopian dream that Wollstonecraft has been pursuing: an unfractured woman, who practices reason and virtue, but who is, nonetheless, an affectionate wife.

I. THE GRAND LIGHT OF HUMAN CREATURES

Before turning our attention to the example of friendship between husband and wife, which Aristotle offers to Wollstonecraft, it is helpful to return to the question of the compatibility between these two thinkers. Scholars have noted the similarity between Wollstonecraft's hope for marriage and Aristotle's notion of friendship. However, they have not pursued this initial observation by looking for further similarities between the ancient Greek philosopher and the ostensibly liberal British thinker. Indeed, Ruth Abbey suggests Wollstonecraft adopts this one element of ancient philosophy in order to shore up her otherwise liberal agenda for political reform. However, I find greater affinity between Wollstonecraft and Aristotle on fundamental tenets of their understanding of political life. To be sure, Wollstonecraft does not explicitly adopt elements of Aristotle's political philosophy, as she does in the cases of Locke and even Rousseau. Nor does Wollstonecraft dispute either explicitly or implicitly elements of Aristotle's political philosophy as she does these two state of nature theorists. Nonetheless, as we have seen in the previous chapter, Wollstonecraft echoes Aristotle's teaching that human beings are rational and that the function and the *telos* of man is to live according to rational principles. Women, considered in "the grand light of human creatures, who in common with men, are placed on this earth to unfold their faculties" (*VRW*, 8). In contrast to state of nature theorists, like Rousseau and Locke, both Aristotle and Wollstonecraft understand the nature of human beings to be determined by their end, rather than their origin. The comparison does not end there. Wollstonecraft does not understand the civil society to be simply a means of protecting ourselves from the aggression of others, as do modern thinkers. For Wollstonecraft, like Aristotle, man's nature is best fulfilled in a political community.

Aristotle begins the *Politics* by describing the generation of the city. Human beings join together because they need each other in order to survive. The first example he cites is the union of man and woman. "First, then, there must of necessity be conjunction of persons who cannot exist without one another: on the one hand, male and female, for the sake of reproduction (which occurs not from intentional choice but—as is also the case with the other animals and plants—from a natural striving to leave behind another that is like oneself); on the other, the naturally ruling and ruled on account of preservation."[3] The development of the city continues by households join-ing to form villages and villages joining to form the city. The city enjoys a degree of self-sufficiency because it does not merely exist for the sake of liv-ing, but for the sake of living well (*Politics*, 1252b9).

> While coming into being for the sake of living, it exists for the sake of living well. Every city, therefore, exists by nature, if such also are the first partnerships. For the city is their end, and nature is an end: what each thing is—for example, a human being, a horse, or a household—when its coming into being is complete is, we assert, the nature of the thing. Again, that for the sake of which [a thing exists], or its end, is what is

best; and self-sufficiency is an end and what is best. From these things it is evident, then, that the city belongs among the things that exist by nature, and that man is by nature a political animal. (*Politics*, 1252b29–1253)

It is important to note that it is not the character of the city, which makes political life conducive to human beings, but the character of human beings that makes political life a necessity.

For, as we assert, nature does nothing in vain; and man alone among the animals has speech. The voice indeed indicates the painful or pleasant, and hence is present in other animals as well; for their nature has come this far, that they have perception of the painful and pleasant and indicate these things to each other. But speech serves to reveal the advantageous and the harmful, and hence also the just and the unjust. For it is peculiar to man as compared to the other animals that he alone has perception of good and bad and just and unjust and other things [of this sort]; and partnership in these things is what makes a household and a city. (*Politics*, 1253a8–19)

If human beings were to live outside of the city, they would be unable to develop and to exercise the faculties, which are unique to them. They could not be considered human. "He who is without a city through nature rather than chance is either a [beast] or a [god]" (*Politics*, 1253a2–4). The implication is, of course, that the independent beings that populate the state of nature would not be considered human by Aristotle.

In the *Ethics*, Aristotle is concerned with the self-sufficiency of human beings. He tells his readers, "we take a self-sufficient thing to mean a thing which merely standing by itself alone renders life desirable and lacking in nothing, and such a thing we deem happiness to be" (*Ethics*, I, vii, 7). Happiness, which has been identified with the Supreme Good, "that at which all things aim" is identified with self-sufficiency. At a first, superficial glance, it may appear as if Aristotle has much in with common modern, state of nature theorists, like Rousseau and Locke, who seek to preserve or to restore human beings' natural independence from other human beings. We should be cautious, however, and appreciate the important difference between this ancient thinker and his modern successors. For the state of nature theorists, human beings' natural independence means the radical autonomy of all individuals in the state of nature. For Rousseau and for Locke, "to be lacking in nothing" means having our physical needs met without the need to cooperate with others. This is especially true of Rousseau. He imagines the state of nature to be so lush and generous that human beings barely have to stir in order to satisfy their very minimal desires. Human beings do not recognize each other, let alone need each other. Aristotle, on the other hand, appreciates that human beings not only need each other, but desire each other's company. His understanding of self-sufficiency takes this into account. "The term self-sufficient, however, we employ with reference not to oneself alone, living a life of isolation, but also to one's parents and children and wife, and one's friends and fellow citizens in general, since man is by nature a social being" (*NE*, I, vii, 6). Human beings may be considered self-sufficient when they posses all the things they would need, rather than living without those things or simply not desiring them at all.

Much of Mary Wollstonecraft's political philosophy resonates with these fundamental Aristotelian principles. The end toward which human beings aim is the use of reason in order to attain virtue and truth. The constant striving toward this aim marks the human with the divine. "Reason is, consequentially, the simple power of improvement; or more properly speaking, of discerning truth . . . More or less may be conspicuous in one being than another; but the nature of reason must be the same in all, if it be an emanation of the divinity" (*VRW*, 53).[4] In her discussion of the natural and unnatural distinctions, Virginia Sapiro notes that Mary Wollstonecraft begins *A Vindication of the Rights of Woman* by establishing order to the universe. "This book about equality begins by defining natural hierarchy within the universe (*VW* 81). Animals and angels serve as the endpoints on a moral continuum by which Wollstonecraft also evaluated people" (Sapiro, 77–78). Wollstonecraft distinguishes angel, human being, and brute by their capacity for reason. "Human rational capacity and passionate nature gives us 'pre-eminence' over animals because they allow us to reach toward virtue. Angels and humans are closer together on this continuum than humans and animals 'because the two former seem capable of improvement' (*Stories*, 372)" (Sapiro, 77–78). I would add to Sapiro's discussion of angels, human beings and brutes by suggesting that Wollstonecraft's understanding of man's place in the natural order is compatible with Aristotle's conception of the natural order. Aristotle also distinguishes man from god and beast on the basis of human capacity to strive for and attain a certain degree of virtue.

Wollstonecraft begins the dedicatory letter of her most famous treatise on the rights of women with a plea for the independence of women. "Independence I have long considered as the grand blessing of life, the basis of every virtue—and independence I will ever secure by contracting my wants, though I were to live on a barren heath" (*VRW*, 4). Wollstonecraft's

understanding of independence has more in common with Aristotle's conception of self-sufficiency than it does with modern thinkers' understanding
of human beings' natural autonomy. As we have seen in our consideration
of Rousseau's and Locke's political philosophy, there is a tension between a
woman's capacity to bear children and her autonomy in the state of nature.
The tension leads Rousseau and Locke to ignore one part of the woman,
either that part which belongs to the human or that part which belongs to
the female sex. The result in both cases is a "wild-chimera" or a "half-being"
(*VRW*, 39). In contrast to Rousseau and Locke, but in comparison to Aristotle, Wollstonecraft's definition of independence allows for woman's attachment to other human beings. "The being who discharges the duties of its
station is independent; and, speaking of women at large, their first duty is
to themselves as rational creatures, and the next in point of importance, as
citizens, is that, which includes so many, of a mother" (*VRW*, 145). Furthermore, scholars have noticed Wollstonecraft's understanding of independence
requires her participation in political life.

> Wollstonecraft's ideal society is therefore not at all the anarchical and
> immoral space that her eighteenth-century and early-nineteenth-cen-
> tury detractors pretended it was: "A truly benevolent legislator always
> endeavors to make it in the interest of each individual to be virtuous;
> and thus private virtue becoming the cement of public happiness, an
> orderly whole is consolidated by the tendency of all parts towards a
> common centre" . . . the cement of societies, domestic or political,
> is not a hierarchal relation of dependence . . . but the independent
> performance of duties and of virtuous actions by citizens who share a
> common social and political goal (Bannet, 156).

Wollstonecraft, in a similar vein to Aristotle, reconciles the individual, in
particular the woman, with spouse, children, and fellow citizens. Without
the other human beings, a woman's life cannot be said to be "desirable and
lacking in nothing, and such a thing we deem happiness to be" (*Ethics*, I, vii,
7).

Because Wollstonecraft's understanding of independence has more
in common with Aristotle's definition of self-sufficiency than it does with
either Rousseau's or Locke's understanding of man's natural independence
or autonomy, it follows that her understanding of the political community
has more in common with Aristotle than with her more immediate, modern
predecessors. Like Aristotle, Mary Wollstonecraft believes that man is best
able to perform his function or fulfill his nature by living in a political

community. Wollstonecraft explicitly criticizes Rousseau's longing for a pristine state of nature.

> Impressed by his view of the misery and disorder which pervaded society, and fatigued with jostling against artificial fools, Rousseau became enamored of solitude, and, being at the same time an optimist, he labours with uncommon eloquence to prove that man was naturally a solitary animal. Misled by his respect for the goodness of God, who certainly . . . gave life only to communicate happiness, he considers evil as positive, and the work of man; not aware that he was exalting one attribute at the expense of another, equally necessary to divine perfection. (*VRW*, 13–14)

Wollstonecraft admonishes Rousseau for his belief that society is the mutation of God's intention. Instead, Wollstonecraft asserts, society is meant to be the fulfillment of the divine plan or, in Aristotle's vocabulary, the end.

> Reared on a false hypothesis his arguments in favor of a state of nature are plausible but unsound; for to assert that a state of nature is preferable to civilization, in all its possible perfections, in other words, to arraign supreme wisdom; and the paradoxical exclamation, that God has made all things right, and that error has been introduced by the creature, whom he formed, knowing what he formed, is as unphilosophical as impious. When that wise Being who created us and placed us here, saw the fair idea, he willed, by allowing it to be so, that the passions should unfold our reason, because he could see that a present evil would produce future good. (*VRW*, 14)

To limit man to the state of nature, even in the pristine form imagined by Rousseau, is to deny man the use of his rational faculties. True to Aristotle's principle that nature does nothing in vain, Wollstonecraft rejects this possibility. "Had mankind remained for ever in the brutal state of nature, which even his magic pen cannot paint as a state in which a single virtue took root, it would have been clear, though not to the sensitive unreflecting wanderer, that man was born to run the circle of life and death, and adorn God's garden for some purpose which could not easily be reconciled with his attributes" (*VRW*, 14).

Wollstonecraft is not simply entering the quarrel between early and late modern thinkers on the character of the state of nature. Her disagreement with Rousseau should not be understood as an alliance with Hobbes or Locke, who argue that civil society is preferable to the state of nature as a means to preserve oneself and calm one's fears. Rather, Wollstonecraft finds civil society preferable to the state of nature because it enables human beings to fulfill their function or strive toward their *telos*.

> It is the pestiferous purple which renders the progress of civilization a curse, and warps the understanding, till men of sensibility doubt whether the expansion of intellect produces a greater portion of happiness or misery. But the nature of the poison points out the antidote; and had Rousseau mounted one step higher in his investigation, or could his eye have pierced through the foggy atmosphere, which he almost disdained to breathe, his active mind would have darted forward to contemplate the perfection of man in the establishment of true civilization, instead of taking his ferocious flight back to the night of sensual ignorance. (*VRW*, 18–19)

Wollstonecraft and Rousseau can agree that human virtue is compromised by eighteenth-century, European society. According to Wollstonecraft, it is the corruption of civilization that discourages man from pursuing virtue, not political community itself.

Upon closer examination, we notice the compatibility between Wollstonecraft's political philosophy and Aristotle's political philosophy. In the previous chapter we noticed that both thinkers understand the end of human beings to unfold their rational faculties and to practice virtue. For Aristotle, the *telos* of human beings is not compromised by generation. Aristotle combines the human and the female sex in a way that forms a whole, unfractured, chimera. Unlike the creatures Wollstonecraft has found by following Rousseau and Locke through the land of chimeras, Aristotle's chimera is not a monstrous "half-being," but resembles Wollstonecraft's utopian dream. The compatibility of these thinkers grows stronger when we consider each ones' understanding of human beings' self-sufficiency or independence and each ones' understanding of the political community. Wollstonecraft insists on the need for political community for the same reason Aristotle does: it allows man to exercise his unique rational capacity and to distinguish himself from the animals. Given her understanding of the political community, Wollstonecraft is disappointed by the failure of eighteenth-century political life to foster women's reason and independence. With Aristotle as our guide through the land of chimeras, we will see friendship, in particular the friendship between husband and wife, puts us on the path to fulfilling Wollstonecraft's utopian dream.

II. FRIENDSHIP

Wollstonecraft sees great promise for political life. Under the right circumstances, woman may be an independent, unfractured human being, who exercises "the soul's faculties in conformity with excellence or virtue" (*Ethics*, I, vii, 15), and still has affection for her husband. In response to the denigrating aristocracies of her time, Wollstonecraft's political treatises are generally viewed as a demand for liberal political reform. However, as we have seen, Wollstonecraft's conceptions of the nature of human beings and the nature of the political community have more in common with Aristotle's understanding of human beings and the polis than they do with human beings' natural independence in the state of nature and the civil society, which emerges from it, as articulated by Rousseau and by Locke. Although Wollstonecraft is dissatisfied with the political regime's ability to promote the virtue of its citizens, in particular, the virtue of women, she spends little time offering suggestions for altering the formal structure of governmental institutions. The most sustained suggestion for political reform is her discussion of national education, which will be treated at length in the next chapter. Otherwise, such efforts seem to Wollstonecraft to be a waste of time. "I may excite laughter, by dropping an hint, which I mean to pursue, some future time, for I really think that women ought to have representatives, instead of being arbitrarily governed without having any direct share allowed them in the deliberations of government" (*VRW*, 147). Not only is Wollstonecraft likely to excite laughter from those who consider women incapable of political deliberation, but she is also likely to arouse a sense of injustice in those that do. Wollstonecraft goes on to quiet both of these responses to her comments. "But, as the whole system of representation is now, in this country, only a convenient handle for despotism, they [women] need not complain, for they are as well represented as a numerous class of hard working mechanics, who pay for the support of royalty when they can scarcely stop their children's mouths with bread?" (*VRW*, 147). Still, Wollstonecraft does not condone Rousseau's retreat to the state of nature. Political reform, which would eventually allow all citizens to deliberate or to practice virtue, begins by eliminating unnatural distinctions among human beings. In the particular case of women, Wollstonecraft places her hopes for improving women's political condition in improving their marriages.[5] "Would men but generously snap our chains, and be content with rational fellowship instead of slavish obedience, they would find us more observant daughters more affectionate sisters, more faithful wives and more reasonable mothers—in a word, better citizens" (*VRW*, 150).

As other scholars have suggested, Aristotle's notion of friendship may be a model for "Wollstonecraft's ideal conception of the relationship between the two sexes" (Tomaselli, xxvi).[6] I would agree that Aristotle provides a model for Wollstonecraft. However, in contrast to Ruth Abbey, who argues Aristotle offers Wollstonecraft "a way to suggest marriage might be reconfigured to realize central liberal values" (Abbey, 79), I would argue Aristotle provides a prescription for happiness as it is understood by classical philosophers, "the active exercise of the soul's faculties in conformity with excellence or virtue" (*NE*, I, vii, 15), rather than "liberal values." The importance Aristotle places on virtue and the equality between friends corrects the vicious relations between man and woman, which Wollstonecraft finds on the pages of Rousseau's books. We had some expectation that Locke's attention to reason and virtue might also be an example to Wollstonecraft. However, Wollstonecraft's conception of human reason is quite different from Locke's. Furthermore, Locke gives us no indication that there is affection between husband and wife. Aristotle's notion of friendship is founded on affection. Aristotle does what neither Rousseau nor Locke was able to do: combine virtue and affection. Or, in other words, Aristotle combines that part of woman, which is common to all human beings, reason and virtue, and that part of woman, which is particular to the female sex, an affection and attachment to others. Aristotle's understanding of friendship, more generally, and the friendship between husband and wife, in particular, is a path through the land of chimeras by which Wollstonecraft may fulfill her utopian dream.

Aristotle's *Nichomachean Ethics* is a practical consideration of human happiness, which is the object of political science. Before beginning his discussion of human happiness, Aristotle promises that it will include a discussion of both the moral and intellectual virtues. By the end of Book VI, Aristotle has, more or less, fulfilled this promise. Yet, there are four books remaining to the *Ethics*. At the start of Book VII, Aristotle self-consciously makes a new beginning. "Let us next begin a fresh part of the subject by laying down that the states of moral character to be avoided are three kinds —Vice, Unrestraint, and Bestiality" (*NE*, VII,i,1). Aristide Tessitore argues, "This new classification is neither identical to, nor different in kind from that provided by virtue and vice (7.1.1145a36–45b2). It is made necessary by the loftiness of the account of ethical excellence."[7] Aristotle's account after Book VI recognizes the need to supplement his discussion of the virtues, both moral and intellectual, by turning to other characteristics of the soul.

> Unlike the beginning, Book VII neither stresses the necessarily imprecise character of ethical inquiry, nor speaks of the need to ascertain the first principles of ethics from the experience provided by a decent upbringing. As will soon become clear, Aristotle's new beginning takes

its bearings from a philosophic problem, specifically, a conflict between the widespread view that human beings sometimes act in ways they know to be wrong and a Socratic teaching that denies this possibility. (Tessitore, 53)

Sometimes human beings act in ways they know to be wrong because these actions give them pleasure (Tessitore, 58). In other words, Book VII of Aristotle's *Nichomachean Ethics* admits into the consideration of human happiness the part of man, which is similar to animals. By the end of Book X, however, Aristotle also admits into his discussion of human happiness that part of man that he shares with the gods. He speaks of the contemplative life, which makes man comparable to the gods, in the following manner.

> And it seems likely that the man who pursues intellectual activity, and who cultivates his intellect and keeps that in the best condition, is also the man most beloved of the gods. For if, as is generally believed, the gods exercise some superintendence over human affairs, then it will be at least reasonable to suppose that they take pleasure in the part of man which is best and most akin to themselves, namely the intellect, and that they recompense with their favors those men who esteem and honor this most, because these care for the things dear to themselves, and act rightly and nobly. Now it is clear that all these attributes belong most of all to the wise man. He therefore is most beloved by the gods; and if so, he is naturally most happy. (*Ethics*, X, viii, 13)[8]

Books VII-X of the *Ethics*, then, move between extremes, between bestiality and divinity, presenting, as it were, the outer limits of man's nature. We have learned in Books I-IV of the *Ethics*, for example, that moral virtue lies in the mean rather than in the extremes, and even more generally that excess is to be avoided. "First of all then we have to observe, that moral qualities are so constituted as to be destroyed by excess and by deficiency—as we see is the case with bodily strength and health (for one is forced to explain what is invisible by means of visible illustrations)" (*Ethics*, II,ii,6).[9] Similarly, in the *Politics*, as we have seen earlier in this chapter, Aristotle explicitly says what is implied throughout the *Nichomachean Ethics*, that human beings are political by nature, occupying a place between beast and god; any who can live outside a city, he says, would be either a beast or god (*Politics*, 1253a2–4). In his *Nichomachean Ethics*, Aristotle places his discussion of friendship (Books VIII and IX) between "bestiality and unrestraint" of Book VII and the divine contemplation of Book X. Not surprisingly, it is through friendship that human beings are able to pursue both pleasure and contemplation. And it is friendship, as we shall see, that both elevates human beings above the beasts, and anchors them in a human world as they engage in contemplation.

Aristotle begins his discussion of friendship by telling his readers, "For friendship is a virtue, or involves virtue; and also it is one of the most indispensable requirements of life" (*NE*, VIII, i, 1). Indeed, a quick comparison of virtue and friendship helps us to appreciate the important place friendship holds in Aristotle's political philosophy. Virtue has been the topic of the *Nichomachean Ethics* since Book I, when Aristotle defines happiness as "the Good of man . . . the active exercise of his soul's faculties in conformity with excellence or virtue, or if there be several human excellences or virtues, in conformity with the best and most perfect among them" (*NE*, I, vii, 15). Aristotle tells us, "[I]t appears that a virtuous friend is essentially desirable for a virtuous man. For as has been said above, that which is essentially good is good and pleasing in itself to the virtuous man." (*NE*, IX,ix,7). Indeed, he ends his discussion of friendship by concluding that friendship is necessary for human happiness (*NE*, IX, ix, 10).

It is for this reason that Aristotle connects friendship with politics. Earlier in Book I Aristotle argued, "to secure the good of one person only is better than nothing; but to secure the good of a nation or a state is a nobler and more divine achievement" (*NE*, I, ii, 8). Thus, "lawgivers make the citizens good by training them in the habits of right action—this is the aim of all legislation, and if it fails to do this it is a failure" (*NE*, II, i, 5). Now in the discussion of friendship Aristotle elaborates the purpose of the lawgiver with reference to friendship: since "friendship appears to be the bond of the state; and lawgivers seem to set more store by it than they do by justice, for to promote concord, which seems akin to friendship, is their chief aim . . . And if men are friends, there is no need for justice between them; whereas merely to be just is not enough—a feeling of friendship also is necessary" (*NE*, VIII, I, 4). Both virtue and friendship are acquired by activity, though both depend on the disposition of the person practicing virtue and friendship (*NE*, VIII, iv, 1).

In his discussion of virtue, Aristotle observes that "pleasures and pains are the things with which moral virtue is concerned" (*NE*, II, iii, 1). "For pleasure causes us to do base actions and pain causes us to abstain from doing noble actions" (*NE*, II, ii, 1–2). However, Aristotle's attention is given more fully to pleasures than to pains with respect to not only virtue, but to friendship as well. For Aristotle, virtue is not simply denying one's pleasure, but rather pursuing pleasure (or avoiding pain) in the right manner and at the right time (*NE*, II, iii, 5). In fact, Aristotle counts among the vicious those who shun every pleasure (*NE*, II, ii, 7). Aristotle observes that human beings are motivated to virtuous action by the noble, the expedient, and the pleasant (*NE*, II, iii, 7). However, pleasure "is a concomitant of all the objects of choice, since both the noble and the expedient appear to us to be pleasant" (*NE*, II, iii, 7). Aristotle started his treatment of virtue with a more explicit link between virtue and pleasure. "And further, the life of active virtue is essentially pleasant. For the feeling of pleasure is an experience of the soul" (*NE*, I, viii, 10).

We may notice a parallel in Aristotle's explanation of friendship. The grounds on which we form our friendships are utility, pleasure, and virtue (*NE*, VIII, iii, 1–9). As we might suspect, Aristotle has the highest regard for those friendships which are based on virtue. Just as pleasure was a concomitant of all objects of choice in the case of virtue, so too is pleasure inseparable from friendship based on virtue. "[T]hough they may put up with what is unpleasant for a short time, no one would stand it continually: you could not endure even the Absolute Good itself for ever, if it bored you" (*NE*, VIII, vi, 4).

In an ancient philosophical treatise on virtue, we would expect a discussion of the great and noble virtues, such as courage and justice. Indeed, Aristotle does devote his attention to such virtues, but his consideration of the moral virtues is not complete until he has offered his reflection on the tendencies, which make human beings "behave in the right manner in society" (*NE*, IV, iv, 6), the "unnamed excellences" (*NE*, IV, vii, 1). Some of the "unnamed excellences" are those very qualities, which make friends pleasant (*NE*, VIII, iii, 1–2). The mean between being obsequious and quarrelsome has no name, Aristotle tells us, "though it closely resembles friendship; for he who exemplifies this middle disposition is the sort of man we mean by the expression 'a good friend,' only that [friendship] includes and element of affection" (*NE*, IV, vi, 4). Affection, Aristotle explains, is marked by intensity and desire, as well as an intimate acquaintance (*NE*, IX, v, 1–2). Among the other "unnamed excellences" is the tendency to avoid exaggeration and understatement of one's own character (*NE*, IV, vii, 2–6). And, finally, Aristotle lists playful conversation or wittiness as a virtue (*NE*, IV, viii, 1).

Aristotle considers the definition of friendship and he concludes, "To be friends therefore, men must (1) feel goodwill for each other, that is, wish each other's good, and (2) be aware of each other's goodwill, and (3) the cause of their goodwill must be one of the loveable qualities mentioned above" (usefulness, pleasure, and virtue) (*NE*, VIII, ii,4). Friendships based on usefulness and pleasure are fleeting because "men love their friend for their own good or their own pleasure, and not as being the person loved, but as useful or agreeable . . . Hence when the motive of the friendship has passed away, the friendship itself is dissolved, having existed merely as a means to that end" (*NE*, VIII, iii, 3). Still, Aristotle recognizes the relative importance of friendships based on usefulness and pleasure. They help the city to function in a respectful and peaceful manner. Like the city itself, friendships come into being for the sake of living and continue to exist for the sake of living well.

Living well is accomplished by the perfect form of friendship: friendship based on virtue or "virtue friendships."[10] It is this type of friendship, which scholars, have suggested is the model for Wollstonecraft's "ideal conception of the relationship between the sexes" (Tomaselli, xxvi).[11] Of course, the perfect form of friendship is defined by the virtue of the friends.

> The perfect form of friendship is that between the good, and those who resemble each other in virtue. For those friends wish each alike the other's good in respect of their goodness, and they are good in themselves; but it is those who wish the good of their friends for their friends' sake who are friends in the fullest sense, since they love each other for themselves and not accidentally. Hence friendship of these lasts as long as they continue to be good; and virtue is a permanent quality. (*NE*, VIII, iii, 6)

Just as virtue is pleasant, so too is this perfect form of friendship. The friendship is rendered pleasant by the particular regard each friend has for the other, and not virtue simply. "Friendship between good men then is the truest friendship, as has been said several times before. For, it is agreed that what is good and pleasant absolutely is loveable and desirable strictly, while what is good and pleasant for a particular person is loveable and desirable relatively to that person; but the friendship of good men for each other rests on both these grounds" (*NE*, VIII, v, 4). Due to the virtue of the friends and the "feeling of friendship" or pleasure that each takes in the other, virtue friendship is the most enduring form of friendship. "Such friendship is naturally permanent, since it combines in itself all the attributes that friends ought to possess" (*NE*, I, iii, 7).

Friendship, as Aristotle articulates it, creates a union of the good for oneself and the good for one's friend. Neither must be sacrificed for the other. Quite the contrary, one's own good and one's friend's good can barely be distinguished. In Book IX of the *Ethics*, Aristotle ticks off five components of the definition for friend. They are consistent with Aristotle's comments on the nature of friendship thus far and his readers do not pause long over these elements of friendship. He then remarks, "But each of them is also found in a good man's feelings towards himself (and in those of all other men as well, in so far as they believe themselves to be good; but, as has been said, virtue and the virtuous man seem to be the standard in everything)" (*NE*, IX, iv, 2). He goes on to demonstrate that the feelings a man has toward himself are the same that he has toward his friend. He lists each point a second time with regard to the self. However, this time Aristotle changes the order. To put it quite simply, the two friends are different, but the same. And, of course, some degree of difference must be acknowledged when considering two separate individuals. Aristotle refers to a friend as "another self" (*NE*, IX, iv, 5). Because the friend is another "self," the good man can be a lover of self, and promote his friend's good with no detriment to his own good. "Therefore the good man ought to be a lover of self, since he will then both benefit himself by acting nobly and aid his fellows" (*NE*, IX, viii,7). His good will be an aid to his fellow because "the good man in becoming dear to another becomes that other's good. Each party therefore both loves his own good and also makes an equivalent return by wishing the other's good" (*NE*, VIII, v, 5). As Aristotle approaches the conclusion to his treatment of friendship, he summarizes the activity of friendship.

> But, as we saw, it is the consciousness of oneself as good that makes existence desirable, and such consciousness is pleasant in itself. Therefore, a man ought to share his friend's consciousness of his existence, and this is attained by their living together and by conversing and my communicating their thoughts to each other; for this is the meaning of living together as applied to human beings, it is not merely feeding in the same place, as it does when applied to cattle. (*NE*, IX, ix, 10).

This highest form of friendship that Aristotle describes here combines pleasure, action, and contemplation. "But if happiness consists in life and activity of a good man, and the activity of a good man, as was said at the beginning, is good and so pleasant in itself, and if the sense that a thing is our own is pleasant, yet we are better able to contemplate our neighbors than ourselves, and their action than our own, and thus good men find pleasure in the actions of other good men who are their friends" (*NE*, IX, ix, 5). Therefore, it follows that "the supremely happy man will require good friends, insomuch as he desires to contemplate actions" (*NE*, IX, ix, 5). The contemplative life, in this formulation, is nothing but the life of friendship. It belongs not to the gods, but to friends, and its pleasures are not those of beasts, but of human beings, even if they are those pleasures—those of contemplation—that might be called divine.

Does Aristotle exclude husbands and wives from this highest sort of friendship that he describes? Tomaselli and Abbey have noticed the compatibility between Aristotle's notion of friendship and Wollstonecraft's hopes for marriage. However, they argue that Aristotle excludes husbands and wives from the perfect form of friendship. In the remainder of this chapter I will argue that Aristotle does consider it possible for husbands and wives to enjoy virtue friendship. Aristotle provides an example of an unfractured woman, who is comprised of the both the human and the female and who is, as a result, both virtuous and affectionate.

III. A NOBLER AMBITION

Aristotle and Wollstonecraft recognize the basis for friendship varies with relationships and both can agree that the friendship based on virtue is most enduring and conducive to human happiness. Though Wollstonecraft appreciates the promise of friendship between husband and wife, the character of woman and her relationship to man in eighteenth-century Britain are quite discouraging. Throughout *A Vindication of the Rights of Woman*, Wollstonecraft criticizes women for their vanity and the scrupulous attention to their bodies that vanity inspires. Gratifying their vanity necessarily distracts women from more virtuous pursuits. "The conduct and manners of women, in fact, evidently prove that their minds are not in a healthy state; for like the flowers which are planted in too rich soil, strength and usefulness are sacrificed to beauty; and the flaunting leaves, after having pleased a fastidious eye, disregarded on the stalk, long before the season when they ought to have arrived at maturity" (*VRW*, 7). As is to be expected, the intellectual deprivation of women affects the relationships they cultivate with others, in particular, their lovers. "The understanding of the sex has been so bubbled by the specious homage, that the civilized women of the present century, with few exceptions, are only anxious to inspire love, when they ought to cherish a nobler ambition, and by their abilities and virtue exact respect" (*VRW*, 7). Wollstonecraft identifies this "nobler ambition" as friendship. "Women, intoxicated by the adoration which men, under the influence of their senses, pay them, do not seek to obtain a durable interest in their hearts, or to become the friends of the fellow creatures who find amusement in their society" (*VRW*, 8). Friendship, which Wollstonecraft sees as "the most holy band of society" (*VRW*, 30), would allow husband and wife to perform their duties and would enable each one to become still more virtuous. "In order to fulfill the duties of life, and to be able to pursue with vigour the various employments which form the moral character, a master and mistress of a family ought not to continue to love each other with passion" (*VRW*, 30). For, "when we are gathering the flowers of the day and reveling in the pleasure, the solid fruit of toil and wisdom should not be caught at the same time" (*VRW*, 31). Although Wollstonecraft understands how it is possible for the friendship between husband and wife to improve the character of woman and to be the occasion for woman to exercise her nature as a "political animal," the moral differences between men and women present an obstacle in her pursuit of her utopian dream. Aristotle offers a path through the land of chimeras from the monstrous "half-beings" to Wollstonecraft's utopian dream of affectionate and virtuous friendships between husband and wife.

Appreciating the great potential for difference among people, Aristotle considers the extent to which friendship is possible between unequal people. Aristotle's own ambivalence on this question is evident in the amount of attention it receives throughout his treatment of friendship. Again and again, he returns to the various ways in which friends may be said to be unequal and the possibility for friendship between them. Virtue friendship, as we have seen, does presume a certain equality of the friends. Abbey suggests that the equality, which Aristotle identifies between the friends, is one reason for Wollstonecraft to incorporate "the major features of the classical notion of higher friendship" into her vision for marriage (Abbey, 79). Abbey argues that the classical notion of higher (or virtue) friendship promotes "liberal values," which are central to Wollstonecraft's political reform. Abbey is correct to identify the equality between man and woman as an important aspiration of Wollstonecraft's work. However, I disagree that Wollstonecraft seeks to establish the equality of men and women on liberal grounds. As we have seen, Wollstonecraft does not share liberal thinkers' understanding of human beings as autonomous creatures, nor does she understand the purpose of the political community to be the protection of human beings' autonomy. The compatibility of Wollstonecraft to Aristotle is much deeper than Abbey argues. For Wollstonecraft, like Aristotle, the extent to which human beings, including man and woman, may be described as equal is determined by the extent to which each human being exercises "his soul's faculties in conformity with excellence or virtue." Given the greater compatibility between Wollstonecraft and Aristotle than initially thought by Abbey, we may be more confident in taking Aristotle as a guide. Aristotle does provide a way of establishing virtue friendship between two seemingly unequal people, husband and wife, which Wollstonecraft has been unable to find while following either Rousseau or Locke through the land of chimeras.

In the course of his consideration of friendship between unequals, Aristotle pauses and states generally the ways in which friends may be said to be unequal. He reminds his readers that there are three kinds of friendships (those based on utility, pleasure, and virtue) and mentions that friendship between unequals may exist in each type. "[I]n each kind there are both friends who are on equal footing and friends on a footing of disparity; for two equally good men may be friends, or one better man and one worse; and similarly with pleasant friends and with those who are friends for the sake of utility, who may be equal or may differ in the amount of benefits which they confer" (*NE*, VIII, xiii, 1). These descriptions of friendships between unequals are of particular importance to us as we move from the fractured woman and her corrupted relation to man described on the pages of the *Vindication* to the virtuous wife, who enjoys friendships with her husband, presented in the same work. We will begin with the last of these friendships, the "pleasant friends," who "may differ in the amount of benefits which they confer." This example of friendship explains the friendship between lovers, according to both Aristotle and Wollstonecraft. We will then consider the second circumstance, which Aristotle mentions, a friendship in which one friend is better and one is worse. In considering the corrupted women of her time, Wollstonecraft would likely admit that this describes many of the relationships between man and woman. Aristotle, however, will offer a way to achieve friendship between two seemingly unequal friends and, therefore, a way to establish friendship between Wollstonecraft's pernicious female contemporaries and their sometimes, relatively more virtuous, male counterparts. Finally, I will argue that, despite the differences between them, husband and wife are an example of Aristotle's virtue friendship. Wollstonecraft echoes Aristotle's example of virtue friendship in articulating her own hopes for marriage.

Both Aristotle and Wollstonecraft identify romantic relationships with pleasure, in particular the beloved's capacity to inspire pleasure in the lover. As the first example of a friendship based on pleasure, Aristotle offers the friendship of lovers, which he will later call "sentimental friendships" (*NE*, IX, i, 2). "With the young . . . the motive of friendship appears to be pleasure, since the young guide their lives by emotion, and for the most part pursue what is pleasant to themselves, and the object of the moment . . . Also the young are prone to fall in love, as love is chiefly guided by emotion, and grounded on pleasure" (*NE*, VIII, iii, 5). These friendships are fleeting and subject to change quickly. Aristotle notices that the lover and the beloved do not always derive the same benefit from each other. "These do not find their pleasure in the same things: the lover's pleasure is in gazing at his beloved, the loved one's pleasure is in receiving the attentions of the lover; and when the loved one's beauty fades, the friendship sometimes fades too, as the lover no longer finds pleasure in the sight of his beloved, and the loved one no longer receives the attentions of the lover (*NE*, VIII, iv, 1). With seemingly little regret, Aristotle suggests that when the lover and the beloved receive unequal benefit from each other or no longer receive any benefit at all, the friendship comes to an end.

Wollstonecraft agrees with Aristotle: "Youth is the season for love in both sexes" (*VRW*, 27). And, like Aristotle, Wollstonecraft knows that attachments based on pleasure are not likely to last. "[B]ut in those days of thoughtless enjoyment provision should be made for the more important years of life, when reflection takes the place of sensation" (*VRW*, 27). The problem is, Wollstonecraft argues, the women of her day make no provision nor do the educational writings, popular in her time, encourage females to do so. Rather, Wollstonecraft regrets, women are encouraged to concern themselves simply with pleasing men. "But Rousseau, and most of the male writers who have followed his steps, have warmly inculcated that the whole tendency of female education ought to be directed to one point:—to render them pleasing" (*VRW*, 27). Wollstonecraft observes that in the absence of rational faculties, the pleasing young woman is given to vice.

> The woman who has only been taught to please will soon find that her charms are oblique sunbeams, and that they cannot have much effect on her husband's heart when they are seen every day, when summer has passed and gone . . . When the husband ceases to be a lover—and the time will inevitably come, her desire of pleasing will then grow languid, or become a spring of bitterness; and love, perhaps, the most evanescent of all passions, gives place to jealousy or vanity. (*VRW*, 27)

Lacking virtue, the creature is dependent on her husband. The qualities of the beloved are feigned to secure the husband's protection, but the woman that Wollstonecraft describes under such circumstances, resembles a monster.

> Gentleness, considered in this point of view, bears on its front all the characteristics of grandeur, combined with the winning graces of condescension; but what a different aspect it assumes when it is submissive demeanour of dependence, the support of weakness that loves, because it wants protection; and is forbearing because it must silently endure injuries; smiling under the lash at which it dare not snarl. (*VRW*, 33)

The disguised, snarling monster may, however, be avoided by following Aristotle's path. "[O]n the other hand many [lovers] do remain friends if as a result of their intimacy they have come to love each other's characters" (*NE*, VIII, iv, 1). Wollstonecraft's correction of the pernicious character of woman adheres to Aristotle's prediction. A woman's "first wish should be to make herself respectable" (*VRW*, 28). In such a case, the friends, who came together for the sake of pleasure, may "come to love each other's characters." The friendship will endure under more virtuous conditions. "This passion, naturally increased by suspense and difficulties, draws the mind out of its accustomed state, and exalts the affections; but the security of marriage, allowing the fever of love to subside, a healthy temperature is thought insipid, only by those who have not sufficient intellect to substitute the calm tenderness of friendship, the confidence of respect, instead of blind admiration, and the sensual emotions of fondness" (*VRW*, 30).

Wollstonecraft is in accord with Aristotle that a friendship based on virtue and the mutual regard of husband and wife should succeed the passion of the lovers. However, Wollstonecraft seems unsure that such a friendship will necessarily follow. Wollstonecraft's uncertainty is due to the seeming inferiority of the women of her day. From the outset of *A Vindication of the Rights of Woman*, Wollstonecraft seems unable to make an unqualified claim that man and woman are equal due to woman's relative physical weakness (*VRW*, 8). The physical superiority of men, Wollstonecraft acknowledges, may contribute to their moral superiority, insofar as virtue is attained by denying our passions. "I have already granted that from the constitution of their bodies, men seem to be designed by Providence to attain a greater degree of virtue" (*VRW*, 26). Having granted the possibility that men and women will attain different degrees of virtue, Wollstonecraft insists that the nature of virtue must be the same in men and women. "If women are by nature inferior to men, their virtues must be the same in quality, if not in degree, or virtue is a relative idea; consequently, their conduct should be founded on the same principles, and have the same aim" (*VRW*, 26).

Although Wollstonecraft allows that her contemporaries may not be virtuous, she does not consider their wretched condition to be natural or beyond repair. Rather, she insists, "men have increased the inferiority till women are *almost* sunk below the standard of rational creatures. Let their faculties have room to unfold, and their virtues to gain strength, and then determine where the whole sex must stand in the intellectual scale" (*VRW*, 35, my emphasis). As for Wollstonecraft, she expects the best. "I will venture to predict that woman will either be the friend or slave of man" (*VRW*, 35).

Again, by considering Aristotle's treatment of friendship, one may find a way out of this predicament. One of the types of friendships Aristotle has mentioned is that form of friendship in which one person is better and one person is worse than the other (*NE*, VIII, xiii, 1). Aristotle suggests a way by which those who seem to be unequal may make themselves commensurate with each other. "Those who are equals must make matters equal by loving each other, etc., equally; those who are unequal by making a return proportionate to the superiority of whatever kind on the one side" (*NE*, VIII, xiii, 1).

In order to appreciate the potential for friendship among unequal persons, it is best to return to the start of Book VIII of the *Ethics*. Aristotle begins by saying that in addition to justice, a feeling of friendship is also needed for human happiness (*NE*, VIII, i, 4). Aristotle goes on to explain that this feeling of friendship is love for a person because that person is useful, pleasant, or virtuous. Affection, we may recall, is similar to a feeling of good will, but it is of greater intensity and desire and it is the result intimate acquaintance (*NE*, IX, v, 1). Affection is the element that produces equality among unequals. "Hence it is friends that love each other as each deserves who continue friends and whose friendship is lasting. Also it is by rendering affection in proportion to desert that friends who are not equals may approach most nearly to true friendship, since this will make them equal" (*NE*, VIII,viii,4–5). It would be easy to mistake the affection between unequal friends as flattery and to assume that affection is a debt paid to the more virtuous of the two friends, but this would be to misunderstand Aristotle's treatment of affection and to underestimate the subtlety of Aristotle's point.

> Affection produces equality between friends because it produces virtue in both of the friends. In order to appreciate this point, affection should be distinguished from honor. Those on the other hand who covet being honored by good men, and by persons who know them, do so from a desire to confirm their own opinion of themselves; so these like honor because they are assured of their worth by their confidence in the judgment of those who assert it. Affection on the other hand men like for its own sake; from which we infer that it is more valuable than honor, and that friendship is desirable in itself. (*NE*, VIII, vii, 2)

And, unlike honor, the nobility of affection lies in giving it, rather than receiving it. "But in its essence friendship seems to consist more in giving than in receiving affection: witness the pleasure that mothers take in loving their children" (*NE*, VIII, vii, 3). The virtuous act of bestowing affection on a good human being may be compared to the virtuous act of a benefactor.

> Benefactors seem to love those whom they benefit more than those who have received benefits conferred them; and it is asked why this is so, as it seems to be unreasonable. The reason is this is that all things desire and love existence; but we exist in activity, since we exist by living and doing; and in a sense he loves his handiwork because he loves existence. This is in fact a fundamental principle of nature: what a thing is potentially, that its work reveals in actuality. (*NE*, IX, vii, 1–4)

By bestowing affection on a friend who is worthy of affection, the "inferior" friend loves existence, and he or she loves the virtue of his or her friend. The person, therefore, shares in virtue by loving it. He or she also shares in virtue in a second way. Virtue, as we may recall, is an activity, as well as a disposition. In bestowing affection on a virtuous and worthy recipient, the action procures him or her virtue that he or she would not have had otherwise had.

Aristotle and Wollstonecraft have both determined that the friendship of lovers is based on pleasure and could not last, unless the two come to love each other for their virtue. Doubting the virtue of the women of her time, Wollstonecraft regrets they are not prepared to form more meaningful friendships with men. Aristotle has offered a way by which two people, one better and one worse, may attain equality and preserve their friendship through affection. The path provided by Aristotle is compatible with Wollstonecraft's expectation for marriage to improve the character of woman and to allow her to fulfill her nature as a human being.

In her distinctive fashion, Wollstonecraft hopes that the superior virtue of one friend (in this case, the male) will encourage the virtue in the other (the female). Regrettable as it may be that Wollstonecraft's female contemporaries form attachments to rakes, Wollstonecraft tells us that it can hardly be surprising. "They who live to please must find their enjoyments, their happiness, in pleasure!" (*VRW*, 119). So, of course, women are quickly and easily drawn to the superficial charms of a rake. "[A] gentleman-like man seldom fails to please them, and their thirsty ears eagerly drink insinuating nothings of politeness . . . Rendered gay and giddy by the whole tenor of their lives, the very aspect of wisdom, or the severe graces of virtue, must have lugubrious appearance to them" (*VRW*, 118). However, if women were to make their choices based on reason, in addition to feeling, they would make matches which have the potential for friendship. "Were women more rationally educated, could they take a more comprehensive view of things, they would be contented to love but once in their lives; and after marriage calmly let passion subside into friendship—into that tender intimacy, which is the best refuge from care" (*VRW*, 119). The friendship between husband and wife allows the woman to become more virtuous by performing the activities of marriage. "[Y]et [friendship] is built on such pure, still affections, that idle jealousies would not be allowed to disturb of the sober duties of life, or to engross the thoughts that ought to be otherwise employed" (*VRW*, 119–120).

Aristotle and Wollstonecraft have both quieted the passions of lovers in favor of the more enduring affection of friends. As a result, marriage, as both Aristotle and Wollstonecraft see it, may be based on the respectable qualities of both the husband and the wife. Wollstonecraft may even hope that women, in choosing husbands, who are reasonable and virtuous may become more virtuous themselves. This brings us farther down the path from the monstrous "half-beings" to the chimera, which has eluded Wollstonecraft: an unfractured woman, who enjoys virtue friendship with her husband. Aristotle, I shall argue, does consider the relationship between husband and wife an example of virtue friendship. Wollstonecraft's hopes for marriage echoes Aristotle's notion of virtue friendship.

IV. THE FRIEND, NOT THE SLAVE OF MAN

Aristotle introduces his readers to the friendship between husband and wife by the way of offering various examples of friendships between unequal persons (*NE*, VIII, vii, 1). This discussion immediately follows Aristotle's treatment of virtue friendship. Aristotle refers to these unequal relationships as a "different kind of friendship" (*NE*, VIII, vii, 1). Recall, we have already noted that Aristotle tells us that in each of the three kinds of friendship (those based on utility, pleasure, and virtue) "there are both friends who are on an equal footing and friends on a footing of disparity" (*NE*, VIII, xiii, 1). Although virtue friendship does presume equality, Aristotle allows for the possibility that friends may be unequal. We should begin by noting the reasons Aristotle considers husband and wife unequal and wonder about the extent to which the inequality between them may be compatible with virtue friendship. Aristotle offers two, though not mutually exclusive, reasons for identifying the friendship between husband and wife as unequal. This relationship "involves superiority of one party over the other" (*NE*, VIII, vii, 1). Aristotle does not explain in what way one may be thought superior to the other. He goes on to offer a further reason for their inequality. These persons are considered unequal "for each of these persons has a different excellence and function" (*NE*, VIII, vi, 1). We may recall from the previous chapter that man and woman have different functions with respect to generation. Yet, their different functions do not preclude either of them from "the active exercise of the soul's faculties in conformity with rational principle" (*NE*, I, vii, 14). Just as in the case of generation, Aristotle seems to suggest that in the case of the family man and woman also have different functions. In her essay, "Aristotle's Child: Development Through *Genesis, Oikos*, and *Polis*," Daryl Tress explains the important role mothers play in the ethical upbringing of their children for Aristotle. To be sure, male and female play somewhat different roles, but these seem to be a practical division of labor. Aristotle does not recommend certain guidelines for this division, suggesting that they are not natural.[12] Perhaps Wollstonecraft best echoes Aristotle's meaning. "Women, I allow, may have different duties to fulfill; but they are human duties, and the principles that should regulate the discharge of them, I sturdily maintain, must be the same" (*VRW*, 51). Husband and wife may be said to differ in superiority in the case of the excellences which are specific to each. Neither husband nor wife may be said to be simply or uniformly superior to the other. This is demonstrated in Aristotle's further discussion of the friendship between husband and wife.

While Aristotle has explained to his readers that husband and wife have different excellences or functions, his further discussion of the friendship between husband and wife, demonstrates how these different excellences establish a certain equality between husband and wife. In treating friendships among unequals, Aristotle returns to the comparison between friendship and justice. "The objects and the personal relationships with which friendship is concerned appear, as was said at the outset, to be the same as those which are the sphere of justice. For in every partnership we find mutual rights of some sort, and also friendly feeling" (*NE*, VIII, ix, 1). Aristotle goes further in establishing the political nature of friendships. He goes on to compare various friendships (in particular, the relationships within the family members) to the three types of regimes: kingship, aristocracy, and timocracy. Kingship describes the parents' relationship to the child; aristocracy describes the relationship of husband and wife; and timocracy describes the relationship of siblings. Aristocracy combines the positive elements of both kingship and timocracy. Like the kingship, the ruling element of the aristocracy is virtue. And, like the timocracy, more than one person rules. This allows for the citizens to rule and be ruled in turn. "Aristocracy is held to be most particularly the distribution of prerogatives on the basis of virtue; for the defining principle of aristocracy is virtue, as that of oligarchy is wealth, and of [rule of] the people freedom" (*Politics*, 1294a, 8–11). Aristotle understands the friendship between husband and wife in the same manner. "The relation of husband to wife seems to be in the nature of an aristocracy: the husband rules in virtue of fitness, and matters that belong to a man's sphere; matters suited to a woman he hands over to his wife" (*NE*, VIII, x, 5). The friendship of husband and wife recognizes the particular qualities of each and rule is determined according to each person's excellence. Aristotle preserves woman's independence —independence as Wollstonecraft understands it. Independence, as we have seen, includes the rational use of her faculties *and* her attachment to her husband. The friendship between husband and wife, despite the differences between them, is marked by both virtue and affection.[13]

Writing *A Vindication of the Rights of Woman* several centuries later, ensconced in liberal political circles, Wollstonecraft echoes Aristotle's notion of virtue friendship in expressing her call for the improved condition of woman. Furthermore, friendship is the occasion for woman to take her place in the intellectual scale. "Let their faculties have room to unfold, and their virtues to gain strength, and then determine where the whole sex must stand in the intellectual scale" (*VRW*, 35). Becoming the friend of her husband, woman fulfills her nature as a "political animal," taking her place between beasts and gods. Above all, Wollstonecraft calls upon woman to practice virtue and use her rational faculties. "Besides, the woman who strengthens her body and exercises her mind will, by managing her family and practicing various virtues, become the friend, and not the humble dependent of her husband" (*VRW*, 29). Wollstonecraft, like Aristotle, allows that woman may practice different virtues. However, they are practiced by the use of her rational faculties. "Woman, I allow, has different duties to fulfill; but they are human duties, and the principles that should regulate the discharge of them . . . must be the same" (*VRW*, 51). By practicing virtue in such a manner, woman will restore that part of her which belongs to all human beings, the fraction of woman ignored by Rousseau, but not by Aristotle.

Restoring the human dignity to woman will place her between animal and god, while preserving what she has in common with each. Our passions are what we have in common with the animals. Nonetheless, we have seen the important place affection holds in Aristotle's understanding of friendship. Affection also has an important place in Wollstonecraft's conception of marriage. By practicing virtue, the female part of woman is no longer dependent on her husband and, therefore,does not resort to cunning in order to secure his affection. Rather, Wollstonecraft expects, the rational and virtuous wife will bestow genuine affection on the deserving husband. "[A]nd if she, by possessing such substantial qualities, merit his regard, she will not find it necessary to conceal her affection, nor pretend to an unnatural coldness of constitution to excite her husband's passions" (*VRW*, 29). In this respect, Aristotle has proven to be a better guide through the land of chimeras than John Locke. Although Locke offers an example of a rational mother to his readers, he gives no indication that she had any affection for her husband. Human beings, according to Aristotle and Wollstonecraft, also have something in common with the divine. Aristotle's notion of virtue friendship allows for that activity, which is most pleasing to the gods: contemplation. Again, this is an instance in which Wollstonecraft resonates more with Aristotle than with Locke, who places decidedly worldly limits on the character of human reason. Marriage, for Wollstonecraft, like Aristotle's virtue friendship, is the occasion for divine contemplation. Incredulous that a creature endowed with reason would be satisfied with woman's current condition, Wollstonecraft wonders, "Gracious Creator of the whole human race! . . . Can she believe that she was only made to submit to man, her equal, a being, who like her was sent into the world to acquire virtue? . . . And can she rest supinely dependent on man for reason, when she ought to mount with him the arduous steeps of knowledge?" (*VRW*, 67). Marriage for Wollstonecraft, as well as virtue friendship for Aristotle, allows woman to fulfill her nature as a complex human being and to take her place as a "political animal" between beasts and gods.

Aristotle's treatment of friendship is the kind of path Wollstonecraft seeks through the land of chimeras. Frustrated that the basis of relationships between male and female is the pleasing qualities of the female, Wollstonecraft laments that the women of her day do not cultivate their human, rational capacities. Aristotle may lead her from these "wild chimeras" to friendships, which are formed between "one better man and one worse" (*NE*, VIII, xiii, 1). Despite woman's corrupt character at the close of the eighteenth century, Wollstonecraft is certain the character of the soul must be the same for both male and female. And, so, woman must be capable of attaining a higher degree of virtue. She seeks a way for woman to eschew vain pleasures and become the more virtuous equal to man. Aristotle shows us how friends, seemingly unequal, may become more equal by the affection one gives to the other. This brings us a bit farther down the path toward Wollstonecraft's utopian dream, "affectionate wives and rational mothers." Aristotle's discussion of the relationship between husband and wife reveals a friendship based on virtue. Both husband and wife rule, each in their turn, according to their particular excellences. This preserves the rational faculties of woman, which belongs to the human species, as well as the affection and attachment she feels for her husband and children, which belongs to the female sex. Aristotle provides a path through the land of chimeras to the fulfillment of Wollstonecraft's utopian dream. However, the dream is not quite realized. Wollstonecraft anticipates that affectionate wives and rational mothers will make better citizens. We have yet to see Wollstonecraft's chimera as a citizen.

Chapter Seven
In a Word, a Better Citizen

A Vindication of the Rights of Woman is Mary Wollstonecraft's most well known political treatise. Yet, much of this work is concerned with the ostensibly private relationships of men and women, in particular the relationship of husband and wife. It is often and rightly seen as Wollstonecraft's refutation of Rousseau's ideal woman, Sophie. However, we should not overlook Wollstonecraft's claim that she "warmly . . . admire[s] the genius of that able writer" (*VRW*, 24). Wollstonecraft, as we have seen in the first chapter, has learned much from the Solitary Walker. Rousseau teaches us, "We are so to speak, born twice: once to exist and once to live; once for our species and once for our sex" (*Emile*, 211). In other words, human beings are comprised of two parts, that part which is human and that part which is male or female. Rousseau tells his readers that this is true of females as well as males. "Everything is equal: girls are children, boys are children; the same name suffices for beings so much alike" (*Emile*, 211). The education that Rousseau designs for Emile is meant to preserve the natural wholeness of man, the proper combination of the two parts of human beings. Even as Rousseau writes his educational treatise, he anticipates that his critics will dismiss his fanciful vision: "For a long while they have seen me in the land of chimeras" (*Emile*, 253). Sharing Rousseau's appreciation of the importance of the female sex to the woman, the family, and the political community, Wollstonecraft follows Rousseau into the land of chimeras pursuing a utopian dream. She expects to find women, who are considered "human creatures" as well as females. Yet, Wollstonecraft knows that chimera has a second meaning. A chimera is a mythological creature comprised of parts of various animals. Wollstonecraft uses both meanings of the word chimera, suggesting the precarious nature of her utopian dream. Women, who are not comprised of both the human and the female, are chimeras in a mythological sense. They are monstrous because they are comprised of only parts of woman and do not fully reflect

human nature. But, it is not Rousseau or even John Locke, two Enlightenment thinkers well known for their egalitarian political philosophies, who
treat woman as human creatures, as well as females. As we have seen in previous chapters, both Rousseau and Locke educate only part of woman, albeit
different fractions. Rousseau's and Locke's "half-beings" result from the state
of nature theorists' inability to account for the biological and the physical
differences between man and woman in a manner that preserves that which
is common to all human beings and that which is particular to the female
sex. Yet, Rousseau has offered another alternative to himself. The inquiry
into the nature of human beings, Rousseau tells his readers, is not "unworthy
of the Aristotles . . . of our century" (*Discourses*, 124). Indeed, Mary Wollstonecraft's political philosophy resonates with Aristotle's. For both thinkers
the soul is central to their understanding of the human condition. Aristotle
puts the human soul together with the female body in a way that is compatible, forming a whole, unfractured woman. Woman may fulfill her nature
as a human being by practicing virtue. Yet, her affection and attachment to
others, which are so often associated with her capacity to bear children, are
not a detriment to her capacity for reason and virtue. Indeed, as we have
already seen in the previous chapter and will see again in this chapter, reason
and affection compliment one another. This is demonstrated in Aristotle's
account of the friendship between husband and wife. It is a model, which
Wollstonecraft does not find on the pages of Rousseau's or Locke's treatises,
but resonates with her own aspirations for marriage. Aristotle points the way
through the land of chimeras to the fulfillment of Wollstonecraft's utopian
dream.

But, Wollstonecraft's fanciful vision is not yet quite realized. In order
to fulfill her utopian dream, it is necessary that this woman, who is comprised of both the human and her sex, fulfill her duties to her family and to
her political community. It is Wollstonecraft's expectation that the improved
character of woman would improve not only her private relationships, but
also her public stature. "Would men but generously snap our chains, and
be content with rational fellowship instead of slavish obedience, they would
find us more observant daughters, more affectionate sisters, more faithful
wives, more reasonable mothers—in a word, better citizens" (*VRW*, 150).
Just as it would be a mistake to simply identify Wollstonecraft's thought with
either Rousseau or Locke, it would be a mistake to conclude our discussion
of Wollstonecraft's political philosophy by noticing only those ways in which
it resonates with Aristotle's. Despite the example of friendship between husband and wife that Aristotle offers to the readers of his *Nicomachean Ethics*,
Aristotle is unable to continue to serve as Wollstonecraft's guide through the

land of chimeras. In order to fulfill her utopian dream, Wollstonecraft must chart a new path, untraveled by Aristotle, Locke, or Rousseau.

In this final chapter I will consider the ways in which Wollstonecraft's political philosophy goes beyond Aristotle's political philosophy. I will begin with a brief consideration of the reasons Aristotle is unable to continue to serve as a guide to Wollstonecraft. Although Aristotle has offered an example of a rational and virtuous woman and Aristotle does point to her importance to the city, he does not introduce her into political life. I will then turn my attention to Wollstonecraft's pursuit of her utopian dream on her own. Wollstonecraft distinguishes herself from Aristotle in two ways. In the first respect, Wollstonecraft elaborates the influence of women and the family on the political community. As we saw in the first chapter, Wollstonecraft like her favorite friend and foe, Rousseau, appreciates the significant ways in which the family may restore the political community. Wendy Gunther-Canada notices that to the extent that male political philosophers have been concerned with women, they have been considered only with respect to marriage. "In the history of political philosophy the stories of women associated with marriage have been subsumed within the masculine quest for the good society" (Gunther-Canada, 19). Mary Wollstonecraft also embeds the story of women in the quest for a good society. But, unlike the masculine quest for the good society, Wollstonecraft does not sacrifice women to it or to marriage. By giving such pride of place to the family, Wollstonecraft levels a critique of the calculating reason and (sometimes enlightened) self-interest, which distinguishes Enlightenment thought from classical philosophy. In putting forth her own plan for educating children, Wollstonecraft elaborates the importance of the affectionate wife and the rational mother to the political community, only hinted at by Aristotle. Wollstonecraft anticipates that "private virtue is the cement of public happiness" (*VRW*, 144).

The second way by which Wollstonecraft distinguishes herself from Aristotle is by introducing the whole, unfractured woman into the public sphere. The education that Wollstonecraft has in mind for girls would encourage them to take an interest in public matters and allow them to earn a living through their own efforts. Such an education will confer independence on women. In this respect, Wollstonecraft goes well beyond Aristotle's hints that women are important part of the city. The education advocated by Wollstonecraft would bring women into the public sphere in a manner Aristotle denies to the women of the polis. Of course, it is not just Aristotle, who has denies women this kind of independence and participation in political life. Rousseau and Locke, for different reasons perhaps, limit woman's participation in political life to the indirect influence she had on her husband and her children. Because Wollstonecraft insists women be allowed to participate in political life, she does advocate a new role for women as citizen, which is unavailable to her in the examples "gathered from books written on this subject by men" (*VRW*, 7). For Wollstonecraft, a whole, unfractured woman is a citizen.

I. HALF OF THE CITY

Aristotle's consideration of the relationship between husband and wife comes during a larger treatment of friendship in the *Ethics*. However, his most well known, and more protracted, consideration of the family—or the household, to use Aristotle's language—comes at the outset of the *Politics*. This discussion of the household is for the sake of understanding the origins of the city. Recall from our discussion of the household in the previous chapter that the city is comprised of many households and households are comprised of various "persons who cannot exist without one another" (*Politics*, 1252a27). The persons, who make up the household, cannot live without one another because each is lacking. They are lacking in ways that prevents them from providing for themselves. "The household is the partnership constituted to by nature for [the needs] of daily life" (*Politics*, 1252b12–13). But, the city does not exist merely for the sake of preservation. "For it is peculiar to man as compared to other animals that he alone has perception of good and bad and just and unjust and other things [of this sort]; and partnership in these things is what makes a household and a city" (*Politics*, 1253a15–19). The *Politics* is Aristotle's contemplation of the best regime. The best regime would not merely provide for the necessities of daily life, but would be organized in such a way as to allow human beings to fulfill their nature as rational animals and to deliberate what is just and unjust. Aristotle surveys political models established in various cities, as well as models put forth by other thinkers, in order to determine what the best regime is.

The relationship of the household to the city has inspired debate among scholars of Aristotle. In her influential work *Public Man, Private Woman*, Jean Bethke Elshtain notices the persistent distinction between the public and private spheres in western political philosophy. Often, the distinction was assumed and went unexamined by male thinkers.[1] The separation of the public and private, Elshtain argues, has its origins in the distinction between nature (*physis*) and culture (*nomos*) in Greek political thought. Politics allows human beings to gain at least partial autonomy from the necessity imposed on them by nature. The household or the private sphere, by Elshtain's account, is marked by necessity. As a result of this difference between public and private life, the household and women are excluded from politics. "Women were silenced in part because that which defines them and to which they are inescapably linked—sexuality, natality, the human body (images of uncleanness and taboo, visions of dependency, helplessness, vulnerability)— was omitted from political speech" (Elshtain, 15). Elshtain considers women's exclusion from political life typical of Greek political thought and certainly true of Aristotle's political philosophy. Women, slaves, and children are unable to participate in the rational deliberations of public life. Yet, they are necessary to it. "Those women, children, slaves, and 'mechanics and labourers' Aristotle distinguishes from free, male citizens are the 'necessary conditions' of the state . . . Although they do not share in public life per se . . . they nevertheless provide the precondition upon which the public life rests" (Elshtain, 46). Women were excluded from the public in order to protect politics from the private.

Other interpretations of Aristotle do not see the separation between the public and the private as starkly as Elsthain. Arlene Saxonhouse devotes her book, *Fear of Diversity,* to "the most profound political challenge: the definition of what distinguishes and what unites, what can both separate out one group, one species, one family, from all others, and yet at the same time unite that group for the sake of the sharing on which the political community is based."[2] While Elshtain finds the exclusion of women necessary to the protection of Aristotle's polis, Saxonhouse argues that such an exclusion is a detriment to political life. *"The balancing of different claims, the order built on compromise and conflict over the meaning of the good life and the just and the unjust—these are the elements of the political world . . .* Aristotle observes the world around him in its great multiplicity of forms, and from that observation, political science emerges" (Saxonhouse, 187, Saxonhouse's emphasis). Still, diversity does threaten the political order and it must be addressed. One way by which we can establish unity out of diversity's potential disorder is to identify a hierarchy. And, Aristotle's treatment of the household does seem to establish a hierarchy among master and slave, male and female, and parent and child. However, Saxonhouse demonstrates the distinctions on which these hierarchies are built are often difficult to discern. Not only does Aristotle show his readers that the difference between master and slave may be hard to distinguish, but he also carefully and subtly leads his readers to recognize occasions when the female soul is superior to the male soul (Saxonhouse, 194).

Saxonhouse turns to Aristotle's critique of Socrates' community of women and children, which Socrates famously puts forth in Plato's *Republic.* Socrates suggests that the city be built on the radical equality of male and female, which would allow both to perform the tasks for which they are best suited, regardless of their sex. In addition, Socrates puts forth the destruction of the family as we know it. No longer would individuals identify themselves as mothers, fathers, children, sisters, or brothers. Aristotle levels a critique of these suggestions in a few ways that are noteworthy for our discussion. Aristotle repudiates the suggestion that human beings are able to transcend their bodies. In doing so Saxonhouse appreciates that "Aristotle allows the female an existence not defined by the male's militaristic or political activities" (Saxonhouse, 196). Saxonhouse quickly reassures those who fear that Aristotle merely defines the female by her capacity to bear children. Aristotle explicitly tells us what the nature or the function of children and slaves are. "Curiously, Aristotle fails to mention the 'function' of the wife or woman. It is clearly neither to grow nor to perform menial tasks, but he does not define the female *ergon* as reproduction. The argument against Socrates' destruction of the family will not rest on the view of the female simply as a baby-producing machine" (Saxonhouse, 198). Such a view of woman would be insufficient for the family provides more to a polis than new human beings to populate it. "Indeed, Aristotle makes it clear that the virtues that concern the male and female, the child and the father, must be addressed in any discussion of the political regimes. 'Since every household is a part of the city, and these things [parts] of the household, it is necessary to look at the virtue of the part with regard to the virtue of the whole'" (Saxonhouse, 198). Aristotle does not exclude women and children from the regime, as Elshtain argues. Saxonhouse reminds us of Aristotle's claim that "women are half part of the free individuals and out of the children comes sharers of the regime" (Saxonhouse, 198; *Politics*, 1260b12–15*).*

There are important reasons that women and children should not be disregarded as parts of the polis. I am concerned with two in particular. First of all Aristotle intimates that the affection one feels for the members of his or her own family serves as the basis for our concern for other citizens. In his further critique of Socrates' community of women and children, Aristotle objects to it on the grounds that it will lead to indifference to all women and children among the citizens, rather than protecting the polis from the private, the love of one's own. "What belongs in common to the most people is accorded the least care: they take thought for their own things above all, and less about things common, or only so much as falls to each individually" (*Politics*, 1261b32–34). Saxonhouse comments, "Far from diluting the care for what is public, as Socrates feared if the divisions are allowed to enter the city, such as love of what is one's own with the context of family is essential for the support of the public realm. The destruction of *philia* though

Socrates' reforms brings apathy" (Saxonhouse, 202). Saxonhouse stops just short of arguing that the family, in allowing for love of one's own, serves as a model or education for our affection for other citizens. And, in fact, Aristotle does not pursue this important function that the family performs for the city as far as he might. Affection, Aristotle acknowledges, is "the greatest good of things for cities, for in this way they would least of all engage in factional conflict" (*Politics*, 1262b7–8). However, the benefit of affection goes beyond merely minimizing conflict. It is the means by which we are attached to and form loyalty to others in the polis. This benefit of the family to the political community is left to later thinkers, such as Rousseau and Wollstonecraft, to contemplate.

Secondly, Aristotle does suggest that virtuous women support the polis and that it is necessary for them to do so in ways that go beyond the "daily needs" of the city. In his treatment of Sparta, Aristotle warns his readers against neglecting the women. "For just as man and woman are a part of the household, it is clear that the city should be held to very nearly divided in two—into a multitude of men and a multitude of women so in regimes where what is connected with women is poorly handled, one must consider that legislation is lacking for half of the city" (*Politics*, 1269b15–18). In order to illustrate his point, Aristotle tells his readers of the mistake made by Lycurgus, Sparta's founder. "[F]or the legislator wished the city as a whole to be hardy, and this is manifest in terms of men, but he thoroughly neglected it in the case of the women, who live licentiously in every respect and in luxury" (*Politics*, 1269b20–22). Aristotle faults Lycurgus for not fostering the same virtues in the Spartan women as he did in the Spartan men. Lycurgus does not make the women "hardy." He goes on to offer the Theban invasion as an example of the harm the Spartan women brought to Sparta. "[T]hey were wholly useless, like women in other cities, but they created more of an uproar than the enemy" (*Politics*, 1269b37–38). Xenophon tells us that the Thebans burned and plundered the houses and "the women could not even endure the sight of the smoke, since they had never seen any enemy."[3] The women did not display the courage and the discipline for which the Spartans are known. Mary Nichols further explains the laxness, which emerged among the Spartan women and which proved to be so harmful to the regime.

> Lycurgus neglected the women to the detriment of the regime. This defect in the regime, however, stems from a more fundamental one: just as he did not adequately incorporate a part into the regime—indeed 'half of the city' (1269b18)—so he failed to incorporate the different aspects of virtue in the regime's end . . . The Spartans knew only how

to conduct war, not how to live in peace. Just as the laws give no attention to women, the men strive for only one side of virtue . . . Failing
to be sufficiently comprehensive, he left his regime prey to chance, the
uncontrolled influence of women in the city's affairs.[4]

I would add to Nichols' observation a concern, which is informed by Rousseau and by Wollstonecraft. Not only should Lycurgus have educated the
Spartan women to practice the same virtues as men and encouraged men
to practice virtues other than those of conducting war, he should have been
more concerned with the virtues that are particular to women. What these
virtues are and how they are to be properly fostered alongside Spartan military
virtue is not discussed by Aristotle. Again, a fuller account of the relationship
of private virtue (or in this case, vice) on politics is left to later thinkers.
Elshtain's strict separation between the public and the private seems to be
too stark. Aristotle hints to his readers that the household has an important
relationship to the polis—beyond providing for its daily needs. Yet, even if
we are persuaded by Saxonhouse's interpretation of Aristotle's treatment of
women and the family, readers of the *Politics* may still like further comment
on the relationship of women and the family to the polis. Wollstonecraft,
on the other hand, does consider more fully what it means for women to be
sharers in the regime and she does elaborate the family's significance to the
political community.

II. PRIVATE VIRTUE THE CEMENT OF PUBLIC HAPPINESS

Recall that *A Vindication of the Rights of Woman* is dedicated to Charles Maurice de Talleyrand-Périgord. Wollstonecraft hopes to persuade Talleyrand to
reconsider his neglect of women—one half of the city—in his recent report
on education. It seems as if the French statesman is in danger of making the
same mistake following the French Revolution as Lycurgus made in Sparta.
Wollstonecraft, like Aristotle, recognizes that women, as well as men, must be
educated in the principles of the regime and to practice virtues, which will
support it. Furthermore, the exclusion of women from politics would contra-
dict the very principles of the French Revolution and reveal a rotting republic.
"But, if women are to be excluded without having a voice, from a participation
of the natural rights of mankind, prove first, to ward off the charge of injustice
and inconsistency, that they want reason—else this flaw in your new constitution will ever shew that man, in some shape, act like a tyrant, and tyranny in
whatever part of society it rears its brazen front, will ever undermine morality"
(*VRW*, 5). In her later plea for the education of women, Wollstonecraft pre-

dicts the gradual decay of both sexes. "Make them free, and they will quickly become wise and virtuous, as men become more so; for the improvement must be mutual, or the injustice which one half of the human race are obliged to submit to, retorting on their oppressors, the virtue of men will be worm-eaten by the insect whom he keeps under his feet" (*VRW*, 175). Denied participation in political life and the conditions, which make it possible, woman is a mere insect. It is in her role as citizen that woman is able to combine that part of her which she shares with all human beings and that which is particular to her sex in order to be whole and independent.

By examining Wollstonecraft's plan for national education, we are able to see the important civic role that Wollstonecraft assigns to wives and to mothers. Although Aristotle had warned his readers against neglecting one half of the city, he does not indicate how that half should be educated in the principles of the regime. Wollstonecraft, on the other hand, does tell her readers how women, who are citizens of a republic, will support that regime, both as females and as human beings. The best means by which to educate children for political life is a combination of public and private education. Wollstonecraft argues that children should spend part of the day in school, but should not attend boarding school. Rather, they should return home at the end of their school day in order to live among their own families. The combination of the public and the private education will encourage the rational faculties to develop and allow affection to grow. Both reason and affection are important facets of citizenship.

As we have seen in previous chapters, Wollstonecraft argues that women, as well, as men "are placed on earth to unfold their faculties" and she indicates human beings are meant to do so in civil society. In this respect, Wollstonecraft's "first principles" resonate more with Aristotle's political philosophy than they do with the tenets of the natural rights doctrine of either Rousseau or of Locke. Aristotle distinguishes human beings from other animals by their ability to deliberate about the just and the unjust. Because it is in their nature to do so, they are, by nature, meant to live in a political community. In addition, the republic is premised on the capacity of human beings for reason and self-government. Children, therefore, should not always defer to the superior reason and wisdom of their parents. This would eventually create a habit of dependence, which is always so reprehensible to Wollstonecraft. And, so, Wollstonecraft points to the first benefit of educating children together in schools. "In order to open their faculties they should be excited to think for themselves; and this can only be done by mixing a number of children together, and making them jointly pursue the same objects" (*VRW*, 157).

The combination of public and private education will also teach children to deliberate about the just and the unjust. As Saxonhouse argues, politics is predicated on the balancing of competing claims. The household or the family, insofar as it is made up of male and female, husband and wife, parents and children, is an example of the balancing of claims, though the family not simply identical to politics. The education that Wollstonecraft advocates and that she expects children to receive at home prepares them for negotiating the competing claims made by different people. "[F]or the domestic affections, that first open the heart to the various modifications of humanity, would be cultivated, whilst the children were nevertheless allowed to spend a great part of their time, on terms of equality, with other children" (*VRW*, 158–159). By returning home from school, the children are exposed to the various claims made by others in the household and, it would seem, the affection children have for them would make the children congenial to those claims. At the same time, children, who are to be the citizens of a republic, must be educated to respect those who are their equals. The time spent with other children at school would encourage practicing the virtue of respect for one's fellow humanity.

Wollstonecraft's plan for national education would also teach children another facet of citizenship: political rule as Aristotle understands it—ruling and being ruled in turn as the virtues of the citizens demand. Spending part of their day at school and part of their day with their families introduces children to natural hierarchy and difference, as well as equality. In her discussion of "natural parental affection," Eileen Hunt Botting reminds us that "Wollstonecraft defines 'natural parental affection' as that which 'makes no difference between child and child, but what reason justifies as pointing out superior merit.' She recognizes this form of parental affection as 'the first source of civilization' because it teaches children to respect each other as equals while honoring the distinctive achievements of one another" (Botting, 205). Although Botting does not put it in these terms, I would suggest this describes political rule. It is the type of rule that characterizes the best regime and the type of relationship that characterizes the friendship between husband and wife as it is understood by both Aristotle and Wollstonecraft. However, Wollstonecraft, not Aristotle, demonstrates the important role the family plays in preparing children for political rule. It is worth noting that the combination of private and public education, which Wollstonecraft suggests, will educate children for citizenship *and* marriage. As we will see throughout Wollstonecraft's treatment of education, what cultivates better citizens also cultivates better husbands and wives. For Wollstonecraft, the citizen is sometimes indistinguishable from the husbands and wives, fathers and mothers.

Wollstonecraft appreciates the salutary effects that affection for one's own family members have on the political community. They go well beyond minimizing conflict. Affection helps to facilitate deliberation and political rule and it also helps to cultivate two additional virtues necessary to citizens of a republic: patriotism and modesty. These are virtues, which Wollstonecraft has promoted since the pages of the dedicatory letter. Throughout her pursuit of her chimera, Wollstonecraft maintains that "virtue is a relative idea; consequently, their [men's and women's] conduct should be founded on the same principles, and have the same aim" (*VRW*, 26). By fostering a traditionally masculine virtue and a traditionally feminine virtue in both sexes, Wollstonecraft reconceives them as human virtues. Nonetheless, she anticipates that theses human virtues may be practiced differently by male and female and, therefore, allows for what is distinctive to each sex. In this way, Wollstonecraft preserves woman's wholeness by combining that which she shares with all human beings with that which is peculiar to the female sex.

The family and, more particularly, a mother cultivate patriotism. Although patriotism is generally considered a public virtue and has often been associated with men, due to their military commitments, Wollstonecraft makes it a private virtue and she attributes it to women. For an example of patriotism Wollstonecraft offers George Washington. "But the days of true heroism are over, when a citizen fought for his country like a Fabricius or a Washington, and then returned to his farm to let his virtuous fervour run in a more placid, but not a less salutary, stream" (*VRW*, 147). Not only is his patriotism an example of public virtue, but it is an example of private virtue. We see that it takes a different cast on the battlefield than the fields of his Virginia farm. Wollstonecraft does not think it is appropriate for women to become soldiers and she does hope to see "the bayonet converted into a pruning hook"(*VRW*, 146). We may notice from Wollstonecraft's mention of Washington, patriotism may be practiced in different manners, depending on the circumstances. Because Wollstonecraft seems to attribute nurturing and benevolent qualities to women, she does not encourage a militaristic patriotism in women. Nonetheless, she expects women to have the same virtue as men, even if it is manifested in a different manner. First of all, a mother should be an example of patriotism to her children. In her dedication to Talleyrand, Wollstonecraft admonishes him for neglecting the education of women. The neglect will prevent her from fulfilling her duties. "And how can woman be expected to co-operate unless she know why she ought to be virtuous? Unless freedom strengthen her reason till she comprehend her duty, and see in what manner it is connected with her real good?" (*VRW*, 4). Her duty and her real good, Wollstonecraft quickly conveys, is to educate

patriots. "If her children are to be educated to understand the true principle of patriotism, their mother must be a patriot; and the love of mankind, from which an orderly train of virtues spring, can only be produced by
considering the moral and civil interest of mankind" (*VRW*, 4). A mother's
patriotism is informed by reason and reflection and it is an example to her
children. In addition to reason, patriotism is also nurtured in children by the
affection they first feel for their family members and, so, it is important to
live at home among them. "Few, I believe, have had much affection for mankind, who did not first love their parents, their brothers, sisters, and even
the domestic brutes, who they first played with. The exercise of youthful
sympathies forms the moral temperature; and it is the recollection of these
affections and pursuits that gives life to those that are afterwards more under
the direction of reason" (*VRW*, 162).

Modesty is the second virtue, which Wollstonecraft anticipates the
family will cultivate in children. Again, it has been Wollstonecraft's concern
since the first pages of the *Vindication*. Modesty, like patriotism, is cultivated through reason and affection. Improving the condition of women will
not only make women patriots, it will make men modest. In her dedication Wollstonecraft informs Talleyrand that the neglect of one half of the
political community will encourage *men* to "seek for pleasure in variety, and
faithless husbands will make faithless wives" (*VRW*, 6). Faithless husbands
and wives undermine public morality. "The box of mischief thus opened in
society, what is to preserve private virtue, the only security of public freedom
and universal happiness?" (*VRW*, 6). Wollstonecraft anticipates that greater
equality between the sexes and the improved condition of women, will result
in greater respect for marriage. It is her hope that a more modest, faithful
husband will encourage a more modest, faithful wife. "The father of a family
will not then weaken his constitution and debase his sentiments, by visiting
the harlot, nor forget, in obeying the call of appetite, the purpose for which
it was implanted. And the mother will not neglect her children to practice
the arts of coquetry, when sense and modesty secure her the friendship of her
husband" (*VRW*, 6). Just as Wollstonecraft attributes a traditionally masculine, public virtue to women, she attributes a traditionally feminine, private
virtue to men. In doing so, Wollstonecraft renders male and female more
similar to each other. This seems to be a lesson learned from Locke. Furthermore, in blurring the distinction between public and private virtues, Wollstonecraft points to the mutual influence of the public and the private and
elaborates a notion only hinted at by Aristotle.

While most eighteenth-century writers are concerned with instilling a
sense of modesty in girls, Wollstonecraft reconceives what she considers to be

a pernicious feminine trait and looks for ways to extend modesty to males. During our discussion of the extent to which Locke may have influenced Wollstonecraft's political philosophy, we saw that Wollstonecraft redefines modesty to be associated with reason, rather than females' sexual charms. In the first meaning of the word, Wollstonecraft understands it as "purity of mind," "the delicacy of reflections" (*VRW*, 122, 123). In her second meaning, it is "that soberness of mind which teaches a man not to think more highly of himself than he ought to think" (*VRW*, 122). Boys are not taught to be modest (in any sense of the word!) at boarding schools. They learn "nasty indecent tricks" from each other "when a number of them pig together in the same bedchamber" (*VRW*, 164). The "nasty indecent tricks" of little boys gradually develops into a disregard for other people, which has negatives consequences on the political community.

> The little attention paid to the cultivation of modesty, amongst men, produces great depravity in all the relationships of society; for . . . all the social affections are deadened by the selfish gratifications, which very early pollute the mind, and dry up the generous juices of the heart. In what an unnatural manner is innocence often violated' and what serious consequences ensue to render private vices a public pest. (*VRW*, 164–165)

The way in which Wollstonecraft educates boys to be more modest is to educate them at home, at least in part. Again, Wollstonecraft relies on our affection for our family. Affection will deter boys from pranks and vice (*VRW*, 165).

However, public education also helps boys and girls to become more modest, particularly in the second meaning that Wollstonecraft gives to the word. "[Yet] to make private support, instead of smothering, public affections, they should be sent to school to mix with a number of equals, *for only by the jostlings of equality can we form a just opinion of ourselves*" (*VRW*, 173, my emphasis). Modesty, in this second meaning of the word, is necessary for self-governing people for they must have a good understanding of their capabilities and the tenacity to live up to them or, alternatively, to step aside for someone of greater capabilities. In other words, modesty, as Wollstonecraft articulates it here, is an important virtue for political rule. In her earlier chapter devoted to the consideration of modesty, Wollstonecraft tells us "[A] modest man often conceives a great plan, and tenaciously adheres to it, conscious of his own strength, till success gives it a sanction that determines its character" (*VRW*, 122). Again, Wollstonecraft names George Washington as an example of virtue, except this time the virtue is modesty. Washington "was not arrogant . . . when he accepted command of the American forces. [He] has always been characterized as a modest man; but had he been merely humble, he would probably have shrunk back irresolute, afraid of trusting to himself the direction of an enterprise, on which so much depended" (*VRW*, 122). It is worth noticing that Wollstonecraft's conception of modesty seems to have something in common with a more traditional conception of feminine modesty, which would have women demure, shrinking from their own worth. It also has something in common with traditional conception of masculine confidence. Modesty, as Wollstonecraft attributes it to Washington, is a combination of the reserve of women and the confidence of men and it may be practiced by both sexes. George Washington, the eighteenth century's new exemplar of republican virtue is distinguished by his capacity for modesty. A virtue, which has traditionally been private and feminine is reconceived as a human virtue and supports political rule.

Keeping in mind the important lessons from both Rousseau and Locke, Wollstonecraft goes beyond Aristotle to demonstrate the significance of the family to the political community. As we saw in the first chapter, Rousseau imparts to Wollstonecraft the importance of the female sex to woman and to the political community. Wollstonecraft could not abide what she considered to be vice to promote the attachment between husband and wife in Rousseau's treatment of marriage. To the extent that Locke encouraged greater similarity between male and female by educating the human half of woman, Locke proved to be influential to Wollstonecraft. However, it is not clear that Locke's rational mother is affectionate. We do not witness any interaction between her and her husband and Locke gives scarcely any attention to the affection she may have for her children. It is Aristotle who is able to combine the human soul with the female body. Such a woman no longer resembles a monster, but peoples Wollstonecraft's utopian dream. She enjoys a friendship with her husband, which allows for both reason and affection. The affection, which she has for her husband and her children and the affection they have for her, is the basis of attachment to other human beings and their fellow citizens. It is an important component in the education of children in citizenship because it facilitates their capacity for deliberation and political rule. Coupled with reason it also helps to foster both patriotism and modesty. Affection, Aristotle is correct in saying, is among the greatest goods of the city, but the salutary effects go well beyond minimizing conflict. Wollstonectaft demonstrates affection's further benefit to the political community and shows us how "private virtue is the cement of public happiness." In this respect, Wollstonecraft elaborates ideas only hinted at by Aristotle.

III. THE CHIMERA, REPRISE

Mary Wollstonecraft's plan for educating children reveals the significant ways the family supports the political community beyond providing for its daily needs. The family—both in the marriage between husband and wife and the relationships children enjoy with their parents and siblings—is central to cultivating reason and affection, which in turns fosters deliberation, political rule, patriotism, and modesty among citizens and future citizens. Wollstonecraft's utopian dream is very nearly fulfilled. In order to realize her dream, Wollstonecraft's unfractured woman must be allowed to participate directly in the public sphere. In making this demand, Wollstonecraft well goes beyond the male philosophers, who have been so instructive. Despite the important lessons in the works of Rousseau, Locke, and Aristotle, the citizen described by them is, at least in some respects, alien to woman. Wendy Gunther-Canada rightly observes, "When a woman reads the works of the great men political philosophy she undergoes an identity crisis as a reader . . . Feminist theorists have recognized that the citizen is a man and a man is everything a woman is not" (Gunther-Canada, 14). The education Wollstonecraft has in mind for females will make the citizens on the pages of these works more recognizable to them for they will practice the virtues of citizenship, which have been mistakenly considered masculine. At the same time, the education will still preserve what has been associated with the female sex, a concern for others. Not only will women be more like the citizens that appear on the pages of these great works of political philosophy, the citizens who populate the republics emerging in the eighteenth century will be more like women—at least those rational and virtuous women, who populate Wollstonecraft's utopian dream. Wollstonecraft even intimates women's involvement in political life will change politics. Wollstonecraft's utopian dream is fulfilled by citizens, who are comprised of both the human and *female* sex.

Because Wollstonecraft insists that mothers be patriots and that fathers be modest, it should come as no surprise that she argues that boys and girls should be educated together, not just in the homes, but in the same schools. Wollstonecraft makes the suggestion for the sake of marriage and for the sake of the political community, as well as for the sake of the individual woman. "If marriage be the cement of society, mankind should all be educated after the same model, or the intercourse of the sexes will never deserve the name of fellowship, nor will women ever fulfill the peculiar duties of their sex, till they become enlightened citizens"(*VRW*, 165). And, just to make sure there is no misunderstanding, Wollstonecraft makes it very clear the extent to which the same model of education should result in "beings so much alike"(*Emile*, 211). There will be no fellowship between men and women nor will women fulfill the duties of their sex "till they become free by being enabled to earn their own subsistence, independent of men; in the same manner, I mean, to prevent misconstruction, as one man is independent of another" (*VRW*, 165). As we have seen, Rousseau disappoints Wollstonecraft because he did not educate that part of Sophie, which she shares with all human beings. Rousseau does not educate Sophie to be independent morally, intellectually, or financially. Denying women an ability to earn their own living leaves them dependent on the opinion of others. "But the sexual weakness that makes woman depend on man for a subsistence, produces a kind of cattish affection which leads a wife to purr about her husband as she would about any man who fed and caressed her" (*VRW*, 175). Dependence renders woman a fraction, less than human.

Throughout this book we have considered Wollstonecraft's plea for the moral and intellectual independence of women. This would, of course, permit woman to be the friend, rather than the slave of man, as well as a participant in political life. However, Wollstonecraft also means to assert woman's financial independence from men. Financial independence, as we saw in the first chapter, is an ability to earn a living through one's own efforts, and not simply having wealth that is independent of one's husband. (We may also remember that Rousseau, Locke, and Wollstonecraft all condemn the peculiar dependence of the wealthy on their riches and abhor the vices, which ensue.) Wollstonecraft makes her strongest case for ensuring the financial independence of women in an earlier chapter of the *Vindication*. Writing about the "pernicious effects," which flow from "unnatural distinctions" she makes a broader critique of all unnatural distinctions, which echoes Rousseau's condemnation corrupt aristocracy, made tyrannical by its weakness. Wollstonecraft appreciates the same propensity of women to become tyrants due to their cultured weaknesses.

"But what have women to do in society?" (*VRW*, 147) Wollstonecraft asks on behalf of her skeptical eighteenth-century readers. She offers several suggestions for their employment outside of the household. The professions she names preserves the wholeness of woman, who is comprised of both the human and the female. On the one hand, they require study and the pursuit of knowledge. On the other hand, they require a concern for other human beings. She argues, "Women might certainly study the art of healing, and be physicians as well as nurses. And midwifery, decency seems to allot to them . . . They might, also study politics, and settle their benevolence on the broadest basis" (*VRW*, 148). Woman's financial independence frees her from the necessity of being pleasing to others and, as a consequence, retains her wholeness.

It is interesting to note that Wollstonecraft likens politics to the medical profession. Through their benevolence, Wollstonecraft anticipates, women would heal the political body just as she might the human body. The capacity to restore politics is not limited to her positive influence on her husband or sons, as many of many of the male philosophers have suggested. Sadly, Wollstonecraft's *Vindication* does not say more about women's capacity to heal the political body through her direct participation in it.

Painfully aware of the precarious existence of her female contemporaries, who do not marry, Wollstonecraft insists that the political regime must allow these women dignified lives. "Is not that government then very defective, and very unmindful of the happiness of one half of its members, that does not provide for honest, independent women, by encouraging them to fill respectable stations?" (*VRW*, 148). As a woman who married relatively late in life and who rescued one sister from a miserable marriage and another sister from their brother's care, Wollstonecraft had an acute appreciation for the humiliating condition of women, who had few ways to support themselves. However, Wollstonecraft's hope that women will find "respectable stations" outside the home is not merely to protect unmarried or the unhappily married women from uncertainty and potential financial hardship. She expects that married women will also seek employment outside of the home.

Wollstonecraft anticipates those critics who argue that educating women in a manner that has been considered masculine will allay her concern for the family, leading her to neglect the duties of wife and mother. Wollstonecraft tells her readers just the opposite is true for those who marry. "It is the want of domestic taste, and not the acquirement of knowledge, that takes women out of their families, and tears the smiling babes from the breast" (*VRW*, 167). Throughout the pages of the *Vindication* Wollstonecraft regrets the education that women receive because it merely cultivates a love of pleasure and vanity. It is the love of pleasure and vanity, which compels women to seek excitement and "men of sense continually lament that an immoderate fondness for dress and dissipation carries the mother of a family for ever from home" (*VRW*, 167). From Wollstonecraft's perspective the duties that are peculiar to their sex do not conflict with the independence that all human beings should enjoy. Quite the contrary, she tells her readers, "Speaking of women at large, their first duty is to themselves as rational creatures, and next, in point of importance, as citizens, is that, which includes so many of a mother" (*VRW*, 145). For Wollstonecraft, woman's duty as a human being, a mother, and as a citizen blend easily together.

By insisting women be properly prepared and allowed to support themselves, Wollstonecraft gives them a public stature they have not enjoyed—not even on the pages of Rousseau's and Locke's egalitarian political treatises. In identifying politics as an occupation that women might pursue, Wollstonecraft goes well beyond Aristotle too. Although he allows women virtue friendship with their husbands, he does not allow them a direct role in political life. This, of course, is true for the male writers who came before (and many, who come after!) Wollstonecraft. Women are prepared for their participation in politics by the development of their reason and virtue—which have long been considered important for citizenship, but which have also been considered masculine. Women are further prepared for political participation because Wollstonecraft reconceives citizenship to include virtues, which have been limited to the private sphere and to women. And, so, while Wollstonecraft is attracted to certain principles in the writing of her male predecessors, it is up to her to write a treatise, in which woman is a citizen and joins man in the quest for a good society.

IV. A NEW GENUS

Moving in the liberal—some say, radical—intellectual and political circles of eighteenth-century Great Britain, Mary Wollstonecraft enters the political discourse of her time with her first political treatise, *A Vindication of the Rights of Men*. Wollstonecraft defends the rights of men, against Edmund Burke who regrets the demise of the French monarchy, symbolized by the conventionally beautiful and charming queen, Marie Antoinette. Wollstonecraft condemns the Queen of France, the exemplar of eighteenth-century feminine virtue, as weak and vicious. Her public demand that women conduct themselves like human beings, rather than hot house flowers, is met with an affront to her humanity and to her femininity. Wollstonecraft is dubbed the Hyena in Petticoats by Horace Walpole (Todd, 168). She is portrayed as a shrill animal in woman's clothing. Walpole's characterization is unfairly nasty, but he is correct *only* insofar as this woman, who dared to write a political treatise, is "a new genus."[5] No longer able to endure the very few ways of earning a living, which were open to women, such as companion or governess, Wollstonecraft embarks on her career as an author. In writing this political treatise and earlier pieces in various genres, Wollstonecraft becomes the first of "a new genus," a woman who earns her living by writing, just as men do. The Hyena in Petticoats soon picks up her pen to vindicate the rights of woman. Although "the woman question" is the occasion for her engagement with male philosophers, Wollstonecraft's contemplation of woman's condition points to a much deeper critique of their political philosophies, most explicitly and caustically that of Rousseau. Her efforts to make women's condition commensurate with her "first principles" also reveal a critique of John Locke's political philosophy. Although her first principles do resonate with Aristotle's political philosophy and the two philosophers share an understanding of marriage as friendship, Wollstonecraft's political philosophy departs from the ancient thinker's too. Wollstonecraft's elaboration of woman's importance to the political community as wife, mother, *and* as citizen points to the limits of Aristotle's treatment of women and the family. Wollstonecraft's serious, critical engagement with the ideas of Rousseau, Locke, and Aristotle (to name just a few), along with the articulation of her own political philosophy establishes Wollstonecraft as the first of a new genus in a second respect. Not only is she a woman writer, she is a female philosopher.[6]

As a new genus of female philosopher, Wollstonecraft conceives a new genus of womanhood. Wollstonecraft begins her treatise on the rights of woman by identifying the source of their miserable condition and by charting a path toward her utopian dream. "[E]ither nature has made a great difference between man and man, or that civilization which has hitherto taken place in the world has been very partial" (*VRW*, 7). Wollstonecraft condemns the education women receive for their "weak and wretched" condition (*VRW*, 7). The education afforded to women, Wollstonecraft regrets, is "gathered from books written by men on this subject, who considering females rather as women than human creatures, have been more anxious to make them alluring mistresses than affectionate wives and rational mothers" (*VRW*, 7). Seduced by the power over men that their beauty affords them, women eschew nobler pursuits. Woman, as Wollstonecraft finds in her own day, is a monstrous "half-being" or a "wild chimera." Considering women as "human creatures," rather than simply as females, and educating them to exercise reason and virtue would restore their wholeness and dignity to them. In *A Vindication of the Rights of Woman*, Wollstonecraft ventures into the land of chimeras, pursing her chimera, her utopian dream of woman, who is comprised of both the human and female.

Considering the dynamic political times in which Wollstonecraft writes and her intellectual pedigree, we would expect that Wollstonecraft's utopian dream would be fulfilled by modern, liberal thinkers. Wollstonecraft is often seen by scholars to have followed in the footsteps of two state of nature theorists: Jean Jacques Rousseau and John Locke. These two philosophers would have been foremost among the thinkers, who articulated the natural equality of human beings to Wollstonecraft's contemporaries. Indeed, Rousseau's and Locke's names are sprinkled throughout the pages of the *Vindication*. However, the equality of human beings in the state of nature is founded on their relative physical similarity and their equal vulnerability. Those think-ers, who subscribe to the state of nature theories, therefore, must account for the physical differences between male and female. For Rousseau, the physical differences between male and female, in particular woman's capacity to bear children, has profound consequences for the nature of woman and the nature of her relationship to man. Locke, on the other hand, does not make much of woman's capacity to bear children. Woman's capacity to bear children does not compromise her use of reason or undermine her indepen-dence. But, Locke's rational mother does not seem to be an affectionate wife. Furthermore, the reason that Locke attributes to human beings has decid-edly worldly limits. It contrasts greatly with human reason as Wollstonecraft understands it. Reason marks human beings with the divine. Despite the promise of these egalitarian thinkers, neither Locke nor Rousseau seems treat the physical differences between male and female in a manner that is satisfac-tory to Wollstonecraft.

Wollstonecraft takes an approach notably different from Rousseau and Locke: she establishes the equality of human beings on their end or *telos* in a way seemingly reminiscent of Aristotle's philosophy. She insists that "wom-en . . . who in common with men, are placed on this earth to unfold their faculties" (*VRW*, 8). It is by fostering their rational capacities and by practic-ing virtue that women will become the "affectionate wives and the rational mothers," who people Wollstonecraft's utopian dream. Given this under-standing of human nature and the relationship between man and woman, it is Aristotle, who proves to be the closest and best traveling companion to Wollstonecraft through the land of chimeras. For both Wollstonecraft and Aristotle, the soul is central to their understanding of the human condition. Wollstonecraft has struggled to combine the human soul with the female body. The imperative to make the female body pleasing seems incompatible with the human soul, capable of aspiring to the divine through its capacity for reason and virtue. "Surely she has not an immortal soul who can loi-ter life away merely employed to adorn her person, that she may amuse the languid hours, and soften the cares of a fellow creature who is willing to be enlivened by her smiles and tricks when the serious business of life is over" (*VRW*, 29). Aristotle's treatment of the physical differences does not compro-mise woman's human character. As I have argued, Aristotle's explanation of friendship provides a model of friendship between husband and wife, which resonates with Wollstonecraft's own. "Besides, the woman who strengthens her body and exercises her mind will, by managing her family and practic-ing various virtues, become the friend, and not the humble dependent of her husband" (*VRW*, 29). Wollstonecraft does not find such an example of friendships between husband and wife with either Rousseau or Locke as her guide.

Friendship between husband and wife makes it possible for Wollstonecraft to replace the monstrous and vicious character of woman with reason, virtue and affection. However, Wollstonecraft's political philosophy goes beyond the political thought of Aristotle in two respects. She elaborates the importance of affection among family members to the political community. Affection, along with reason, fosters deliberation, political rule, patriotism, and modesty. Affection is an important facet in preparing children for citizenship and practicing citizenship as an adult. Furthermore, Wollstonecraft goes well beyond Aristotle and other male philosophers in identifying women as citizens. Educated to be rational and virtuous, the chimera Wollstonecraft has pursued, is capable of entering political life. Yet, the benevolence Wollstonecraft attributes to her suggests the woman retains what is distinctive to the female sex. Wollstonecraft's utopian dream is fulfilled by a whole, unfractured woman who is a citizen.

Along with the new genus of womanhood, Wollstonecraft introduces us to a new genus of citizen. Wollstonecraft, in contrast to her male predecessors, brings woman into the public sphere, insisting that she support herself through her own efforts and participate in politics. However, we should be careful not to miss Wollstonecraft's full contribution to a discussion of republican citizenship. Wollstonecraft does not merely add women to the collection of citizens—male citizens—and expect that they will simply act in a manner that had generally be considered masculine. Rather, citizenship is reconceived to reflect the virtues of woman. Although Wollstonecraft expects women to emulate the patriotism of George Washington, albeit in a manner appropriate for them, Wollstonecraft also expects patriots, like George Washington, to emulate virtuous women! The proper combination of reason and affection allows a self-governing people to deliberate, practice political rule, and to cultivate the important virtues of patriotism and modesty.

As "a new genus" of a female philosopher, Wollstonecraft is among the first to "plead for her sex." But, she does so out of "an affection for the whole human race" (*VRW*, 3). And, so, Wollstonecraft's sometimes scathing critiques of male thinkers' treatments of women have pointed to the tension and the limits of their political philosophies. Identifying the ways by which the male philosophers have proven to be instructive, but also a hindrance, to Wollstonecraft reveals her smart, critical engagement with male philosophers. We gain an appreciation for her thought, but also a deeper understanding of the thought of those male philosophers. *A Vindication of the Rights of Woman* is not merely a critique of the others' thought, however. Mary Wollstonecraft successfully navigates the land of chimeras and fulfills her dream with a woman, who is unfractured by her vicious social passions. The new path that the female philosopher charts leads to a new genus of womanhood and new genus of citizenship.

Notes

NOTES TO THE INTRODUCTION

1. Mary Wollstonecraft, *A Vindication of the Rights of Man* and *A Vindication of the Rights of Woman*. Edited by Sylvana Tomaselli. (New York: Cambridge University Press, 1995), 30. Parenthetical citations to *A Vindication of the Rights of Man* refer to this edition.
2. Janet Todd, *Mary Wollstonecraft: A Revolutionary Life*. (New York: Columbia University Press, 2000),168. Parenthetical citations refer to this edition.
3. Mary Wollstonecraft, *A Vindication of the Rights of Woman*. Edited by Carol Poston. (New York: W.W. Norton & Company, 1988), 3. Parenthetical citations refer to this edition.
4. Barbara Taylor, *Mary Wollstonecraft and the Feminist Imagination*. (Cambridge: Cambridge University Press, 2003), 10. Parenthetical citations refer to this edition.
5. Susan Khin Zaw, "The Reasonable Heart: Mary Wollstonecraft's View of the Relation Between Reason and Feeling in Morality, Moral Psychology, and Moral Development." *Hypatia*, Vol. 13, no. 1 (Winter 1998), 79. Parenthetical citations refer to this edition.
6. Ralph M. Wardle, *Mary Wollstonecraft: A Critical Biography*. (Lincoln: University of Nebraska Press, 1951), 118. Parenthetical citations refer to this edition.
7. Michael Zuckert begins the introduction of his book, *Natural Rights and the New Republicanism* by telling his readers, "In the beginning all the English were Christian Aristotelian, more or less" (p. xv). Throughout the seventeenth century, the British political climate adopted the thought of John Locke.
8. Virginia Sapiro, *A Vindication of Political Virtue: the Political Theory of Mary Wollstonecraft*. (Chicago: The University of Chicago Press, 1992), 77–78. Parenthetical citations refer to this edition.

9. Wendy Gunther-Canada, *Rebel Writer: Mary Wollstonecraft and Enlight-enment Politics.* (DeKalb: Northern Illinois Press, 2001), 9. Parenthetical citations refer to this edition.
10. Virginia Sapiro, "Wollstonecraft, Feminism, and Democracy: 'Being Bastilled'" in *Feminist Interpretations of Mary Wollstonecraft,* ed. Maria J. Falco. (University Park, PA: The Pennsylvania State University Press, 1996), 36.
11. George S. Fraser, *Alexander Pope* (London: Routledge & Kegan Paul, 1978), 36. Wollstonecraft quotes Alexander Pope quite often and seems to be well acquainted with his poetry. While Pope is revered for his witty satire, he is not considered a particularly original philosopher. His general ideas are that of Aristotle.
12. Jean-Jacques Rousseau, *Discourse on the Origin and the Foundations of Inequality Among Men,* in *The Discourses and Other Political Writings.* Edited by Victor Gourevitch (Cambridge: University of Cambridge, 1997), 113. Parenthetical citations refer to this edition.

NOTES TO CHAPTER ONE

1. Carol Blum, *Rousseau and the Republic of Virtue: the Language of Politics in the French Revolution* (Ithaca: Cornell University Press, 1986), 137. Parenthetical citations refer to this edition.
2. Mary Seidman Trouille, *Sexual Politics in the Enlightenment: Women Writers Read Rousseau* (Albany: State University of New York Press, 1997), 56–57. Parenthetical citations refer to this edition.
3. Jean Grimshaw, "Mary Wollstonecraft and the Tensions in Feminist Philosophy," *Socialism, Feminism, and Philosophy: A Radical Reader.* Edited by Sean Sayers and Peter Osbornee. (London: Routledge, 1990), 14. Parenthetical citations refer to this edition.
4. Gary Kelly's *Revolutionary Feminism: The Mind and Career of Mary Wollstonecraft* (New York: St. Martin's Press, 1996), 41.
5. Syndy Conger, *Mary Wollstonecraft and the Language of Sensibility* (London: Associated University Presses, 1994), xxxi. Parenthetical citations refer to this edition.
6. Eileen Hunt Botting, *Family Feuds: Wollstonecraft, Burke, and Rousseau on the Transformation of the Family* (Albany, State University of New York Press, 2006), 12. Parenthetical citations refer to this edition.
7. Jean-Jacques Rousseau, *Emile or On Education.* Introduction, Translation and Notes by Allan Bloom (New York: Basic Books, 1979), 211. Parenthetical citations refer to this edition.
8. Jean-Jacques Rousseau, *The Discourses and Other Early Political Writings,* Edited and Translated by Victor Gourevitch (New York: Cambridge University Press, 1997), 148. Parenthetical citations refer to this edition.

9. Laurence Cooper. *Rousseau, Nature & the Problem of the Good Life.* (University Park: The Pennsylvania State University Press, 1999). Parenthetical citations refer to this edition.

10. Following Cooper, I will refer to the human being in the state of nature as the Savage. To call him natural man would be confusing and misleading, as natural refers to the quality of an individual's soul and not his or her physical location. I do not intend any negative connotation with this designation.

11. Roger Masters, *The Political Philosophy of Rousseau* (Princeton: Princeton University Press, 1968), 4. Parenthetical citations refer to this edition.

12. In his book, *Love and Friendship*, Allan Bloom notes that the problem of Book V of the *Emile* is how to care for another person as one cares for him or herself. Bloom suggests that this is the equivalent to the political problem of the *Social Contract*: how obedience to the law one gives oneself guaranteed (p. 91).

13. Mary Wollstonecraft, *The Collected Letters of Mary Wollstonecraft.* Edited by Ralph M. Wardle (Ithaca: Cornell University Press, 1979), 145. Wollstonecraft's emphasis. Parenthetical citations refer to this edition.

14. Jean- Jacques Rousseau, *On the Social Contract.* Edited by Roger D. Masters and Translated by Judith R. Masters. (New York: St Martin's Press: 1978), 46. Parenthetical citations refer to this edition.

15. Rousseau returns to women's roles as mothers in Book V in the *Emile*. He is adamant that it is women's "proper purpose to produce [children]" (*Emile*, 362). In a footnote to this passage, Rousseau explains that it is necessary for each woman to bear four children, given the infant mortality rate, in order to maintain the current population. While today we are liberated from this concern for the survival of the species, Rousseau's treatment of women is very much informed by this practical concern.

16. See Denise Schaeffer, "Reconsidering the Role of Sophie in Rousseau's *Emile, Polity*, Vol. XXX, no. 4, Summer 1998. Schaeffer acknowledges that Sophie is a failure of the unified soul as it is attributed to the Savage in the state of nature. However, Sophie's fractional character contributes to the wholeness of the family. Considering the rich and complex wholeness of the family results in a better understanding of Rousseau's view of wholeness. Schaeffer's thoughtful and convincing defense of Sophie would fall on Wollstonecraft's deaf ears. Wollstonecraft would not accept the premise that the sacrifice of Sophie's wholeness or independence is necessary for the happiness of the family.

17. This is not to imply, however, that Wollstonecraft agrees with Rousseau in every respect about which a good education consists. As we shall see in the next chapter of this section, Wollstonecraft and Rousseau differ fundamentally in the place they accord to virtue and reason.

18. Mary P. Nichols, "Rousseau's Novel Education in the *Emile*," *Political Theory*, Vol. 13, No. 4, November 1985.

19. In her book, *Gendered Community: Rousseau, Sex and Politics*, Penny Weiss suggests that feminist critics of Rousseau exaggerate the difference between

a craftsman, a carpenter in the case of Emile, and a wife. Weiss minimizes the difference between the two roles by suggesting the wife is more free of social convention than is usually recognized and by arguing that the craftsman is less free than Rousseau would have us believe. The exclusion of the wife or household manager from the public sphere also leaves her independent of it. Furthermore, in managing a house, a woman learns a set of skills which is easily transferred to various circumstances. Should a woman's father or husband die, she is able to use her skills in her new home and is not dependent on any one man. Although the craftsman is presented as a free man, who must only rely on his own hands in order to learn a living, Weiss reminds her readers that the craftsman is part of a larger *social* scheme that requires the division of labor. From the point of view, the craftsman is equally dependent on social convention as the wife or household manager (Weiss, 20).

20. Although Rousseau designates some as trades more appropriate for women than men, Rousseau does not encourage women to seek employment outside the home. Rousseau is clear that their virtue is best preserved as wives and mothers. Nonetheless, it is worth noting that one of the qualities which characterizes Rousseau's ideal woman, Sophie, is her love of sewing. "What Sophie knows best and has been most carefully made to learn are the labors of her own sex, . . . like cutting and sewing her own dresses. There is no needlework which she does not know how to do and which she does with pleasure. But the work she prefers to every other is lacework, because there is none which results in a more agreeable pose" (the pose struck while doing needlework) (*Emile*, 394).

21. Rousseau does not describe Sophie as natural when describing her compatibility to the natural man, Emile. See also *Emile*, 363.

NOTES TO CHAPTER TWO

1. Claudia L. Johnson, *Equivocal Beings: Politics, Gender, and Sentimentality in the 1790s* (Chicago: Chicago University Press, 1995), 32.

2. The only natural right that Wollstonecraft ascribes to woman in *A Vindication of the Rights of Woman* is the love that a dutiful wife deserves from her husband (*VRW*, 67).

3. Rousseau begins the *Emile* with this very declaration. "Everything is good as it leaves the hands of the Author of things; everything degenerates in the hands of man" (*Emile*, 37).

4. Because Wollstonecraft is committed to reason and virtue as the defining traits of human beings, we might expect Wollstonecraft to condemn Emile. After all, Emile is meant to embody man's natural qualities. He is independent and good. Rather than cultivate reason and virtue in his young pupil, Rousseau deters the awakening of Emile's passions and limits them

in order to preserve his natural independence and goodness. Contrary to our expectations, Wollstonecraft does not pursue this line of critique. She is relatively silent on the character of Emile and reserves her ire for Sophie. Perhaps the most obvious reason for this is that her treatise is written for the benefit of women. We may also notice that Emile, though lacking in reason and virtue, is not vicious. Therefore, he is not as offensive to the integrity of human beings or the political community as a fractional creature would be. Nonetheless, Wollstonecraft's critique of Sophie is instructive. As we shall see, Wollstonecraft points to the vicious character of natural woman and calls into question the consistency of Rousseau's account of the state of nature.

5. Rousseau begins Book V of the *Emile* with the announcement that it is time to introduce Emile (and Rousseau's readers) to his companion, Sophie. He then begins describing women and young girls more generally. Wollstonecraft concentrates her criticism of Rousseau on the initial descriptions. Although Rousseau may mean to distinguish his ideal woman, Sophie, from them, Wollstonecraft understands Rousseau's discussion in the first part of Book V to be representative of Sophie. I think that the objections Wollstonecraft raises to Rousseau's characterization of women and little girls, may also be leveled against the young lady Rousseau identifies as Sophie. I will point out the important similarities in the notes. To demonstrate the consistency between women and little girls, more generally, and Sophie, in particular, would be a distraction from Wollstonecraft's objections to Rousseau's understanding of the female and a distraction from her implicit critique of Rousseau's natural rights theory.

6. Joel Schwartz, *The Sexual Politics of Jean-Jacques Rousseau* (Chicago: The University of Chicago Press, 1984), 33. Parenthetical citations refer to this edition.

7. Wollstonecraft refers to the Greek legend of Procrustes. According to this legend, Procrustes made his guests fit his iron bed by stretching them if they were to short or chopping off their legs if too tall.

8. Rousseau was born in Geneva. Throughout his corpus Rousseau draws many unfavorable comparisons between Paris and this small, virtuous republic. He takes various opportunities to claim that he is a citizen of Geneva. For Wollstonecraft to identify Rousseau with the corrupt, aristocratic France, rather than Rousseau's beloved republic, is not an ignorant mistake on Wollstonecraft's part. Elsewhere in the *Vindication of the Rights of Woman*, Wollstonecraft refers to Rousseau as "the citizen of Geneva" (15). Rather, Wollstonecraft's identification of Rousseau with France should be taken as a criticism of the Solitary Walker.

9. Despite Rousseau's claim to distinguish himself from other educational writers by not educating Emile with a view to his adult life, Rousseau does

just that. The difference being that Rousseau educates Emile to be a natural man, rather than an eighteenth century-civil man.

10. It is worth noting that "modesty" does not have the same connotations for Wollstonecraft as it does for Rousseau. For Wollstonecraft, modesty is the means by which *both* men *and* women quiet the sexual passions. It is associated with chastity and fidelity. For Rousseau, on the other hand, modesty is woman's most important virtue. It requires the love of adornment and a knack for covering one's charms so that they are imagined by the opposite sex (*Emile*, 394). Modesty is the force by which women gain empire over men. It is the particular domain of women. In fact Rousseau condemns the men that are so foolish to become fashion merchants. "Oh, let each make and sell the arms of his own sex!" (*Emile*, 200).

11. When we meet Sophie as a young lady, Rousseau describes her superior figure. We soon find out that Sophie was not born with that figure. "Sophie was a glutton. She was naturally so" (*Emile*, 395). It was only by appealing to Sophie's vanity that her mother was able to correct Sophie's eating habits. "Her mother surprised her, scolded her, punished her, and compelled her to fast. She finally succeeded in persuading Sophie that bonbons spoil the teeth and eating too much fattens the figure. Thus Sophie mended her ways" (*Emile*, 395).

12. Though it is instructive to notice a comparison between the little girl and the female Savage (and Emile and the Savage), we have already seen significant differences between the little girl and Emile. The same will be said of the male and female Savage. Rousseau himself warns us of this possibility. "Women's judgment is formed earlier than men's. Since almost from infancy women are on the defensive and entrusted with a treasure that is difficult to protect, good and evil are necessarily known to them sooner . . . Maturity is not everywhere the same at the same time" (*Emile*, 397).

13. Perhaps offspring do not wander off to forage for themselves as soon as Rousseau, and Weiss, have suggested.

14. Over and over again, Rousseau tells us in one way or another that "Everything is good as it leaves the hands of the Author of things; everything degenerates in the hands of man" (*Emile*, 37). Despite nature's design that man eat only vegetation, man introduces meat into his diet. For a further example of man being his own worst enemy, see Rousseau's discussion of fire. Although "Nature had taken precautions to withhold this fatal secret from us" (*Discourses*, 168), man learned to use it and, in turn, invented metallurgy and agriculture. Rousseau attributes man's civilization and ruin to these two arts.

15. Rousseau begins his description of Sophie as a young lady with a statement of his expectations for all virtuous women. "The woman who is at once decent loveable, and self-controlled, who forces those about her to respect her, who has reserve and modesty, who, in a word, sustains love by means

of esteem, sends her lovers with a nod to the end of the world, to combat, to glory, to death, to anything she pleases. This seems to me to be a noble empire, and one well worth the price of purchase" (*Emile*, 393). Rousseau immediately tells his reads, "This is the spirit in which Sophie has been raised" (*Emile*, 393). In the state of nature, like childhood, the female has relatively few passions and is concerned for physical needs. Therefore, the female Savage and the Little Glutton use their charms to obtain food. However, in civil society human beings' passions have multiplied and they are now concerned with moral distinctions. Woman is not content with food and employs her charms in order to satisfy her desire to rule. All of the three females that we have considered "consider the people who surround them as instruments depending on them to set in motion, they make use of people to follow their inclination and supplement their weakness" (*Emile*, 67).

16. Just as Rousseau gives us an example of the Little Glutton obtaining food by use of her charm, Rousseau allows his readers to witness Sophie charm Emile. Sophie claims to run as quickly as Emile. Rousseau describes Sophie preparing for her race with Emile, "trussing up her dress on both sides and, more concerned to display a slender leg to Emile's eyes than to vanquish him in his combat" (*Emile*, 437). Emile underestimates Sophie. "She takes the lead with such rapidity that Emile has just enough time to catch this new Atalanta when he perceives her so far ahead of him" (*Emile*, 437). And like the little glutton and the female Savage, Sophie allows Emile to treat her as if she were weaker than she actually is. "Gently putting his left arm around her, he lifts her like a feather and, pressing this sweet burden to his heart, completes the course. He makes her touch the goal first and then, shouting, 'Sophie is the winner,' puts his knee to the ground before her and admits that he is conquered" (*Emile*, 437). Immediately following the account of the race, the reader learns Sophie's compensation for her presumed and feigned weakness. Rousseau tells us that Sophie visits Emile in the carpentry shop. The sight of Emile working "does not make Sophie laugh. It touches her; it is respectable. Woman, honor the head of your house. It is he who works for you, who wins your bread, who feeds you. This is man" (*Emile*, 437).

17. Again, we can draw a comparison between the female and male Savage in this degenerating stage of the state of nature. Having encountered the vices of the city, Sophie and Emile decide to settle in the country. Rousseau describes the scene. "They vivify and reanimate the extinguished zeal of the unfortunate village folk. I believe I see the people multiplying, the fields fertilized, the earth taking on a new adornment. The crowd and the abundance transform work into festivals, and cries of joy and benedictions arise from the midst of the games which center on the lovable couple who brought them back to life. The golden age is treated like a chimera, and it will always be one for anyone whose heart and taste have been spoiled" (*Emile*, 474). At

first glance, Rousseau's description of Sophie and Emile's life together seems ideal. However, readers of the *Second Discourse* know that the greater contact with an ever increasing number of people and agriculture foster vice in human beings, who are naturally good. Rousseau knows the danger that the chimera he describes may dissolve into a monstrous account of this community. It requires the continued presence of Rousseau. In the end, he does not leave the young man to his bride as he had promised to do. Emile's dependence is painfully obvious.

NOTES TO CHAPTER THREE

1. In the *Emile*, Rousseau faults Locke for, among other things, concluding his educational treatise at the time of awakening passions, the birth of the sex (*Emile*, 357). And, in the *Second Discourse*, Rousseau criticizes Locke for claiming to describe human beings as they are by nature, but failing to do so (*Second Discourse*, 132).

2. John Locke, *Two Treatises of Government*, Edited by Peter Laslett (Cambridge: Cambridge University Press, 1988), 271, 307. Parenthetical citations refer to this edition.

3. The influence of John Locke on Wollstonecraft's early career is rather clear. The title of her first published work, *Thoughts on the Education of Daughters* implies Wollstonecraft's intention to imitate John Locke. Wollstonecraft makes her intention explicit in her discussion of moral discipline. She writes, "To be able to follow Mr. Locke's system (and this may be said of almost all treatises on education) the parents must have subdued their own passions."

4. John Locke, *Some Thoughts Concerning Education* and *Of the Conduct of Human Understanding*, Edited by Ruth W. Grant and Nathan Tarcove (Indianapolis: Hackett Publishing Company, 1996), 7. Parenthetical citations refer to this edition.

5. Nathan Tarcov, *Locke's Education for Liberty* (Chicago: University of Chicago Press, 1984), 2. Parenthetical citations refer to this edition.

6. Jean Bethke Elshtain's *Public Man, Private Woman: Women in Social and Political Thought* (Princeton: Princeton University Press, 1981). Parenthetical citations refer to this edition.

7. For example, Locke advises parents that their children's diets should be very plain. Should a child complain of hunger between meals, Locke suggests he be given dry bread. If he is truly hungry, this will satisfy him (*STCE*, 16–17) and the child will not develop sophisticated, insatiable passions.

8. Locke goes on to tell us that the child's mother, as well as his or her father, deserves respect and the father's authority cannot undermine the respect owed to the child's mother. "But all the *Duty of Honour*, the other part,

remains never less entire to them; nothing can cancel that. It is so insepa-rable from them both, that the Father's Authority cannot dispossess the Mother of this right, nor can any Man discharge his Son from *honouring her that bore him*" (*TT*, 313). In addition to the respect the mother earns by fulfilling her obligation to her offspring, Locke suggests here that she deserves respect having given birth to the child. However, Locke does not pause to elaborate the difference between father and mother in this respect, treating them as similarly as possible. We shall see in this chapter that Locke treats boys and girls as "beings so much alike." We shall see in the next chapter that Locke also understands men and women to be "beings so much alike" that their equality rests on similarity.

9. Robert Horowitz, "John Locke and the Preservation of Liberty: A Peren-nial Problem of Civic Education," *The Political Science Reviewer*, Volume VI, fall 1976, 340. Parenthetical citations refer to this article.

10. See for example *A Vindication of the Rights of Woman*, 39–40, 69.

11. Moira Ferguson and Janet Todd, *Mary Wollstonecraft* (Boston: Twayne Publishers, 1984), 19. Parenthetical citations refer to this edition.

12. Virginia Sapiro reminds us that education has a broader meaning to Wollstonecraft and her eighteenth century contemporaries. It is not sim-ply the formal education that is received at schools, but rather the early and informal cultivation of habits and tempers. Today we would refer to this broader understanding of education as "socialization" (Sapiro, 238–240).

13. Keep in mind that we are talking about the games of little girls and their dolls. As we have seen in considering Wollstonecraft's relationship to Rousseau, women have a natural instinct to care for their own children, albeit a relatively weak instinct that must be and *should* be nurtured, according to Wollstonecraft.

14. Tarcov argues that the Lockean virtues, such as self-denial, civility, and liberality, counter human beings propensity for cruelty and love of dominion. See *Locke's Education for Liberty*, chapter 3.

15. Locke hopes that this rational and industrious mother will "avoid under-standing them [the Gospels] in Latin if she can" (*STCE*, 135). Locke is not simply discouraging women from attempting metaphysical knowl-edge that is beyond the capacity of the female sex. As we will see in the next chapter, Locke also discourages his male pupil from using human reason to think about God. It would seem Locke does not want the ratio-nal mother (or the father, for that matter) to understand or contemplate the Gospels deeply in Latin or English.

16. Wollstonecraft promises her readers that she will treat the "peculiar duties of women" in a second volume (*VRW* 7, 63, 145). Wollstonecraft never writes this planned treatise. Perhaps her treatment would not have been as tentative as we find it in *A Vindication of the Rights of Women*.

NOTES TO CHAPTER FOUR

1. Mary Wollstonecraft, *Thoughts on the Education of Daughters, The Works of Mary Wollstonecraft*, Volume 4. Edited by Janet Todd and Marilyn Butler (New York: New York University Press, 1989), 9. Parenthetical citations refer to this edition.

2. John Locke, *An Essay Concerning Human Understanding*. Collated and annotated by Alexander Campbell Fraser. (New York: Dover Publications, Inc.), 37. Parenthetical citations refer to this edition.

3. At this point, Locke seems to come very close to contradicting himself, wishing to attribute natural tendencies to human beings, which "may be observed in all persons and all ages, steady and universal" (*ECHU*, 67). For a thorough treatment of this apparent contradiction, see Peter Myers' *Our Only Star and Compass: Locke and the Struggle for Political Rationality* (Lanham, MD: Rowman & Littlefield Publishers, 1998). Meyers explains, "Locke's natural-historical inquiry represents a delicate attempt to preserve a commonsense understanding of the nonarbitrariness of our ideas, while yet promoting a spirit of openness to scientific progress grounded in the incompleteness of those ideas" (Meyers, 68).

4. Thomas L. Pangle, *The Spirit of Modern Republicanism: the Moral Vision of the American Founders and the Philosophy of Locke*. (Chicago: University of Chicago Press, 1988),184. Parenthetical citations refer to this edition.

5. This language is similar to the language Locke uses in the *Essay*. The attributes of human beings are "stamped" on or "planted" in their souls. How or by what, Locke does not say. As we will see later in this chapter, there are some things, which Locke considers beyond the capacity of human beings to comprehend.

6. John Locke, *Two Treatises of Government*. Edited by Peter Laslett (Cambridge: Cambridge University Press, 1988), 270–271. Parenthetical citations refer to this edition.

7. Locke notices this propensity in children and suggests it be taken into consideration when assigning tasks to them. "What they do cheerfully of themselves, do they not presently grow sick of and can no more endure as soon as they find it is expected of them as a duty? Children have as much a mind to show that they are free, that their own good actions come from themselves, that they are absolute and independent, as any of the proudest of you grown men, think of them as you please" (*STCE*, 51).

8. In his article, "John Locke and the Preservation of Liberty: A Perennial Problem of Civic Education," Robert Horwitz makes a similar argument. Horwitz notices that "These new-born infants and young children described by Locke possess natures better suited for the existence in either the state of nature or Hobbesian despotisms than for an education designed to prepare them for citizenship within civil society" (343). The Lockean educator is

to make these children capable of creating and *preserving* a civil order that protects the life and liberty of its citizens.

9. I do not mean to suggest that Rousseau and Locke have the same understanding of human nature nor of human reason. However, in responding to Rousseau, Wollstonecraft does put forth her epistemological principles, which may then be compared and contrasted to Locke's.

10. The autonomous character of man and woman is necessary to Locke's larger project of establishing the natural freedom and equality of all human beings. Pangle argues, "The fact is, the human family is the most obvious stumbling block in the path of any philosophy which attempts to conceive of man as essentially an independent individual. It is therefore only by offering a convincing explanation of the family—of man's commonest, and usually strongest, social inclinations— that Locke can with any color of plausibility claim to have given an adequate proof for—and explanation of—the "State of Nature" (Pangle, 172).

NOTES TO CHAPTER FIVE

1. In her treatment of feminism, Daryl Tress notes the radical distinction between mind and body, which is typical of modern thought, was already firmly established by the time that Wollstonecraft writes the *Vindication*. "So when Wollstonecraft made her seemingly innocuous proposal, that women and men both possess minds so both require education, I believe that she herself was aware, to some extent, at least, of how implausible this would sound to her contemporaries. 'Mind' had already become evidently masculine, in ways that the classical soul which it replaced had not been, and her proposal was bound to strike her audience as bizarre" (Tress, 1991, 297).

2. Aristotle, *Nichomachean Ethics*. Translated by H. Rackham. (Cambridge: Harvard University Press, 1994), I, I, 1–20. Parenthetical citations refer to this edition.

3. Aristotle, *De Anima* in *The Complete Works of Aristotle*. Edited by Jonathan Barnes. (Princeton: Princeton University Press, 1984), 415a26–415b1. Parenthetical citations refer to this edition.

4. Aristotle, *Generation of Animals*. Translated by A.L. Peck. (Cambridge: Harvard University Press, 1990), 715b13–18. All parenthetical citations refer to this edition.

5. It may even be suggested that it is contrary to Aristotle's own teaching. In the *Politics*, Aristotle puts forth the notion that "Nature makes one thing for one purpose" and each performs its task best if it has only one task to do" (*Politics*, 1252b1–5). In her treatment of this passage, Mary Nichols explains that the complexity of the soul and body makes this principle nearly impossible to uphold. Furthermore, the desirability of upholding this principle

is questionable. See *Citizens and Statesmen*, pages 19–35. The immediately following discussion of *Generation of Animals* in this papers offers evidence that it is not contrary to Nature's purpose for human being's to perform more than one function, albeit not simultaneously.

6. It is important to note the significance that Aristotle gives to sensation. It is a pathway to knowledge. Even if "the men of genius" Wollstonecraft condemns are correct and women do lack reason, but not sensibility (which would mean Aristotle is incorrect), Wollstonecraft can still demand the improvement of education because women still have access to knowledge through sensation.

7. Much of Aristotle's consideration of current theories of generation is an attempt of afford *both* men and women a significant role in generation. Implicit in this discussion is the principle that Nature does nothing in vain. In lines 739b16–21, Aristotle explicitly states this principle.

8. Semen is the English word used by the translator to refer to the generative fluid that produces the offspring. It does not necessarily refer to the male generative fluid. At the outset of the *Generation of Animals*, Aristotle has not definitively decided that the semen is simply a male contribution to generation. As Aristotle proceeds and does distinguish the male and female generative fluids, semen will also refer to the male's generative fluid and the menstrual fluid will refer to the female's generative fluid.

9. Daryl McGowan Tress, "The Metaphysical Science of Aristotle's *Generation of Animals* and Its Feminist Critics," *Review of Metaphysics*, Vol. XLVI, no. 2 (December 1992), 311. Parenthetical citations refer to this edition.

10. Today's radical feminists would join Aristotle in wondering why a woman doesn't "accomplish generation all by itself and from itself." Believing that the power of generation has been usurped from the woman by patriarchy, the radical feminists see "no need of the male in addition." And, yet, like Aristotle, the radical feminist cannot explain how a woman can accomplish generation by herself. Technology has rendered sexual intercourse between men and women unnecessary. Nonetheless, the woman is unable to conceive a child without a contribution from outside of herself.

11. G.E.R. Lloyd, "Aristotle's Psychology and Zoology," *Essays on Aristotle's De Anima*. Edited by M. Nussbaum and A. Rorty (New York: Oxford University Press, 1992), 151. Parenthetical citations refer to this edition.

12. Aristotle, *Metaphysics* in *The Complete Works of Aristotle*. Edited by Jonathan Barnes. (Princeton: Princeton University Press, 1984), 1045b18–21. Parenthetical citations refer to this edition.

NOTES TO CHAPTER SIX

1. Ruth Abbey, "Back to the Future: Marriage as Friendship in the Thought of Mary Wollstonecraft," *Hypatia*, vol. 14, no. 3 (Summer 1999), 79. Parenthetical citations refer to this edition.

2. Like Sapiro and Tomaselli, Abbey discusses "the classical notion of higher friendship" in a general way. However, it is Aristotle's *Nichomachean Ethics* that is the classical text, which discusses friendship in greatest detail. Indeed, it is the only classical text to appear in Abbey's bibliography. Therefore, I will discuss Abbey's comparison of Wollstonecraft to classical philosophy by turning to Aristotle in specific.

3. Aristotle, *Politics*. Translated by Carnes Lord. (Chicago: University of Chicago Press, 1985), 125ab27–32). Parenthetical citations refer to this edition.

4. In her book on Mary Wollstonecraft, *A Vindication of Political Virtue: The Political Theory of Mary Wollstonecraft*, Virginia Sapiro points out that Wollstonecraft uses the terms First Cause, God, or nature interchangeably. Sapiro provides evidence from the reviews Wollstonecraft wrote that interchanging these terms was self conscious on her part. The First Cause, God, or Nature "are synonymous in her vocabulary. 'The substitution of the word *nature* instead of a more intelligible phrase, *the first cause*, or simply *God*, is a mere play on words' (*Revs* 1789:151)" (Sapiro, p. 43). Because contemporary Aristotelian scholars continue to debate the relationship between the First Cause and the divine, I allow Wollstonecraft to use these phrases interchangeably. Though she seems satisfied with her understanding of these principles, I would suggest that this is an instance when an education similar to her male counterparts, which included the study Aristotle, would have refined her philosophical understanding. Since the publication of Sapiro's work, other scholars have done excellent studies on Wollstonecraft's theology. *Mary Wollstonecraft and the Feminist Imagination* by Barbara Taylor and *Family Feuds* by Eileen Hunt Botting are two such examples.

5. By placing her hopes for political reform in marriage, Wollstonecraft has placed her hope for political reform in a private institution. Recall Tarcov's observation that Locke's *Some Thoughts Concerning Education* is often overlooked by political theorists because education is no longer a political concern in modern thought. By concentrating on a private institution to improve political life, Wollstonecraft has violated the separation of the public and the private and has already departed from liberalism. Fundamental to liberalism is the relatively small sphere of public or political life. Liberal political thought is marked by the vigilant protection of private life from public life and the strict separation of the two. The separation, which was meant to protect the private sphere, some have argued, has been to the detriment of women as the separation has prevented women from participating in political life.

6. Friendship is used to describe many relationships. For both Aristotle and Wollstonecraft, it also describes the relationship among citizens of a regime. For Wollstonecraft, though, there is a sense that the friendship between husband and wife is foundational to the proper friendship among citizens. See

for example *Vindications*, page 140. In the context of this chapter, I am primarily concerned with the friendship between husband and wife and will use marriage and friendship interchangeably.

7. Aristide Tessitore, *Reading Aristotle's Ethics: Virtue, Rhetoric, and Political Philosophy*. (Albany: State University of New York Press, 1996), 51. Parenthetical citations refer to this edition.

8. In the Greek text, Aristotle does not use the word for male human being (*aner*). Rather, he relies on the substantive use of an adjective, where the article, plus a gendered adjective can stand for a noun or for a generalization or abstraction. So, for example, the Greek may refer to "the good," but the translator often offers a noun to make it more pleasing to English speakers and translates the construction as "the good man." Aristotle's substantive use of the adjective with masculine ending can be translated as "the good man," but it would also be appropriate to translate it as "the good person." Given the ambivalence of the Greek and that Aristotle does explicitly identify females in various forms of friendship, such as that between husband and wife, I believe that friendship, as Aristotle conceives it, even in its highest form, is not limited to men.

9. Ronna Burger argues in her essay, "Aristotle's 'Exclusive' Account of Happiness: Contemplative Wisdom as a Guise of the Political Philosopher" (in *The Crossroads of Norm and Nature: Essays on Aristotle's Ethics and Metaphysics*, ed. May Sim), that the contemplative life is impossible for human beings. Just as form is not separable from matter in this world, so the noetic soul is incapable of separation from the sentient and nutritive soul in human beings.

10. Julie K. Ward, "Aristotle on *Philia*," *Feminism and Ancient Philosophy*. Edited by Julie K. Ward. (New York: Routledge, 1996), 163. Parenthetical citations refer to this edition.

11. Tomaselli and Abbey identify this form of friendship, virtue friendship, with the relationship between men (Tomaselli, xxvi and Abbey, 79). From the outset, we should notice that Aristotle himself does not make that distinction. As we shall see later in this chapter, the perfect form of friendship may occur between man and woman, husband and wife.

12. Daryl McGowan Tress, "Aristotle's *Child*: Development Through *Genesis, Oikos*, and *Polis*," *Ancient Philosophy* 17 (1997), 75. Parenthetical citations refer to article.

13. For either spouse to assume complete rule over the other would be a perversion of the relationship "When the husband controls everything, he transforms the relationship into oligarchy, for he governs in violation of fitness, and not in virtue of superiority. And sometimes when the wife is an heiress it is she who rules. In these cases then authority goes not by virtue but by wealth and power, as in an oligarchy" (*NE*, VIII, x, 5). In the case that the aristocratic relationship degenerates into an oligarchic relationship and the

friendship no longer exists for the sake of practicing virtue, the friendship no longer constitutes human happiness. Happiness depends on the virtue or independence of husband and wife.

NOTES TO CHAPTER SEVEN

1. Jean Bethke Elshtain, *Public Man, Private Woman: Women in Social and Political Thought*, Second Edition (Princeton: Princeton University Press, 1981), 9. Parenthetical citations refer to this edition.
2. Arlene W. Saxonhouse, *Fear of Diversity: The Birth of Political Science in Ancient Greek Thought* (Chicago: Chicago University Press, 1992), 186. Parenthetical citations refer to this edition.
3. Xenophon, *Hellenica*. Edited by T.E. Page. (Cambridge: Harvard University Press, 1947),VI, 5, 28.
4. Mary Nichols, *Citizens and Statesmen: A Study of Aristotle's Politics* (Savage, MD: Rowman & Littlefield, 1992), 47.
5. Mary Wollstonecraft, *The Collected Letters of Mary Wollstonecraft*. Edited by Ralph M. Wardle (Ithaca: Cornell University Press, 1979), 164.
6. In her recent biography of Mary Wollstonecraft, *Vindication*, Lyndall Gordon, portrays Mary Wollstonecraft's life as revolutionary. Although I am concerned with Wollstonecraft's philosophic and political originality, Gordon chronicles Wollstonecraft's many roles throughout her life, each one, Gordon explains, Wollstonecraft reinvented.

Bibliography

PRIMARY WORKS

Aristotle. *The Generation of Animals.* Translated by A.L. Peck. Cambridge: Harvard University Press, 1990.

Aristotle. *De Partibus I and De Generatione Animalium I.* Translated and commentary by D.M. Balme Oxford: Clarendon Press, 1992.

Aristotle. *Nichomachean Ethics.* Translated by H. Rackham. Cambridge: Harvard University Press, 1994.

Aristotle. *The Politics.* Translated with an introduction by Carnes Lord. Chicago: The University of Chicago Press, 1984.

Barnes, Jonathan, ed. *The Complete Works of Aristotle.* Numerous translators. Princeton, NJ: Princeton University Press, 1984.

Burke, Edmund. *A Philosophical Enquiry into the Origin of Our Ideas of the Sublime and the Beautiful.* Edited with an introduction by James T. Boulton. Notre Dame: University of Notre Dame Press, 1968.

Burke, Edmund. *Reflections on the Revolution in France.* Edited by J.G.A. Pocock. Indianapolis: Hackett Publishing Company, 1987.

Burke, Edmund. *A Vindication of Natural Society.* Edited by Frank N. Pagano. Indianapolis: Liberty Fund Press, 1982.

Crittenden, Danielle. *What Our Mothers Didn't Tell Us: Why Happiness Eludes the Modern Woman.* New York: Simon and Schuster, 1999.

Fox-Genovese, Elizabeth. *"Feminism Is Not the Story of My Life:" How Today's Feminist Elite Has Lost Touch with the Real Concerns of Women.* New York: Anchor Books, 1996.

Friedan, Betty. *The Feminine Mystique.* New York: Bantam Doubleday Dell Publishing Group, 1983.

Locke, John. *Some Thoughts Concerning Education* and *Of the Conduct of Understanding.* Edited and with an introduction by Ruth W. Grant and Nathan Tarcov. Indianapolis: Hackett Publishing Company, 1996.

Locke, John. *Two Treatise of Government.* Edited by Peter Laslett. New York: Cambridge University Press, 1992.

Price, Richard. *Political Writings.* Edited by D.O. Thomas. New York: Cambridge University Press, 1991.

Price, Richard. 1948. *Review of the Principle Questions in Morals.* Edited by D. Daiches Raphael. Cambridge: Oxford University Press.

Priestley, Joseph. 1993. *Political Writings.* Edited by Peter N. Miller. New York: Cambridge University Press.

Priestley, Joseph. *Jesus and Socrates Compared.* Montana, USA: Kessinger Publishing Company.

Roiphe, Anne. *Fruitful: A Real Mother in the Modern World.* Boston: Houghton Mifflin Company, 1996.

Rousseau, Jean-Jacques. *The Discourses and Other Early Political Writings.* Edited by Victor Gourevitch. New York: Cambridge University Press, 1997.

Rousseau, Jean-Jacques. *Emile or On Education.* Translated and with an introduction by Allan Bloom. New York: Basic Books, 1979.

Rousseau, Jean-Jacques. *Politics and the Arts: Letter to M. D'Alembert on the Theatre.* Translated and with an introduction by Allan Bloom. Ithaca, NY: Cornell University Press, 1996.

Rousseau, Jean-Jacques. *The Reveries of the Solitary Walker.* Translated by Charles E. Butterworth. Indianapolis: Hackett Publishing Company, 1992.

Shalit, Wendy. *Return to Modesty: Discovering the Lost Virtue.* New York: The Free Press, 1999.

Todd, Janet & Butler, Marilyn, ed. *The Complete Works of Mary Wollstonecraft.* New York: New York University Press, 1989.

Wollstonecraft, Mary. *A Vindication of the Rights of Woman.* Edited by Carol H. Poston. New York: W. W. Norton & Company, 1988.

Wollstonecraft, Mary. *A. Vindication of the Rights of Men* and *A Vindication of the Rights of Woman.* Edited by Sylvana Tomaselli. New York: Cambridge University Press, 1995.

Wardle, Ralph, ed. *The Collected Letters of Mary Wollstonecraft.* Utica, NY: Cornell University Press, 1979.

Young, Cathy. *Ceasefire!: Why Women and Men Must Join Forces to Achieve True Equality.* New York: The Free Press, 1999.

SECONDARY WORKS

Abbey, Ruth. "Back to the Future: Marriage as Friendship in the Thought of Mary Wollstonecraft." *Hypatia*, 199, Volume 14, no. 3.

Alexander, Meena. *Women in Romanticism: Mary Wollstonecraft, Dorothy Wordsworth, and Mary Shelley.* Savage, MD: Barnes and Noble Books, 1989.

Barker-Benfield, G.J. "Mary Wollstonecraft: Eighteenth Century Commonwealthwoman." *Journal of the History of Ideas* 50 (1989).

Benstock, Shari, ed. *The Private Self: Theory and Practice of Women's Autobiographical Writings.* Chapel Hill: University of North Carolina, 1988.

Bloom, Allan. *Love and Friendship.* New York: Simon and Schuster, 1993.

Blum, Carol. *Rousseau and the Republic of Virtue: The Language of Politics in the French Revolution.* Ithaca, NY: Cornell University Press, 1986.

Botting, Eileen Hunt. *Family Feuds: Wollstonecraft, Burke, and Rousseau on the Transformation of the Family.* Albany: State University of New York Press, 2006.

Brody, Miriam. "Mary Wollstonecraft: Sexuality and Women's Rights" in *Feminist Theory:* Three *Centuries of Key Women Thinkers.* Edited by Dale Spender. New York: Pantheon Books, 1983.

Browne, Alice. The *Eighteenth Century Feminist Mind.* Detroit: Wayne State University Press, 1987.

Burger, Ronna. "Aristotle's 'Exclusive' Account of Happiness: Contemplative Wisdom as a Guise of the Political Philosopher" in *Crossroads of Norm and Nature: Essays on Aristotle's Ethics and Metaphysics.* Edited by May Sim. Lanham, MD: Rowman & Littlefield, 1995.

Conger, Syndy McMillen. Mary Wollstonecraft and the Language of Sensibility. Cranberry, NJ: Associate University Press, 1994.

Cooper, Laurence. *Rousseau, Nature & the Problem of the Good Life.* University Park, Pennsylvania: The Penssylvania State University Press, 1999.

Crafton, Lisa Plummer. *The French Revolution Debate in English Literature and Culture.* Westport, CT: Greenwood Press, 1997.

Davis, Michael. *The Autobiography of Philosophy: Rousseau's The Reveries of a Solitary Walker.* MD: Rowman & Littlefield Publishers, 1999.

Davis, Michael. *The Politics of Philosophy: A Commentary on Aristotle's Politics.* Lanham, MD: Rowman & Littlefield Publishers, 1996.

Deane, Seamus. *The French Revolution and Enlightenment in England.* Cambridge, MA: Harvard University Press, 1988.

Eisenstein, Zillah R. *The Radical Future of Liberal Feminism.* New York: Longman, 1981.

Elshtain, Jean Bethke. *Public Man, Private Woman: Women in Social and Political Thought.* Princeton, NJ: Princeton University Press, 1981.

Falco, Maria J., ed. *Feminist Interpretation of Mary Wollstonecraft.* University Park, PA: The Pennsylvania State University Press, 1996.

Ferguson, Moira and Todd, Janet. *Mary Wollstonecraft.* Boston: Twayne Publishers, 1984.

Flexner, Eleanor. *Mary Wollstonecraft: A Biography.* New York: Coward, McCann & Geoghegan, 1972.

Fraser, George S. *Alexander Pope.* London: Routledge & Kegan Paul, 1978.

Freeland, Cynthia, ed. *Feminist Interpretations of Aristotle.* University Park, PA: The Pennsylvania State University Press, 1992.

Gatens, Moira." 'The Oppressed State of My Sex': Wollstonecraft on Reason, Feeling and Equality" in *Feminist Interpretation and Political Theory.* Edited by Mary Lyndon Shanley and Carole Pateman. University Park: Pennsylvania University Press, 1991.

George, Margaret. *One Woman's Situation:* Urbana: University of Illinois Press, 1970.

Gordon, Lyndall. *Vindication: A Life of Mary Wollstonecraft.* New York: Harper Collins, 2005.

Grimshaw, Jean. "Mary Wollstonecraft and the Tensions in Feminist Philosophy" in *Socialism, Feminism, and Philosophy: A Radical Reader.* Edited by Sean Sayers and Peter Osbornee. London: Routledge, 2005.

Gunther-Canada, Wendy. *Rebel Writer: Mary Wollstonecraft and Enlightenment Politics.* DeKalb: Northern Illinois University Press, 2001.

Horowitz, Robert. "John Locke and the Preservation of Liberty: A Perennial Problem of Civic Education." *The Political Science Reviewer* 6 (1996).

Hudson, W.D. *Reason and Right: A Critical Examination of Richard Price's Moral Philosophy.* San Francisco: Freeman, Cooper & Company, 1970.

Hunt, Eileen. "The Family as Cave, Platoon and Prison: the Three Stages of Wollstonecraft's Philosophy of the Family. *Review of Politics* 64 (2002).

Jensen, Pamela Grande, ed. *Finding a New Feminism: Rethinking the Woman Question for Liberal Democracy.* Lanham, MD: Rowman & Littlefield, 1996.

Johnson, Claudia L. *Equivocal Beings: Politics, Gender, and Sentimentality in the 1790's.* Chicago: University of Chicago Press, 1995.

Kelly, Gary. *Revolutionary Feminism: The Mind and Career of Mary Wollstonecraft.* New York: St. Martin's Press, 1996.

Lloyd, G.E.R. "Aristotle's Psychology and Zoology," *Essays on Aristotle's De Anima.* Edited by M. Nussbaum and A. Rorty. New York: Oxford University Press, 1992.

Lovejoy, Arthur O. *The Great Chain of Being.* Cambridge, MA: Harvard University Press, 1964.

MacIntyre, Alasdair. *After Virtue: A Study in Moral Theory.* Notre Dame: University of Notre Dame Press, 1984.

Masters, Roger. *The Political Philosophy of Rousseau.* Princeton: Princeton University Press, 1968.

Masugi, Ken. "Another Peek at Aristotle and Phyllis: The Place of Women in Aristotle's Argument on Equality." *Natural Right: Essays in Honor of Harry V. Jaffa.* Edited by Thomas B. Silver and Peter W. Schramm. Durham, NC: Carolina Academic Press, 1984.

Meyers, Mitzi. "Reform or Ruin: 'A Revolution in Female Manners'" *Studies in Eighteenth-Century Culture* 11 (1982).

Myers, Peter. *Our Only Star and Compass: Locke and the Struggle for Political Rationality.* Lanham, MD: Roman & Littlefield Publishers, 1998.

Nichols, Mary. "Rousseau's Novel Education in the *Emile.*" *Political Theory* 13 (1985), no. 4.

Nichols, Mary. *Citizens and Statesmen: A Study of Aristotle's Politics.* Savage, MD: Rowman & Littlefield Publishers, 1992.

Okin, Susan Moller. *Women in Western Political Thought.* Princeton, NJ: Princeton University Press, 1979.

Pangle, Thomas L. *The Spirit of Modern Republicanism: the Moral Vision of the American Founders and the Philosophy of Locke.* Chicago: University of Chicago Press, 1988.

Rogers, Katherine M. *Feminism in Eighteenth-Century England.* Urbana: University of Illinois Press, 1982.

Rorty, Amelie Oksenberg, ed. *Essays on Aristotle's Ethics.* Berkeley: University of California Press, 1980.

Ruderman, Anne Crippen. *The Pleasures of Virtue: Political Thought in the Novels of Jane Austen.* Lanham, MD: Rowman & Littlefield Publishers, 1995.

Salkever, Stephen G. *Finding the Mean: Theory and Practice in Aristotelian Political Philosophy.* Princeton, NJ: Princeton University Press, 1990.

Sapiro, Virginia. *A Vindication of Political Virtue: The Political Theory of Mary Wollstonecraft.* Chicago: The University of Chicago Press, 1992.

Saxonhouse, Arlene W. *Fear of Diversity: The Birth of Political Science in Ancient Greek Thought.* Chicago: University of Chicago Press, 1992.

Saxonhouse, Arlene W. "Family, Polity, & Unity: Aristotle on Socrates' Community of Wives." *Polity* 15 (1982), no. 2.

Schaeffer, Denise. "Reconsidering the Role of Sophie in Rousseau's *Emile.*" *Polity* 30 (1998), no.4.

Schwartz, Joel. *The Sexual Politics of Jean-Jacques Rousseau.* Chicago: The University of Chicago Press, 1984.

Strauss, Leo. *The City and Man.* Chicago: The University of Chicago Press, 1978.

Sunstein, Emily W. *A Different Face: The Life of Mary Wollstonecraft.* New York: Harper & Row Publishers, 1975.

Swanson, Judith A. *The Public and the Private in Aristotle's Political Philosophy.* Ithaca, NY: Cornell University Press, 1992.

Tarcov, Nathan. *Locke's Education for Liberty.* Chicago: The University of Chicago Press, 1989.

Taylor, Barbara. *Mary Wollstonecraft and the Feminist Imagination.* Cambridge: Cambridge University Press, 2003.

Tessitore, Aristide. *Reading Aristotle's Ethics: Virtue, Rhetoric, and Political Philosophy.* Albany: State University of New York Press, 1996.

Thomas, D.O. The *Honest Mind: The Thought and Work of Richard Price.* Oxford: Clarendon Press, 1977.

Todd, Janet. *Mary Wollstonecraft: A Revolutionary Life.* New York: Columbia University Press, 2000.

Tomalin, Claire. *The Life and Death of Mary Wollstonecraft.* New York: Penguin Books, 1992 .

Tress, Daryl. "Feminist Theory and Its Discontents," *Interpretation* 18 (1991), no. 2.

Tress, Daryl. "Aristotle's *Child:* Development Trough *Genesis, Oikos,* arid *Polis."* *Ancient Philosophy* 17 (1997).

Trouille, Mary Seidman. *Sexual Politics in the Enlightenment: Women Writers Read Rousseau.* Albany: State University of New York Press, 1997.

Ward, Julie K., ed. *Feminism and Ancient Philosophy.* New York: Routledge, 1996

Wardle, Ralph M. *Mary Wollstonecraft: A Critical Biography.* Lincoln: University of Nebraska Press, 1951.

Weiss, Penny. *Gendered Community: Rousseau, Sex, and Politics.* New York: New York University Press, 1993.

Willey, Basil. *The Eighteenth Century Background: Studies on the Idea of Nature in the Thought of the Period.* Boston: Beacon Press, 1961.

Winthrop, Delba. "Aristotle and Theories of Justice." *American Political Science Review* 72 (1978).

Zaw, Susan Khin. "The Reasonable Heart: Mary Wollstonecraft's View of the Relation Between Reason and Feeling in Morality, Moral Psychology, and Moral Development." *Hypatia* 3 (1998).

Zuckert, Michael. *Natural Rights, and New Republicanism.* Princeton, NJ: Princeton University Press, 1994.

Index

For Product Safety Concerns and Information please contact our EU
representative GPSR@taylorandfrancis.com
Taylor & Francis Verlag GmbH, Kaufingerstraße 24, 80331 München, Germany

www.ingramcontent.com/pod-product-compliance
Lightning Source LLC
Chambersburg PA
CBHW070412270326
41926CB00014B/2793

9 781138 879867